Contributions to Economics

More information about this series http://www.springer.com/series/1262

Ronney Aamoucke

Innovative Start-Ups and the Distribution of Human Capital

The Role of Regional Knowledge

Springer

Ronney Aamoucke
GSBC EIC "The Economics of Innovative Change"
Jena, Germany

ISSN 1431-1933 ISSN 2197-7178 (electronic)
Contributions to Economics
ISBN 978-3-319-44461-1 ISBN 978-3-319-44462-8 (eBook)
DOI 10.1007/978-3-319-44462-8

Library of Congress Control Number: 2016952090

Printed on acid-free paper

This Springer imprint is published by Springer Nature
The registered company is Springer International Publishing AG Switzerland

Acknowledgments

I am deeply indebted to many people who supported me during my study and work on this thesis. First, I am extremely grateful to my supervisor, Prof. Dr. Michael Fritsch, for providing me with scientific support. I benefited from many discussions with colleagues as my thesis developed. I thank my colleagues at the chair of "Business Dynamics, Innovation, and Economic Change," most especially Michael Wyrwich for his constant support and Mathias Pionthek and Moritz Zöllner for fruitful discussion. Moreover, I thank the supervisors of my thesis. I very much appreciate the engaging and encouraging discussions during my presentations at the Jena Economic Research Workshops with Prof. Dr. Uwe Cantner, doctoral students, and postdoctoral researchers from the Graduate College "Economics of Innovative Change" at the FSU Jena.

Contents

List of Figures

List of Tables

List of Abbreviations and Acronyms

CAE	Conseil d'Analyse Économique
CFI	Comparative fit index
EU	European Union
HEIs	Higher education institutions
Max	Maximum
Min	Minimum
OECD	Organisation for Economic Co-operation and Development
OLS	Ordinary least square
R&D	Research and development
RMSEA	Root mean squared error of approximation
SEM	Structural equation modeling
Std. Dev.	Standard deviation
SUR	Seemingly unrelated regression
SVR	Sachverständigenrat zur Begutachtung der gesamtwirtschaftlichen Entwicklung
UNDP	United Nations Development Programme
US	United States
USA	United States of America
WHO	World Health Organization

Chapter 1
Introduction

Economic progress and development—that is, the permanent improvement of the conditions of life—is the most important issue, and the greatest challenge, for human societies. What really drives economic progress? For a long time, religious beliefs dominated the human worldview, meaning that economic well-being was believed due to supernatural causes. In the modern age, however, the human worldview is changed. This change took place initially in Europe. European societies experienced radical change in the late Middle Ages (Herlihy 1997; Bennett 2010). Geographic explorations widened the human worldview. European adventurers explored the globe, acquiring new knowledge and resources (Love 2006). The "Scientific Revolution," the "Enlightenment," and the "Industrial Revolution" influenced society to see the world in terms of reason and to value knowledge of its workings. Unprecedented economic progress was made in Western countries (Clark 2007).

This "brief history" provides a possible answer to the question posed above: it is knowledge that drives economic progress. This fundamental hypothesis is the backbone of my thesis. Knowledge, of course, comes in many forms. In this thesis, I analyze two of its manifestations: entrepreneurship in the form of innovative start-ups and human capital in form of highly educated people. Empirical studies show that the geography of both innovative start-ups and human capital is highly uneven (Harhoff 1999; Bade and Nerlinger 2000; Glaeser et al. 1995; Moretti 2004b). Based on this empirical evidence, the question I ask and answer here is: What are the determinants behind the uneven distribution of innovative start-ups and human capital?

The remainder of this introductory chapter is organized as follows. Section 1.1 discusses the emergence of entrepreneurship theory as well as the impact of new business formation on economic progress. Section 1.2 covers the rise of human capital theory and its impact on economic development. Section 1.3 explains the major purpose of this thesis and details its structure.

R. Aamoucke, *Innovative Start-Ups and the Distribution of Human Capital*,
Contributions to Economics, DOI 10.1007/978-3-319-44462-8_1

1.1 Entrepreneurship

1.1.1 The Rise of Entrepreneurship Theory

The word "entrepreneur" comes from the French verb "entreprendre," which means to "do something" or "to undertake."[1] The word "entrepreneur" was used for the first time in an economic sense by the Irish-born banker and economist Richard Cantillon (1755). Cantillon argued that there are often discrepancies between supply and demand that give rise to a profit-making opportunity by buying cheap and selling high. A person alert to such opportunities and willing to undertake such a venture, with full knowledge that success is uncertain, is an "entrepreneur." Jean-Baptiste Say (1803) refined the concept of "entrepreneur" by defining an entrepreneur as a person who combines the available factors to bring to market products that satisfy human needs in a process that requires knowledge and risk-taking. Nevertheless, during the nineteenth century, entrepreneurship did not play a significant role in economic thought, although there were a few exceptions such Jeremy Bentham and John Stuart Mill (Hébert and Link 2006; Carlsson et al. 2013).

The clearest explanation of the role of entrepreneurship in economic progress was made by the Austrian-born economist Joseph Alois Schumpter (1934). Although not the first to identify the process, Schumpeter was instrumental in bringing to prominence the idea of "creative destruction" and considered entrepreneurs to be the most basic agents of economic progress.[2] Schumpeter argued that economic progress occurs when a state of equilibrium is disrupted by a wave of discoveries instantiated as new products and production methods that are introduced by entrepreneurs. Moreover, Schumpeter argued no human society has ever or will ever be short of new ideas. For example, even the ancient Egyptians had a concept of the steam engine. What they were missing, however, was entrepreneurship: the process of introducing this new ideas into the economy. Nevertheless, Schumpeter's ideas took a long time to find a foothold in economic analysis and, indeed, received their first real attention in the field of economic history. Generally, the concept and study of entrepreneurship penetrated the economic sciences relatively late. Indeed, to begin with, it had a stronger presence in the study of management and behavioral sciences. For instance, McClelland (1961) identified entrepreneurship as one of four driving forces behind economic growth, along with technology, population growth, and the division of labor. He argued that the norms and values that prevail in any given society, particularly with regard to the need for achievement, are decisive for economic progress.

---

[1]For a general overview on the development of the definition of entrepreneurship and research on the subject, see, for instance, Hébert and Link (1989, 2006),Cornelius et al. (2006), and Carlsson et al. (2013).

[2]For more information on earlier instances of the idea of creative destruction, see Reinert and Reinert (2006).

During the 1970s, Western economies experienced a period of stagflation, crises, and institutional reform. In such a climate, Kirzner (1973) identified the economic role entrepreneurs play in the reestablishment of market equilibrium. Near the end of the 1970s, economic research on entrepreneurship received a boost from the work of David Birch (1979, 1987) who showed that it is not large corporations but small firms that are responsible for the majority of new jobs in the USA.[3] Since the late 1970s, the entrepreneurship research has grown rapidly, covering topics such as personal traits of entrepreneurs, entrepreneurial opportunities, new firms and market entries, small business, and family firms (Carlsson et al. 2013, pp. 922–927). Despite this "boom" in entrepreneurship research, the field still lacks a standard definition of entrepreneurship (Gartner 1990). Nevertheless, economists and policymakers agree that "entrepreneurs are agents of change and growth in a market economy and they can act to accelerate the generation, dissemination and application of innovative ideas" (OECD 1998a, p. 11).

In the framework of this thesis, entrepreneurship is understood as new business formation. In Chaps. 2 and 3, I distinguish between four types of start-ups based on the R&D intensity of their industries. High-technology start-ups have an R&D intensity of more than 8.5 %; technologically advanced start-ups have an R&D intensity between 3.5 and 8.5 %. Technology-oriented services offer services related to innovation activity. The remainder of the start-ups are classified as "non-innovative."

1.1.2 The Impact of New Business Formation

There is a general consensus among scholars and policymakers that new business formation is conducive to regional development (Carree and Thurik 2010; Fritsch 2008, 2011, 2013). Moreover, its positive influence is not found only in actual market entries or successful start-ups; even intended market entries and failed start-ups can have a laudatory impact on regional development (Baumol et al. 1988).

Several studies suggest that start-ups contribute to regional development by fostering technical progress, especially in the early stages of a product lifecycle (Acs and Audretsch 1990; Audretsch 1995b; Winter 1984). Baumol (2004) attributes young and small businesses with a crucial role in the radical innovations of the twentieth century. Geroski (1995, p. 431) suggests that high rates of start-ups are associated with high rates of innovation. He argues that new business are less reluctant to introduce innovations than established firms, which are more interested

[3]David Birch claimed that 66 % of all new jobs between 1969 and 1976 in the USA were created by firms with fewer than 20 employees. Birch's work was not without its critics, of course (Davis et al. 1996a, b; Storey 1994; Neumark et al. 2011); however, Birch's undeniable contribution is that he initiated a fervent debate over entrepreneurship, one that continues to the present day. David Birch won the first Global Award for Entrepreneurship Research in 1996 for having identified the key role of new and small firms in job creation.

in protecting existing profits than in searching for new profit opportunities. Bosma et al. (2011) find that high market entries in service sectors are associated with high regional productivity growth in Netherlands.

New business formation can facilitate the concentration of industries in space and trigger the so-called Marshall-Arrow-Romer (MAR) externalities (Marshall 1890/1920; Arrow 1962; Romer 1986). The geographic proximity of firms in the same industry often facilities the flow of knowledge and the exchange of ideas that lead to key innovations.[4] One of the most important mechanisms for concentrating industries in space is "spinoffs." Spinoffs are start-ups by employees who leave their established firms in order to start up an own business in the same sector as the established firm. Klepper and Thompson (2007) explain the emergence of spinoffs as due to disagreement between employees and their bosses over the potential of an employee's innovative idea. Moreover, Klepper (2007) attributes the concentration of the automobile industry around Detroit to spinoffs.

The empirical evidence on the impact of new business formation on employment growth in subsequent years is mixed. Some studies (e.g., Fritsch 1996, 1997) find no significant positive relationship between the level of start-ups and regional employment growth; other studies find a positive impact for certain countries (see Reynolds (1994, 1999) and Acs and Armington (2002, 2004b) for the US, Ashcroft and Love (1996) for the United Kingdom, and Piergiovanni et al. (2012) for Italy).[5] Fritsch and Schroeter (2011a) find an inverse U-shaped relationship between the level of start-up activity and employment change in West Germany. Generally, the mechanism by which new business formation influences regional development can be viewed as a process of challenge-response interaction between start-ups and established firms. This view is based on the ideas of Joseph Schumpeter and the concept of "creative destruction."[6] According to this idea, start-ups enter the market and compete with the established firms, with two main effects: they create new jobs[7] and they force established firms to adapt—or not. Firms that fail to adapt to the new market environment will either shrink or exit the market.[8]

Moreover, in the face of this more competitive environment, start-ups and established firms should become more creative, for example, by introducing yet more innovations or engaging in product differentiation. In the long term, the supply side of the market becomes more productive, more innovative, and more efficient. This type of effect, sometimes called "supply-side effects," occurs indirectly as a by-product of increased competition. Several empirical studies show that

---

[4]However, some scholars challenge this view. For instance, Huber (2012) finds that technological knowledge spillovers within the Cambridge Information Technology Cluster are highly limited.

[5]For more information, see Fritsch (2013).

[6]Another mechanism by which new business formation contributes to regional development is "nondestructive creation," a process in which start-ups search for new applications of existing products (Hubbard 2008).

[7]These effects are sometimes called "direct effects." See Fritsch and Weyh (2006) for more details on the direct effects of start-ups in West Germany for the period 1984–2002.

[8]These effects are sometimes called "replacement" effects.

these effects are considerably more effective for regional development than any other type of effect (Fritsch 2008, pp. 4–5; Fritsch and Noseleit 2013a, b). However, the market must be working according to the "survival of the fittest" scenario as a condition for "supply-side effects" to be triggered.

The competitive pressure of start-ups increases with their quality. High-quality start-ups pose a serious challenge to established firms and force them to either adapt or exit. With start-ups of higher quality, the supply-side effects become quantitatively larger and deeper. There are several indicators of start-up quality, of which innovativeness is the most important. However, identifying innovative start-ups is not a simple task. One way to identify innovative start-ups, and the one employed in this thesis, is to look at the share of inputs devoted to research and development (R&D) activity. Alternatively, innovative start-ups can be identified by venture capital (VC) investment because this sort of investment is made only after a detailed assessment of the start-up's quality (Fritsch 2011). However, this method can be problematic. First, VC investors may select start-ups with a particularly high level of innovativeness. Second, there is a possible bias toward firms located in spatial proximity (Lutz et al. 2013; Fritsch and Schilder 2008). Third, VC investors are a heterogeneous group of investors (Schäfer and Schilder 2009), meaning that unobserved factors play a role in their investment decisions.

Schumpeter suggested that innovative entrepreneurs are rare because undertaking "new things is difficult and constitutes a distinct economic function, first because they lie outside of the routine tasks which everybody understands, and secondly, because the environment resists in many ways" (Schumpeter 1942, p. 13). Indeed, empirical data show that the number of innovative start-ups is small. Table 1.1 shows the average number of start-ups in different industries. The share of start-ups in high-technology industries relative to all start-ups is only 0.39 %, while the share of start-ups in technology-advanced industries is only 0.66 %. Despite their rarity, innovative start-ups are of special importance for regional development. Audretsch et al. (2006) find that output and labor productivity in a neoclassical production function is influenced by start-up rates in the high-tech industry as an additional production factor. Fritsch and Schroeter (2011b) demonstrate that innovative start-ups do have an employment effect and quality does make a difference. Baptista and Preto (2011) find for Portuguese regions that the impact

Table 1.1 Average yearly number of start-ups in innovative and knowledge-intensive industries in the period 1995–2008

	Mean	Min	Max	Std. dev.
All start-ups	246,451	206,679	270,103	19,588
High-technology industries[a]	971	657	1232	234.36
Technologically-advanced industries[b]	1632	1232	2169	243.45
Technology-oriented services[c]	16,191	13,906	19,891	1822.38

Source: Own calculations based on the ZEW Founder Panel
[a]Manufacturing industries that have R&D intensity more than 8.5 %
[b]Manufacturing industries with an R&D intensity between 3.5 and 8.5 %
[c]Firms that offer certain services to industries closely related to innovation and new technology

of knowledge-based start-ups on regional employment is considerably larger than the impact of start-ups in other industries.

Other studies suggest that the impact of start-ups on regional development depends on their ability to remain in the market for a relatively long time (Falck 2007; Fritsch and Noseleit 2013b). The empirical evidence on whether innovative start-ups have a relatively higher likelihood of surviving for longer periods is ambiguous. In a study of the USA, Audretsch (1995a) shows that the survival likelihood of start-ups in innovative industries is significantly lower than that of start-ups in industries where innovative activity is less important. However, if start-ups survive the first several years, they later exhibit relatively higher growth rates. Audretsch et al. (2000) find for the Netherlands that the likelihood of survival is positively influenced by the age and size of firms, and negatively influenced by the intensity of R&D in the industry. Areason for the higher propensity of failure for more innovative firms (i.e., those spending more on R&D) may be due to the great risk involved in the technical and market success of new products. In contrast, Metzger and Rammer (2009) suggest that innovative start-ups in Germany have slightly higher survival rates. Fritsch et al. (2014) find that start-ups in innovative industries have higher survival rates than start-ups in other industries.

1.2 Human Capital

1.2.1 The Rise of Human Capital Theory

Economists have known about the importance of human capital for a long time (Kiker 1966). Adam Smith (1776/1976, p. 118) suggested that the acquired abilities of a society's members are an important source of the wealth of nations. Alfred Marshall (1890/1922, p. 564) noted that "the most valuable of all capital is that invested in human beings." However, despite this early recognition of the importance of human capital, its incorporation into mainstream economic theory was delayed until the second half of the twentieth century.[9] There are several reasons for this. First, for a long time, mainstream economics was dominated by neoclassical theory, which relied on optimality conditions and neglected the role of human capital as well that played by entrepreneurs (Baumol 1968). Generally, two major assumptions were problematic for the incorporation of human capital into mainstream theory: the homogenous labor assumption and the restriction of the concept of capital to physical goods. The second obstacle for human capital's entry into mainstream economics was the crises in the first half of the twentieth century and the subsequent emergence of Keynesian economics, which paid more attention to

[9]Marginson (1997) identified four stages for the development of human capital theory: the First Wave Human Capital Theory (1960s), the Screening Theory Phase (1970s–1980s), the Second Wave Human Capital Theory (1980s), and the Market liberal human capital theory (1980s–1990s).

short-run economics and aggregate demand. A third problem may have been simple terminology—perhaps economists balked at viewing human beings as "capital" (Schultz 1961, p. 2).[10]

However, during the 1960s, a number of empirical findings challenged mainstream theory. For instance, empirical research found that output grew more than labor and capital after World War II and that labor income explains the major part of personal income inequality (Mincer 1981; Becker 1992). Such observations motivated a number of scholars to introduce the concept of human capital into mainstream economic theory. Schultz (1961) argued that both knowledge and skills represent a form of capital that can be increased by deliberate investment, leading to increased personal income and economic progress.[11] Becker (1962, 1964) argued that higher individual levels of education increase income, and that people's decisions to invest in human capital are based on a rational cost-benefit assessment.[12] Mincer (1958, 1974) defined human capital as acquired capabilities that are developed through formal and informal education. Accordingly, human capital includes the embodiment and transmission of knowledge as well as the production of new knowledge that paves the way for innovation and technical progress.[13]

The 1950s witnessed some progress in macroeconomic growth theory (Barro and Sala-i-Martin 2004, pp. 16–21). Solow (1956) and Swan (1956) introduced a neoclassical model with homogenous labor and physical capital as production factors. The model predicted that growth ceases without technological progress. The obvious shortcoming of the model was the exogenous nature of technological progress.[14] Henceforth, macroeconomists tried to incorporate human capital into the growth model. In the mid-1980s, researchers such Romer (1986, 1990) and Lucas (1988) included human capital and knowledge spillovers to reduce the problem of diminishing returns to the accumulation of capital. Accordingly, two approaches were developed in macroeconomic growth theory to capture the role played by human capital in the process of economic growth (Aghion and Howitt 1998, chapter 10).[15] Under the first approach, human capital is viewed as another production factor of production that should be accumulated to drive economic growth. For instance, Lucas (1988) introduced human capital in the production function as a further production factor and assumed that the rate of human capital

[10]A jury of German linguists deemed the term—*Humankapital*—the German Un-Word of the year 2004 because it implies that people would be degraded and their abilities classified according to economically relevant quantities (http://www.unwortdesjahres.net/index.php?id=18).

[11]See Bouchard (1998) for a criticism of Schultz's work.

[12]Many scholars suggest that in addition to education and skills the concept of human capital should include other dimensions such as health (Becker 2002, 2007; McFadden 2008).

[13]For more details on definition and measurement of human capital, see OECD (1998b), Mulligan and Sala-i-Martin (2000), Le et al. (2003).

[14]Solow (1957, p. 317) himself acknowledged the role of human capital when he noted that "a lot of what appears as shifts in the production function must represent improvement in the quality of the labor input, and therefore a result of real capital formation of an important kind."

[15]This difference in views is sometimes called the "Lucas versus Nelson-Phelps controversy."

accumulation determines the growth rate per capita. In the second approach, human capital is believed to drive economic growth by facilitating innovation and the adoption of new technologies. For instance, Nelson and Phelps (1966) suggested two ways for the stock of human capital to drive growth. First, human capital increases the ability of economies to adapt to change and import technologies from more developed economies. Second, human capital affects the ability of economies to introduce innovations.[16] Benhabib and Spiegel (1994) in a study of more than 75 countries found that human capital does have a significant impact on total factor productivity but not on growth in per capita income. Benhabib and Spiegel suggested that education influence productivity growth by increasing the rate of domestic innovation, increasing the rate of technology adoption from abroad, and attracting physical capital to from abroad.

1.2.2 The Impact of Human Capital

There is now a general consensus that human capital is a fundamental driver of economic progress, basically due to the role knowledge plays in economic growth (Glaeser et al. 2004). People with higher levels of education have more knowledge and greater ability to absorb and generate new knowledge. Indeed, some scholars argue that human capital played a pivotal role in initiating and perpetuating the Industrial Revolution (van Zanden 2009; Clark 2005). Moreover, there is evidence that human capital accumulation results in agriculture-based economies becoming industry based (Tamur 2002).

At the regional level, two types of studies analyze the impact of human capital. One type concentrates on different regions in the same country so as to compare regions; the other type looks at regions in different countries. For instance, Gennaioli et al. (2013) investigate the determinants of regional development by using a database of 1569 sub-national regions from 110 countries covering 74 % of the world's surface. The authors find that human capital, as measured by educational attainment, is the most important determinant of regional growth. Acemoglu and Dell (2010) examine sub-national data from North and South America and find that about half the within-country variation in levels of income is accounted for by education.

Systematic research into the impact of human capital on regional growth began during the 1950s. Ullman (1958) investigated the concentration of economic activity and noted the important role of human capital for regional development. Jane Jacobs (1961, 1969) emphasized the role of cities in generating human capital,

[16]There is vast literature on both approaches. For more discussion, see, for instance, Mankiw et al. (1992), Coe and Helpman (1995), Benhabib and Spiegel (1994, 2005), Gemmell (1996), Topel (1999), De La Fuente and Donénech (2001), Krueger and Lindahl (2001), Pritchett (2001), Engelbrecht (2003), Klenow and Rodriguez-Clare (2005), Caselli and Coleman (2006), Ciccone and Papaioannou (2009), and Wolff (2012).

showing that cities increase the connections between economic actors and facilitate the process of knowledge generation and diffusion. Over the last two decades, a great deal of research has been devoted to analyzing in more detail the impact of human capital on different indicators of regional development, such as population growth, employment growth, income, productivity, lower crime, greater civic involvement, and the like. For instance, Glaeser et al. (1995) show that income growth and population growth were correlated to each other across US cities in the period 1960–1990 and that initial schooling rate affected both positively. Similarly, Simon (1998) finds a positive and persistent relationship between initial levels of human capital and subsequent employment growth for the period 1940–1986. Simon and Nardinelli (1996, 2002) argue that regions with initially higher levels of human capital in the USA and UK grow faster in the long run. Winters (2013) shows that human capital levels have positive external effects on labor force participation and employment and that less educated employees receive the largest external benefits. Gottlieb and Fogarty (2003) find significant relationship between educational attainment in 1980 and per capita growth rate of income and employment during the 1990s.

The main reasons for the positive effects of human capital on employment growth are due to the effects human capital has on productivity and the supply of consumer amenities. Glaeser and Saiz (2004) suggest that at the metropolitan-area level, human capital influences productivity growth but not consumer amenities. At the very local level, human capital affects both productivity and amenities. Shapiro (2006) argues that increasing productivity is not the only channel by which human capital generates employment growth. Roughly 60 % of the employment growth effect of human capital is due to enhanced productivity growth, while the other 40 % is due to growth in consumer amenities.

Moretti (2004a, b) argues that the impact of human capital on regional development is transmitted by various externalities. First, human capital raises regional productivity by making other employees more productive. Accordingly, if the regional share of people with a tertiary degree increases by 1 percentage point, the wages of high school drop-outs, high school graduates, and university graduates increases by 1.9 %, 1.6 %, and 0.4 %, respectively. Second, higher regional levels of human capital can reduce the likelihood of engaging in activity that generates negative externalities, such as criminality. Lochner and Moretti (2004) estimate the social savings from crime reduction achieved by one additional high school graduate at about $1170–$2100. Third, highly educated people are more likely to make better decisions on policy issues (Milligan et al. 2004; Dee 2004). Fourth, Currie and Moretti (2003) find that higher maternal education improves infant health.

Similar evidence of human capital's positive impact on regional development is found for several countries. Suedekum (2008) suggests that West German regions with a large initial share of human capital experienced higher total employment growth for the period 1977–2002. Eaton and Eckstein (1997) find for France between 1876 and 1990, and for Japan between 1925 and 1985, that urban growth was driven by the acquisition of human capital. Polasek et al. (2011) analyze the effects of human capital on productivity in Swiss cantons, measuring it as average years of schooling as well as shares of employees with tertiary education. Average years of schooling did not show any robust effect on productivity growth; share of people with a tertiary education was the main driving force for productivity growth. De La Fuente (2002) shows that regional convergence across Spanish regions is caused mainly by the equalization of education levels, as well as by the diffusion of technology.

In a study of Italy, Di Liberto (2008) finds, surprisingly, that increased education contributes to growth only in the southern part of the country and that the most important level of education is primary education, while tertiary education tends to have a negative effect on regional growth. A similarly surprising result is found for regions of Portugal by Pereira and St. Aubyn (2009). There are basically three theories for why, in certain cases, human capital has no or a negative influence on regional development. First, higher education may not necessarily reflect higher productivity, but could be acting more as a signaling function in the labor market (Psacharopoulos 1985). Second, the institutional framework might reward productive activity less well than it does rent-seeking activity, a pursuit that tends to increase with additionally acquired qualifications (Murphy et al. 1991). Third, it could be that the positive impact of human capital is restricted to countries and regions close to the technological frontier. That is, if highly educated people lived in places far from the technological frontier, their human capital would have no effect on regional development (Vandenbussche et al. 2006).

1.2.3 Human Capital and New Business Formation

This section reviews the literature on the relationship between the two cornerstones of the thesis—innovative start-ups and human capital. Several studies demonstrate a positive impact of human capital on the emergence and performance of new business ventures, a result thought to be due to the process of entrepreneurship, which involves knowledge creation, absorption, and commercialization. Highly educated people are assumed to have more knowledge and have greater ability to absorb and create new knowledge. Therefore, they are assumed to have a strong influence on the emergence and success of new business formation.

Figure 1.1 shows the relationship between the number of people with a tertiary degree and the amount of high-technology and technologically-advanced manufacturing in West Germany for the period 2001–2008. The correlation coefficient between human capital and innovative start-ups is 0.7381, a clear evidence of the importance of human capital for new business formation. The strong propensity of highly educated people to start new business ventures has a two-part theoretical base. First, the knowledge spillover theory of entrepreneurship assumes that new business formation requires knowledge, which predominantly resides in HEIs and incumbents. Entrepreneurs draw on this knowledge stock and commercialize it in the form of a new business venture (Acs et al. 2009, 2013). The second

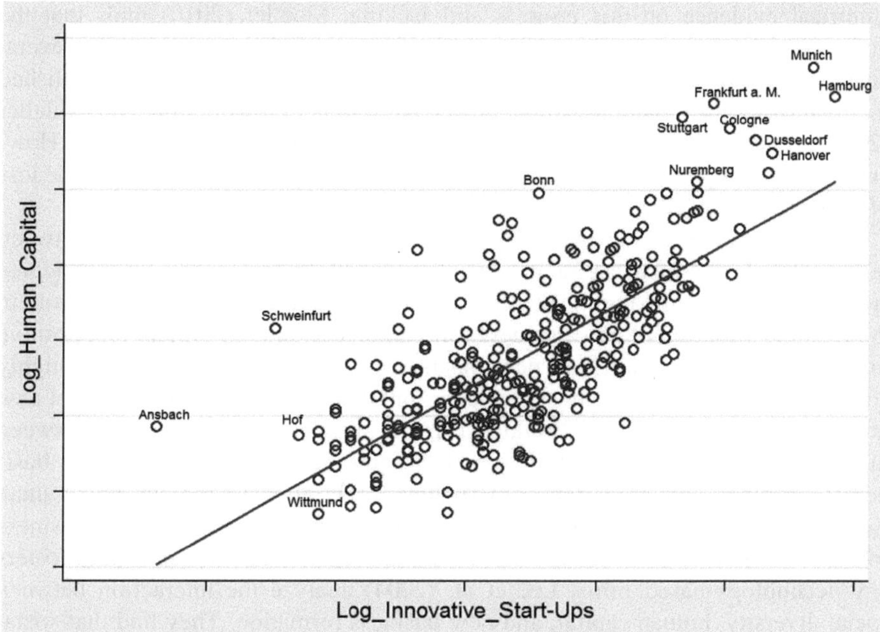

Fig. 1.1 Scatter plot of human capital and innovative start-ups

theoretical underpinning is the concept of absorptive capacity, that is, people vary in their ability to recognize the value of new information and commercialize it (Cohen and Levinthal 1990). Combining these two ideas results in the "absorptive capacity theory of knowledge spillover entrepreneurship," which can summarized by stating that the process of knowledge commercialization by entrepreneurs does not rely only on the level of new knowledge or the speed of knowledge creation, but also on entrepreneurial absorptive capacity (Qian and Acs 2011). Accordingly, absorptive capacity, that is, individual ability to absorb external knowledge, is decisive for new business ventures. Human capital is one of the most important determinants of entrepreneurial absorptive capacity (Cohen and Levinthal 1990; Mowery and Oxley 1995; Mokyr 1990).

Qian et al. (2013) develop a three-phase structural model for regional systems of entrepreneurship built on the absorptive capacity theory of knowledge spillover entrepreneurship and find that the human capital aspect of entrepreneurial absorptive capacity is one of the most important driving forces for innovative new business formation. However, it could be argued that finding positive effects on new business formation of human capital when the same is defined as educational attainment is problematic because the type of knowledge acquired in HEIs seldom suffices as a basis for setting up a new business venture. This argument gave rise to a line of research that attempts to discover whether founders set up their new ventures directly after graduation or whether they instead prefer to work in an established firm before founding a new venture (Fritsch 2013). To date, strong empirical evidence on this issue is still lacking. Mueller (2010) finds that the majority of the founders of academic spin-offs start up their new ventures several years after graduation. Moreover, Mueller (2009) shows that start-ups established 3–5 years after the founders have graduated have higher growth. Moreover, Mueller (2009) argues that academic knowledge depreciates rapidly after graduation. However, the gained practical on-the-job experience more than compensates for the loss of academic knowledge.

Acs and Armington (2004a, 2006) empirically explore the relationship between regional levels of human capital in form of the share of people with a tertiary degree and new business formation. They find that human capital plays a decisive role in the regional variation of new business formation. The authors explain this positive influence of human capital on new business formation by the ability of highly educated people to acquire new knowledge and their awareness of the value of new ideas. Moreover, Harhoff (1999) finds a significantly positive relationship between highly qualified regional workforce and the emergence of innovative new businesses. Baptista and Mendonça (2010) find for Portuguese regions that human capital in the form of university graduates fosters knowledge-based new business formation, and Piva et al. (2011) find for Italian regions that human capital fosters new technology-based firms. Lee et al. (2004) analyze the interaction between social diversity, human capital, and new business formation. They find that social and cultural diversity attract a particular kind of human capital that, in turn, fosters innovative new business formation. Arvanitis and Stucki (2012) find that founders of innovative start-ups are characterized by university education and prior experience in R&D.

A great many studies analyze the impact of human capital on the success of new business formation (Storey 1994). Different indicators are used to reflect the performance and quality of start-ups, including initial size, employment growth, profits, survival, and the like. Moreover, two types of human capital are distinguished: generic human capital and specific human capital. Generic human capital is knowledge and qualification acquired predominantly through formal education. Specific human capital involves capabilities and skills necessary for running a new business, such as industry-specific knowledge and managerial experience (Becker 1964; Colombo et al. 2004).

Almus and Nerlinger (1999) find evidence of a positive correlation between founders' human capital and the employment growth of innovative start-ups in Germany. Almus (2002) and Brüderl and Preisendöfer (2000) argue that start-ups by founders with high academic degrees are more likely to be fast-growing firms. Koeller and Lechler (2006) find for a sample of German innovative start-ups that employment growth is significantly higher for ventures started by founders with more managerial experience. Gottschalk et al. (2010) show that the initial size of start-ups increases with higher levels of founder human capital.

Cooper et al. (1994) find for a sample of US start-ups that human capital in the form of education and industry-specific knowledge makes a positive contribution to their survival and growth. Åstebro and Bernhardt (2005) show that entrepreneurs with a high level of human capital have more greater amounts of start-up capital. Mata (1996) finds for a sample of Portuguese start-ups that highly educated entrepreneurs establish larger start-ups. In a recent study for Portugal, Baptista et al. (2014) find that a start-up's probability of surviving for 3 years on the market is positively influenced by it founder having both generic and specific forms of human capital as well as having been previously employed.

In a sample of Italian high-tech start-ups, Colombo et al. (2004) find that the initial size of start-ups is influenced by specific human capital in the form of professional, managerial, and entrepreneurial experience. In another study of Italian high-tech start-ups, Colombo and Grilli (2005, 2010) attribute start-ups' growth directly to the founders' higher education and industry-specific experience. The authors suggest that higher education in economics and management has more impact than higher education in technical fields. In contrast, technical work experience is more conducive to start-ups' growth than commercial experience. Moreover, they find an indirect effect of human capital on start-ups' growth via access to venture capital.

In a sample of Dutch start-ups, Pennings et al. (1998) find evidence suggesting that industry-specific human capital contributes to firm survival. Similarly, Van Praag and Cramer (2001) show a strong influence of education on start-up success. Bosma et al. (2004) show that although human capital influences all performance measures, the most important component of human capital is former experience in the industry in which the founder starts up the business venture. Moreover, more highly educated founders made more profit, while founders with experience as an employee created more employment. Van Praag (2003) shows that experience as an employee has a positive effect on the hazard of voluntary exits, and that experience in the industry has a significantly negative effect on hazard rate.

1.3 Aim and Structure

Empirical evidence shows that innovative start-ups and human capital tend to be concentrated in certain regions, suggesting that region-specific characteristics play a role in this phenomenon (Harhoff 1999; Bade and Nerlinger 2000; Berry and Glaeser 2005; Moretti 2004b). This thesis contributes to the literature concerned with this uneven geographic distribution of innovative start-ups and human capital.

Chapters 2 and 3 address the emergence and distribution of innovative start-ups. The theoretical framework behind the analyses in Chaps. 2 and 3 is the "knowledge spillover theory of entrepreneurship." This theory assumes that new business formation requires knowledge that resides in HEIs and incumbents (Acs et al. 2009, 2013). Knowledge spillovers from these institutions manifest as start-ups and, consequently, the geographic proximity to these institutions is important because of the "sticky" nature of knowledge (Anselin et al. 1997; Adams 2002; Asheim and Gertler 2005; Boschma 2005). The analyses in Chaps. 2 and 3 are based on a database rich with information about the regional knowledge base. The database includes information on all newly founded independent firms set up in German regions in the period 1995–2008. Innovative start-ups are identified by their affiliation with certain industries, based on the ZEW foundation panel.

Previous research has found strong indications that regional academic knowledge has a positive effect on innovative start-ups (Audretsch and Lehmann 2005; Audretsch et al. 2005; Baptista and Mendonça 2010; Hülsbeck and Pickavé 2014); however, the strength and significance of these positive effects varies across different innovative industries as well as across regions and the reasons for this variation remain undiscovered. Chapters 2 and 3 address this gap in the literature. Both chapters analyze the specific characteristics of HEIs that are most important for the emergence of innovative start-ups. Chapter 2 concerns itself with different characteristics of HEIs, such as their presence in the region, their size, and their quality. Chapter 3 explores the relative importance of various disciplines to the emergence of innovative business and also investigates the impact of different types of HEIs as well as of different transmission channels such as professors, students, external funds, etc.

Based on detailed information about the regional knowledge base, particularly about universities, the analysis in Chap. 2 finds that regional public research and education have a strong positive impact on new business formation in innovative industries but not in industries classified as non-innovative. Measures for the presence of public academic institutions have more of an impact on the formation of innovative new businesses than indicators reflecting the quality of these institutions. Moreover, there is relatively weak evidence for the interregional spillover of these effects. These results clearly demonstrate the importance of localized knowledge and, especially, of public research for the emergence of innovative new businesses.

Chapter 3 deepens the analyses of Chap. 2 by including other aspects of HEIs and their effects on innovative start-ups. Previous research provides sparse evidence for the influence of three HEI characteristics on innovative start-ups: discipline, type of HEI, and transmission channel (Audretsch et al. 2004; Audretsch and Lehmann 2005; Baptista and Mendonça 2010). Moreover, previous research distinguishes between only two research fields and ignores others. Furthermore, these studies are based on limited information about HEI activity in these fields and do not consider all types of HEIs. In addition, the question as to how exactly the knowledge that resides in HEIs spills over to new businesses remains unanswered. Who is it that transforms the academic knowledge into an innovative start-up—former students, faculty, or former researchers? (Zucker et al. 1998; Åstebro et al. 2012).

Chapter 3 investigates the role played by different fields of academic knowledge and various types of higher education institutions in the emergence of innovative start-ups in a region. This chapter shows that education and research in the applied and natural sciences have the strongest effect on the emergence of new businesses in innovative industries. When looking at the various indicators for these types of knowledge, the strongest effects are found for the number of professors, followed by the number of students and the amount of external funds attracted. Moreover, universities have the highest impact on innovative start-ups, presumably due to their research intensity.

Chapter 4 analyzes the geographic distribution of human capital across West German regions. Human capital is defined by educational attainment. Thus, regional human capital is the share of people with at least a tertiary degree relative to total employment force in the region. Since the concept of human capital centers on human beings, quality of life seems an appropriate explanation for the geography of human capital. Quality of life is a topic of increasing interest to the media, political circles, academia, and international organizations(Rappaport 2009; UNDP 2013; OECD 2011; WHO 2012). In the media, ranking cities and regions based on quality of life is a "hot" topic. For instance, a yearly report published in Europe—the "European Cities Monitor"—ranks the attractiveness of major European cities based on six broad categories: demographics, labor force, business costs, access to markets, operating environment, and quality of life (Cushman and Wakefield 2011). The consulting firm Mercer issues a yearly report that evaluates the quality of life in more than 200 cities worldwide based on criteria such as housing, climate, education, infrastructure, crime, communication, recreation, consumer services, and political and social environment. In political circles, quality of life is of great interest, being viewed as an instrument for improving the competitiveness of regions and countries. Comparisons (such as the rankings discussed above) between countries, regions, and cities in regard to economic, social, and environmental aspects can put a lot of public opinion pressure on policymakers. Thus, improving the quality of life offered by a region can be viewed as a strategy for attracting valuable assets such as human capital and firms to the region. For instance, in 2008, the former president of France, Nicholas Sarkozy, commissioned three economists—Joseph Stiglitz, Amartya Sen, and Jean-Paul Fitoussi—to make statistical information about the economy and society look better by assessing the feasibility of alternative measurement tools and indicators of economic and social progress in addition to GDP. Similarly, at the EU policy-making level, one of the basic goals in the framework of sustainable development is to achieve some degree of convergence among European regions and improvement of the quality of life. To this end, a palette of indicators has been established to inform policymakers (EU Committee of the Regions 1999; Moreno et al. 2005).

Although previous research has provided important insight into the forces that shape the geography of human capital, it has two major shortcomings. First, it relies on single factors such as the presence of universities, availability of consumer services, or tolerance (Berry and Glaeser 2005; Florida et al. 2008; Abel and Deitz 2012). Work employing a general framework that includes all relevant factors is rare, even though focusing on single factors may be inappropriate and result in misleading conclusions. Along these lines, Florida et al. (2008) note that universities, consumer services, and tolerance are more complementary than competitive in explaining the geography of human capital. If these factors are indeed complementary, then it is more accurate to use them together as several components of the quality of life. Second, in economics, the concept of quality of life is usually

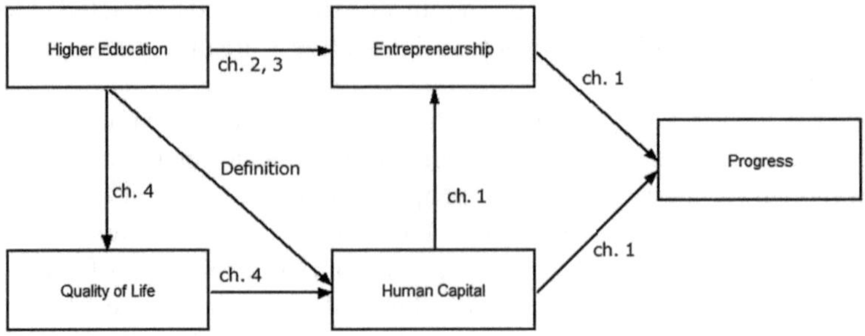

Fig. 1.2 Structure of the thesis

restricted to include only consumer services and amenities such as mild weather, recreation, and healthcare. In contrast, psychology and related fields of study employ a broad concept of quality of life that includes all relevant factors that make life more enjoyable.

Chapter 4 addresses both of this shortcomings. It discusses the concept of quality of life from different points of view. Specifically, it begins with fundamental human needs and builds a bridge from them to the concept of quality of life. In Chap. 4, quality of life is viewed as a multidimensional concept that has the power to explain the geography of human capital. The quality of life concept employed in Chap. 4 includes 27 elements that cover six major dimensions of human life. Analyzing the impact of all these elements simultaneously is not without difficulty; there are severe endogeneity problems that prevent causal interpretation of the empirical results. However, starting from fundamental human needs has the advantage of providing a theoretical basis for the empirical results. Moreover, the best available techniques—path models and structural equations—are used to analyze the impact of different elements of quality of life on the geography of human capital.

Figure 1.2 illustrates the broad structure of this thesis. The cornerstones upon which it is built are economic progress, innovative entrepreneurship, human capital, higher education, and quality of life. The main take-away point of the thesis is that higher education and public research in a region are the chief sources of economic progress. Both factors contribute to educating people and providing them with the qualifications necessary to perform valuable economic functions. They foster the emergence of innovative start-ups, which are important agents of change and progress. Finally, they improve the quality of life, which influences the geography of valuable assets for economic progress, including human capital.

References

Abel JR, Deitz R (2012) Do colleges and universities increase their region's human capital? J Econ Geogr 12:667–691

Acemoglu D, Dell M (2010) Productivity differences between and within countries. Am Econ J Macroecon 2:169–188

Acs ZJ, Armington C (2002) The determinants of regional variation in new firm formation. Region Stud 36:33–45
Acs ZJ, Armington C (2004a) The impact of geographic differences in human capital on service firm formation rates. J Urban Econ 56:244–278
Acs ZJ, Armington C (2004b) Employment growth and entrepreneurial activity in cities. Region Stud 38:911–927
Acs ZJ, Armington C (2006) Entrepreneurship, geography, and American economic growth. Cambridge University Press, New York, NY
Acs ZJ, Audretsch DB (eds) (1990) Innovation and small firms. MIT Press, Cambridge, MA
Acs ZJ, Braunerhjelm P, Audretsch DB, Carlsson B (2009) The knowledge spillover theory of entrepreneurship. Small Bus Econ 32:15–30
Acs ZJ, Audretsch DB, Lehmann E (2013) The knowledge spillover theory of entrepreneurship. Small Bus Econ 41:767–774
Adams JD (2002) Comparative localization of academic and industrial spillovers. J Econ Geogr 2:253–278
Aghion P, Howitt P (1998) Endogenous growth theory. MIT Press, Cambridge, MA
Almus M (2002) What characterizes a fast-growing firm? Appl Econ 34:1497–1508
Almus M, Nerlinger EA (1999) Growth of new technology-based firms: which factors matter? Small Bus Econ 13:141–154
Anselin L, Varga A, Acs ZJ (1997) Local geographic spillovers between university research and high technology innovations. J Urban Econ 42:422–448
Arrow KJ (1962) The economic implications of learning by doing. Rev Econ Stud 29:155–173
Arvanitis S, Stucki T (2012) What determines the innovation capability of firm founders? Indus Corp Change 21:1049–1084
Ashcroft B, Love JH (1996) Firm births and employment change in the British Counties: 1981–1989. Papers Region Sci 25:483–500
Asheim BT, Gertler MS (2005) The geography of innovation: regional innovation systems. In: Fagerberg J, Mowery DC, Nelson RR (eds) The Oxford handbook of innovation. Oxford University Press, Oxford, pp 291–317
Åstebro T, Bernhardt I (2005) The winner's curse of human capital. Small Bus Econ 24:63–78
Åstebro T, Bazzazian N, Braguinsky S (2012) Startups by recent university graduates and their faculty: implications for university entrepreneurship policy. Res Policy 41:663–677
Audretsch DB (1995a) Innovation and industry evolution. Int J Indus Organ 13:441–457
Audretsch DB (1995b) Innovation and industry evolution. MIT Press, Cambridge, MA
Audretsch DB, Lehmann EE (2005) Does the knowledge spillover theory of entrepreneurship hold for regions? Res Policy 34:1191–1202
Audretsch DB, Houweling P, Thurik AR (2000) Firm survival in the Netherlands. Rev Indus Organ 16:1–11
Audretsch DB, Lehmann EE, Warning S (2004) University spillovers: does the kind of science matter. Industry Innov 11:193–205
Audretsch DB, Lehmann EE, Warning S (2005) University spillovers and new firm location. Res Policy 34:1113–1122
Audretsch DB, Keilbach M, Lehmann EE (2006) Entrepreneurship and economic growth. Oxford University Press, Oxford
Bade F-J, Nerlinger EA (2000) The spatial distribution of new technology-based firms: empirical results for West-Germany. Papers Region Sci 79:155–176
Baptista R, Mendonça J (2010) Proximity to knowledge sources and the location of knowledge-based start-ups. Ann Region Sci 45:5–29
Baptista R, Preto MT (2011) Regional and business dynamics. Small Bus Econ 36:419–442
Baptista R, Karaöz M, Mendonça J (2014) The impact of human capital on the early success of necessity versus opportunity-based entrepreneurs. Small Bus Econ 42:831–847
Barro RJ, Sala-i-Martin X (2004) Economic growth, 2nd edn. MIT Press, Cambridge, MA
Baumol WJ (1968) Entrepreneurship in economic theory. Am Econ Rev Papers Proc 58:64–71

Baumol WJ (2004) Entrepreneurial enterprises, large established firms and other components of the free-market growth machine. Small Bus Econ 23:9–21

Baumol WJ, Panzar JC, Willig RD (eds) (1988) Contestable markets and the theory of industry structure, rev. ed. Harcourt Brace Jovanovich, San Diego, CA

Becker GS (1962) Investment in human capital: a theoretical analysis. J Polit Econ 70:9–49

Becker GS (1964) Human capital, 1st edn. Columbia University Press, New York, NY

Becker GS (1992) The economy of looking at life. Nobel lecture. http://www.nobelprize.org/nobel_prizes/economic-sciences/laureates/1992/becker-lecture.pdf

Becker GS (2002) The age of human capital. In: Lazear EP (ed) Education in the twenty-first century. Hoover Institution Press, Palo Alto, CA, pp 3–8

Becker GS (2007) Health as human capital: synthesis and extensions. Oxf Econ Papers 59:379–410

Benhabib J, Spiegel MM (1994) The role of human capital in economic development: evidence from aggregate cross-country data. J Monet Econ 34:143–173

Benhabib J, Spiegel MM (2005) Human capital and technology diffusion. In: Aghion P, Durlauf SN (eds) Handbook of economic growth, vol 1A. Elsevier, Amsterdam, pp 935–966

Bennett JM (2010) Medieval Europe: a short history. McGraw-Hill, New York, NY

Berry C, Glaeser EL (2005) The divergence of human capital levels across cities. Papers Region Sci 84:407–444

Birch DL (1979) The job generation process. MIT Program on Neighborhood and Regional Change (mimeo), Cambridge, MA

Birch DL (1987) Job creation in America: how our smallest companies put the most people to work. The Free Press, New York, NY

Boschma R (2005) Proximity and innovation: a critical assessment. Region Stud 39:61–74

Bosma N, Praag M, van Thurik R, de Wit G (2004) The value of human and social capital investments for the business performance of startups. Small Bus Econ 23:227–236

Bosma N, Stam E, Schutjens V (2011) Creative destruction and regional productivity growth: evidence from the Dutch manufacturing and services industries. Small Bus Econ 36:401–418

Bouchard P (1998) Training and work: myths about human capital. In: Scott S, Spencer B, Thomas A (eds) Learning for life: Canadian readings in adult education. Thompson Educational Publishing, Toronto, pp 128–139

Brüderl J, Preisendöfer P (2000) Fast growing businesses: empirical evidence from a German study. Int J Sociol 30:45–70

Cantillon R (1755/2010) Essai sur la Nature du Commerce en Général. Ludwig von Mises Institute, Auburn, English translation: An essay on economic theory

Carlsson B, Braunerhjelm P, McKelvey M, Olofsson C, Persson L, Ylinenpää H (2013) The evolving domain of entrepreneurship research. Small Bus Econ 41:913–930

Carree MA, Thurik R (2010) The impact of entrepreneurship on economic growth. In: Acs ZJ, Audretsch DB (eds) Handbook of entrepreneurship research, 2nd edn. Springer, New York, NY, pp 557–594

Caselli F, Coleman JW (2006) The world technology frontier. Am Econ Rev 96:499–522

Ciccone A, Papaioannou E (2009) Human capital, the structure of production, and growth. Rev Econ Stat 91:66–82

Clark G (2005) Human capital, fertility, and the industrial revolution. J Eur Econ Assoc 3:505–515

Clark G (2007) A farewell to Alms: a brief economic history of the world. Princeton University Press, Oxfordshire

Coe D, Helpman E (1995) International R&D spillovers. Eur Econ Rev 39:859–887

Cohen WM, Levinthal DA (1990) Absorptive capacity: a new perspective on learning and innovation. Admin Sci Quart 35:128–152

Colombo MG, Grilli L (2005) Founders' human capital and the growth of new technology-based firms: a competence-based view. J Bus Venturing 25:610–626

Colombo MG, Grilli L (2010) On growth drivers of high-tech start-ups: exploring the role of founders' human capital and venture capital. Res Policy 34:795–816

Colombo MG, Delmastro M, Grilli L (2004) Entrepreneurs' human capital and the start-up size of new technology-based firms. Int J Indus Organ 22:1183–1211
Cooper AC, Gimeno-Gascon FJ, Woo CY (1994) Initial human capital and financial capital as predictors of new venture performance. J Bus Venturing 9:371–395
Cornelius B, Landström H, Persson O (2006) Entrepreneurial studies: the dynamic research front of a developing social science. Entrepreneurship Theory Pract 30:375–398
Currie J, Moretti E (2003) Mother's education and the intergenerational transmission of human capital: evidence from college openings. Quart J Econ 118:1495–1532
Cushman & Wakefield (2011) European cities monitor 2011. http://www.cushmanwakefield.co.uk/en-gb/research-and-insight/2012/european-cities-monitor-2011/
Davis SJ, Haltiwanger JC, Schuh S (1996a) Job creation and destruction. MIT Press, Cambridge, MA
Davis SJ, Haltiwanger JC, Schuh S (1996b) Small business and job creation: dissecting the myth and reassessing the facts. Small Bus Econ 8:297–315
De la Fuente A (2002) On the sources of convergence: a close look at the Spanish regions. Eur Econ Rev 46:569–599
De la Fuente A, Donénech R (2001) Schooling data, technological diffusion, and the neoclassical model. Am Econ Rev 91:323–327
Dee TS (2004) Are there civic returns to education? J Publ Econ 88:1697–1720
Di Liberto A (2008) Education and Italian regional development. Econ Educ Rev 27:94–107
Eaton J, Eckstein E (1997) Cities and growth: theory and evidence from France and Japan. Reg Sci Urban Econ 27:443–474
Engelbrecht H-J (2003) Human capital and economic growth: cross-section evidence for OECD countries. Econ Rec 79:40–51
EU Committee of the Regions (1999) Evaluation quality of life in European regions. Commission of the European Communities, Brussels
Falck O (2007) Mayflies and long-distance runners: the effects of new business formation on industry growth. Appl Econ Lett 14:1919–1922
Florida R, Mellander C, Stolarick K (2008) Inside the black box of regional development – Human capital, the creative class and tolerance. J Econ Geogr 8:615–649
Fritsch M (1996) Turbulence and growth in West-Germany: a comparison of evidence by regions and industries. Rev Indus Organ 11:231–251
Fritsch M (1997) New firms and regional employment change. Small Bus Econ 9:437–447
Fritsch M (2008) How does new business formation affect regional development? Introduction to the special issue. Small Bus Econ 30:1–14
Fritsch M (2011) Start-ups in innovative industries—Causes and effects. In: Audretsch DB, Falck O, Heblich S, Lederer A (eds) Handbook of innovation and entrepreneurship. Elgar, Cheltenham, pp 365–381
Fritsch M (2013) New business formation and regional development—A survey and assessment of the evidence. Found Trends Entrepreneurship 9:249–364
Fritsch M, Noseleit F (2013a) Investigating the anatomy of the employment effects of new business formation. Cambridge J Econ 37:349–377
Fritsch M, Noseleit F (2013b) Start-ups, long- and short-term survivors, and their contribution to employment growth. J Evol Econ 23:719–733
Fritsch M, Schilder D (2008) Does venture capital investment really require spatial proximity? An empirical investigation. Environ Plann A 40:2114–2131
Fritsch M, Schroeter A (2011a) Why does the effect of new business formation differ across regions? Small Bus Econ 36:383–400
Fritsch M, Schroeter A (2011b) Does quality make a difference? Employment effects of high- and low-quality start-ups. Jena Economic Research Papers # 001–2011, Friedrich Schiller University and Max Planck Institute of Economics Jena
Fritsch M, Weyh A (2006) How large are the direct employment effects of new businesses? – An empirical investigation. Small Bus Econ 27:245–260

Fritsch M, Noseleit F, Schindele Y (2014) Surviving against the tide: the role of region and industry performance for new business survival. Friedrich Schiller University (mimeo), Jena

Gartner WB (1990) What are we talking about when we talk about entrepreneurship? J Bus Venturing 5:15–28

Gemmell N (1996) Evaluating the impacts of human capital stocks and accumulation on economic growth: some new evidence. Oxf Bull Econ Stat 58:9–28

Gennaioli N, La Porta R, Lopez-De-Silanes F, Shleifer A (2013) Human capital and regional development. Quart J Econ 128:105–164

Geroski P (1995) What do we know about entry? Int J Indus Organ 13:421–440

Glaeser EL, Saiz A (2004) The rise of the skilled city. Brooking-Wharton Papers Urban Aff 5:47–94

Glaeser EL, Scheinkman JA, Shleifer A (1995) Economic growth in a cross-section of cities. J Monet Econ 36:117–143

Glaeser EL, La Porta R, Shleifer A (2004) Do institutions cause growth? J Econ Growth 9:271–303

Gottlieb PD, Fogarty M (2003) Educational attainment and metropolitan growth. Econ Dev Quart 17:325–336

Gottschalk S, Müller K, Niefert M (2010) Entry strategies, founder's human capital and start-up size. Int J Entrepreneurship Small Bus 11:403–423

Harhoff D (1999) Firm formation and regional spillovers – Evidence from Germany. Econ Innov New Technol 8:27–55

Hébert RF, Link AN (1989) In search of the meaning of entrepreneurship. Small Bus Econ 1:39–49

Hébert RF, Link AN (2006) Historical perspectives on the entrepreneur. Found Trends Entrepreneurship 2:261–408

Herlihy D (1997) The black death and the transformation of the west. Harvard University Press, Cambridge

Hubbard RG (2008) Nondestructive creation: entrepreneurship and management research in the study of growth. J Policy Model 30:595–602

Huber F (2012) Do clusters really matter for innovation practices in information technology? Questioning the significance of technological knowledge spillovers. J Econ Geogr 12:107–126

Hülsbeck M, Pickavé EN (2014) Regional knowledge production as determinant of high-technology entrepreneurship: empirical evidence for Germany. Int Entrepreneurship Manag J 10:121–138

Jacobs J (1961) The death and life of great American cities. Random House, New York, NY

Jacobs J (1969) The economy of cities. Vintage, New York, NY

Kiker BF (1966) The historical roots of the concept of human capital. J Polit Econ 74:481–499

Kirzner I (1973) Competition and entrepreneurship. University of Chicago Press, Chicago, IL

Klenow P, Rodriguez-Clare A (2005) Externalities and growth. In: Aghion P, Durlauf S (eds) Handbook of economic growth, vol 1A. Elsevier, Amsterdam, pp 817–861

Klepper S (2007) Disagreements, spinoffs, and the evolution of Detroit as the capital of the US automobile industry. Manag Sci 53:616–636

Klepper S, Thompson P (2007) Spinoff entry in high-tech industries: motives and consequences. In: Malerba F, Brusoni S (eds) Perspectives on innovation. Cambridge University Press, Cambridge, pp 187–218

Koeller CT, Lechler TG (2006) Employment growth in high-tech new ventures. J Labor Res 27:135–147

Krueger A, Lindahl M (2001) Education for growth: why and for whom? J Econ Lit 49:1101–1136

Le T, Gibson J, Oxley L (2003) Cost- and income-based measures of human capital. J Econ Surv 17:271–307

Lee SY, Florida R, Acs ZJ (2004) Creativity and entrepreneurship: a regional analysis of new firm formation. Region Stud 38:879–891

Lochner L, Moretti E (2004) The effect of education on crime: evidence from prison inmates, arrests, and self-reports. Am Econ Rev 94:155–189
Love RS (2006) Maritime exploration in the age of discovery, 1415–1800. Greenwood, Westport, CT
Lucas RE Jr (1988) On the mechanics of economic development. J Monet Econ 22:3–42
Lutz E, Bender M, Achleitner AK, Kaserer C (2013) Importance of spatial proximity between venture capital investors and investees in Germany. J Bus Res 66:2346–2354
Mankiw NG, Romer D, Weil D (1992) A contribution to the empirics of economic growth. Quart J Econ 107:407–437
Marginson S (1997) Markets in education. Allen & Unwin, St. Leonard's
Marshall A (1890/1920) Principles of economics, 8th edn. MacMillan, London
Mata J (1996) Markets, entrepreneurs and the size of new firms. Econ Lett 52:89–94
McClelland DC (1961) The achieving society. D. van Nostrand, Princeton, NJ
McFadden D (2008) Human capital accumulation and depreciation. Appl Econ Perspect 30:379–385
Metzger G, Rammer C (2009) Unternehmensdynamik in Forschungs- und Wissensintensiven Wirtschaftszweigen in Deutschland (English: Firm Dynamics in Research- and Knowledge Intensive Industries in Germany). Studien zum deutschen Innovationssystem Nr. 05-2009, ZEW, Mannheim (mimeo)
Milligan K, Moretti E, Oreopoulos P (2004) Does education improve citizenship? Evidence from the United States and the United Kingdom. J Publ Econ 88:1667–1695
Mincer J (1958) Investment in human capital and personal income distribution. J Polit Econ 66:281–302
Mincer J (1974) Schooling, earnings, and experience. Columbia University Press, New York, NY
Mincer J (1981) Human capital and economic growth. National Bureau of Economic Research (NBER), Working Paper no. 803
Mokyr J (1990) The lever of riches. Oxford University Press, New York, NY
Moreno R, Royuela V, Vayá E (2005) Monitoring the Lisbon Strategy's targets. Investigaciones Regionales 7:155–192
Moretti E (2004a) Estimating the social returns to higher education: evidence from longitudinal and repeated cross-section data. J Economet 121:175–212
Moretti E (2004b) Human capital externalities in cities. In: Henderson JV, Thisse JF (eds) Handbook of urban and regional economics, vol 4. Elsevier, Amsterdam, pp 2244–2291
Mowery DC, Oxley JE (1995) Inward technology transfer and competitiveness: the role of national innovation systems. Cambridge J Econ 19:67–93
Mueller K (2009) Employment growth in newly established firms – Is there evidence for academic entrepreneur's human capital depreciation? ZEW Discussion Papers no. 09-050, Mannheim (mimeo)
Mueller K (2010) Academic spin-off's transfer speed—Analyzing the time from leaving university to venture. Res Policy 39:189–199
Mulligan CB, Sala-i-Martin X (2000) Measuring aggregate human capital. J Econ Growth 5:215–252
Murphy KM, Shleifer A, Vishny RW (1991) The allocation of talent: implications for growth. Quart J Econ 106:503–530
Nelson RR, Phelps ES (1966) Investment in humans, technological diffusion, and economic growth. Am Econ Rev 56:69–75
Neumark D, Wall B, Zhang J (2011) Do small business create more jobs? New evidence for the United States from the national establishment time series. Rev Econ Stat 93:16–29
OECD: Organisation for Economic Co-operation and Development (1998a) Fostering entrepreneurship. OECD, Paris
OECD: Organisation for Economic Co-operation and Development (1998b) Human capital investment: an international comparison. OECD, Paris

OECD: Organisation for Economic Co-operation and Development (2011) How's life? Measuring well-being. OECD, Paris
Pennings L, Lee K, van Witteloostuijn A (1998) Human capital, social capital, and firm dissolution. Acad Manag J 41:425–440
Pereira J, St. Aubyn M (2009) What level of education matters most for growth? Evidence from Portugal. Econ Educ Rev 28:67–73
Piergiovanni R, Carree MA, Santarelli E (2012) Creative industries, new business formation, and regional economic growth. Small Bus Econ 39:539–560
Piva E, Grilli L, Rossi-Lamastra C (2011) The creation of high-tech entrepreneurial ventures at the local level: the role of local competences and communication infrastructures. Industry Innov 18:563–580
Polasek W, Scharzbauer W, Sellner R (2011) Human capital and regional growth in Switzerland. Rev Econ Anal 3:46–58
Pritchett L (2001) Where has all the education gone? World Bank Econ Rev 15:367–391
Psacharopoulos G (1985) Education for development: an analysis of investment choices. Oxford University Press, Oxford
Qian H, Acs ZJ (2011) An absorptive capacity theory of knowledge spillover entrepreneurship. Small Bus Econ 40:185–197
Qian H, Acs ZJ, Stough RR (2013) Regional systems of entrepreneurship: the nexus of human capital, knowledge and new firm formation. J Econ Geogr 13:559–587
Rappaport J (2009) The increasing importance of quality of life. J Econ Geogr 9:779–804
Reinert H, Reinert ES (2006) Creative destruction in economics: Nietzsche, Sombart, Schumpeter. Eur Heritage Econ Social Sci 3:55–85
Reynolds PD (1994) Autonomous firm dynamics and economic growth in the United States, 1986–90. Region Stud 27:429–442
Reynolds PD (1999) Creative destruction: source or symptom of economic growth? In: Acs ZJ, Carlsson B, Karlsson C (eds) Entrepreneurship, small and medium-sized enterprises and the macroeconomy. Cambridge University Press, Cambridge, pp 97–136
Romer P (1986) Increasing returns and long-run growth. J Polit Econ 94:1002–1037
Romer P (1990) Human capital and growth: theory and evidence. Carnegie-Rochester Conf Ser Publ Policy 32:251–286
Say JB (1803/1880) A treatise on political economy: the production, distribution, and consumption of wealth. Batoche Books, Kitchener, ON
Schäfer D, Schilder D (2009) Smart capital in German start-ups – An empirical analysis. Venture Capital 11:163–183
Schultz TW (1961) Investment in human capital. Am Econ Rev 51:1–17
Schumpeter JA (1934) The theory of economic development. Cambridge University Press, Cambridge, German Original Edition (1911) Die Theorie Wirtschaftlicher Entwicklung. Berlin: Duncker & Humblot
Schumpeter JA (1942) Capitalism, socialism and democracy. Harper and Row, New York, NY
Shapiro JM (2006) Smart cities: quality of life, productivity, and the growth effects of human capital. Rev Econ Stat 88:324–335
Simon CJ (1998) Human capital and metropolitan employment growth. J Urban Econ 43:223–243
Simon C, Nardinelli C (1996) The talk of the town: human capital, information and the growth of English cities, 1861–1961. Explor Econ Hist 33:384–413
Simon CJ, Nardinelli C (2002) Human capital and the rise of American cities, 1900–1990. Reg Sci Urban Econ 32:59–96
Smith A (1776/1976) An inquiry into the nature and causes of the wealth of nations. Glasgow Edition. Clarendon Press, Oxford
Solow RM (1956) A contribution to the theory of economic growth. Quart J Econ 70:65–94
Solow RM (1957) Technical change and the aggregate production function. Rev Econ Stat 39:312–320
Storey DJ (1994) Understanding the small business sector. Routledge, London

Suedekum J (2008) Convergence of the skill composition across German regions. Reg Sci Urban Econ 38:148–159

Swan TW (1956) Economic growth and capital accumulation. Econ Rec 32:334–361

Tamur R (2002) Human capital and the switch from agriculture to industry. J Econ Dyn Control 27:207–242

Topel R (1999) Labor markets and economic growth. In: Ashenfelter O, Card D (eds) Handbook of labor economics, vol 3. Elsevier, Amsterdam, pp 2943–2984

Ullman EL (1958) Regional development and the geography of concentration. Papers Proc Region Sci Assoc 4:179–198

UNDP: United Nations Development Programme (2013) Human development report. United Nations, New York, NY

van Praag CM (2003) Business survival and success of young small business owners. Small Bus Econ 21:1–17

van Praag CM, Cramer JS (2001) The roots of entrepreneurship and labour demand: individual ability and low risk aversion. Economica 68:45–62

van Zanden JL (2009) The skill premium and the "Great Divergence". Eur Rev Econ Hist 13:121–153

Vandenbussche J, Aghion P, Meghir C (2006) Growth, distance to frontier and composition of human capital. J Econ Growth 11:97–127

WHO: World Health Organization (2012) Mental health: evidence and research. Department of Mental Health, WHO

Winter SG (1984) Schumpeterian competition in alternative technological regimes. J Econ Behav Organ 5:287–320

Winters JV (2013) Human capital externalities and employment differences across metropolitan areas of the USA. J Econ Geogr 13:799–822

Wolff E (2012) Spillovers, linkages, and productivity growth in the US economy, 1958–2007. In: Andersson M, Johansson B, Karlsson C, Lööf H (eds) Innovation and growth. Oxford University Press, Oxford, pp 233–265

Zucker LG, Darby MR, Brewer MB (1998) Intellectual human capital and the birth of US biotechnology enterprises. Am Econ Rev 88:290–306

Chapter 2
Regional Public Research, Higher Education, and Innovative Start-Ups

2.1 Introduction

New businesses are an important source of economic growth (Fritsch 2013), especially those start-ups that pose a competitive threat to incumbent firms by introducing a significant innovation. The available data suggest that only a small fraction of all start-ups is of such quality and that their geographic distribution is highly uneven (Fritsch 2011). According to the knowledge spillover theory of entrepreneurship (Acs et al. 2009), new businesses in general, and highly innovative start-ups in particular, are manifestations of knowledge spillover from extant knowledge sources. Hence, the number and the types of new business are shaped considerably by the regional knowledge base, and the emergence of innovative start-ups can be especially expected in regions with significant amounts of knowledge, private or public.

This chapter analyzes the role played by regional knowledge, particularly academic knowledge, in the emergence of innovative start-ups in Germany. This study makes several significant contributions to this field of research.[1] First, all start-ups in innovative and knowledge-intensive industries are included.[2] Second, the used data comprise much more detailed information about higher education institutes (HEIs), such as universities, which allows to identify those parts and features of a region's academic knowledge base that are most relevant for

[1]Earlier studies for Germany are Harhoff (1999), Bade and Nerlinger (2000), Audretsch and Lehmann (2005), Audretsch et al. (2005), and Hülsbeck and Pickavé (2014).

[2]Harhoff's (1999) analysis is limited to start-ups in electrical machinery and the mechanical engineering industry. Audretsch and Lehmann (2005) and Audretsch et al. (2005) focus on 281 firms that made an initial public offering (IPO) in Germany between March 1997 and March 2002. Since these firms may have been set up considerably in advance of making an IPO, their founding date is only vaguely defined.

R. Aamoucke, *Innovative Start-Ups and the Distribution of Human Capital*, Contributions to Economics, DOI 10.1007/978-3-319-44462-8_2

innovative start-ups.[3] Third, while nearly all the earlier studies are based on pure cross-sections, the analysis in this chapter uses relatively long time series data that allow to employ panel estimation techniques. Fourth, the used data include more recent periods. Hence, given the changing nature of German universities, the results and conclusions of this chapter are not only more up to date but also more relevant than the results of studies that investigate the start-ups of the early 1990s. Fifth, the analyses of this chapter include Eastern Germany, the part of the country that was under a socialist regime until 1989 and a region that is neglected in some of the earlier studies (Harhoff 1999; Bade and Nerlinger 2000).

The following section (Sect. 2.2) highlights the theoretical relationship among the three cornerstones of the analysis—innovative start-ups, geography, and knowledge—and reviews previous research on the spatial determinants of innovative new business formation. Section 2.3 discusses the data and provides an overview of the geographic distribution of innovative start-ups in Germany. Section 2.4 introduces the estimation approach; the results of the multivariate analysis are presented in Sect. 2.5. Section 2.6 concludes.

2.2 Knowledge, Innovative Start-Ups, and Geography

2.2.1 Theory: Innovative Start-Ups as Knowledge Spillovers

The knowledge spillover theory of entrepreneurship (Acs et al. 2009) is based on the assumption that starting an innovative venture requires a combination of knowledge and entrepreneurial talent. Since a large part of the necessary knowledge resides in incumbent firms, universities, and non-university public research organizations, this approach regards innovative start-ups as a form of knowledge spillover, that is, the institutional knowledge spills over into the newly founded business. The microeconomic assumption behind this process is that employees of the incumbent organizations try to commercialize certain parts of the incumbent's knowledge by starting a venture of their own. Empirical research shows that a typical motivation for many such spin-offs is disagreement between management and the potential entrepreneur over the realization of an idea, be it because of different perceptions of the idea's economic potential, the risk involved in bringing the innovation to the marketplace, or for other reasons (Klepper 2009).Hence, it is further assumed that the knowledge commercialized by the innovative start-up would not be exploited if left in the incumbent organization.[4]

[3]Information about the non-university research institutions in the region are also included, which are neglected in Audretsch and Lehmann (2005), Audretsch et al. (2005), and Hülsbeck and Pickavé (2014).

[4]For the researcher, starting an own business is often the only way to have an idea realized. For a more detailed discussion of this point, see Audretsch et al. (2006) and Acs et al. (2009).

In the process of entrepreneurial knowledge spillover, there are at least two reasons why the regional dimension, in terms of geographic proximity, should be relevant. First, new knowledge does not flow freely across space but tends to be regionally bound (Anselin et al. 1997; Adams 2002; Asheim and Gertler 2005; Boschma 2005). Second, founders show a pronounced tendency to locate their firm in close spatial proximity to their former workplace or to the place where they reside (Figueiredo et al. 2002; Dahl and Sorenson 2009). Hence, innovative entrepreneurship is a "regional event" (Feldman 2001; Sternberg 2009), meaning that the regional knowledge stock is an important source for the emergence of new businesses.

There are a number of features of the regional knowledge base that—according to the knowledge spillover theory of entrepreneurship—can be expected to be particularly conducive to the emergence of innovative new businesses. One of these features is the level of research and development (R&D), which plays an important role in the creation of entrepreneurial opportunities. Hence, there should be a pronounced correspondence between the spatial distribution of R&D activity and innovative start-ups. The presence of universities, as well as of non-university public research institutes, may be particularly relevant in at least two respects. First, these institutes collect, generate, and store knowledge and make it available in the region, e.g., by providing innovation-related services and by cooperating with private firms. Second, in fulfilling their purpose of educating students, these institutions are transferring knowledge and, eventually, making it available in the labor market. Since the vast majority of founders of innovative businesses have had at least some higher education (Fritsch 2011), universities can be regarded as an important source of innovative start-ups. Since some knowledge is specific to certain industries and technologies, the regional industry structure is an important characteristic of the regional knowledge stock.[5] Hence, the employment share in innovative industries can be expected to be significantly linked to the number of start-ups in this type of industry.

Based on the assumption that the emergence of innovative new businesses is a knowledge spillover, a positive relationship between the size of the respective knowledge base and the number of innovative start-ups is expected. Specifically, the amount of resources devoted to the creation of new knowledge via R&D activity should be related to the number of innovative start-ups. Two more factors may have a positive impact on the likelihood that such a knowledge spillover by start-ups will occur: the employment share of small businesses and the size and density of the region.

There are three reasons why the share of small and, especially, young business employment could be important for the emergence of start-ups. First, on average, small-firm employees have a higher propensity to start their own business than do employees of larger firms (Parker 2009; Elfenbein et al. 2010). Second, a high share

[5]This corresponds to the observation that founders are likely to set up their business in the industry in which they previously worked (Fritsch and Falck 2007).

of small-firm employment in a region indicates a high share of industries with low minimum efficient size, which implies low barriers to entry. Accordingly, the high start-up rates found in regions with high shares of small-firm employment may be explained by the prevalence of industries with low minimum efficient size (Fritsch and Falck 2007). Third, a high share of employment in small firms implies the presence of relatively many entrepreneurial role models, which may have some influence on the decision to start an own business (Bosma et al. 2012).

The size and density of a region should have a positive effect on the number of innovative start-ups for at least two reasons. First, due to the limited mobility of knowledge across space, the potential for knowledge spillovers in a region rises with the number of potential recipients located in spatial proximity. Second, large agglomerations often provide an abundant supply of other important resources required for starting a business, such as financial resources and qualified labor.

2.2.2 Previous Work on the Geographic Distribution of Innovative Start-Ups

Most empirical studies on innovative new businesses identify them by their affiliation with certain industries that are classified as being innovative. A well-known classification of industries based on innovativeness is that of the OECD (2005), which chiefly categorizes industries by their R&D intensity. The OECD classification deals only with manufacturing industries, but certain service-sector industries, the "knowledge-intensive services," may also be regarded as being innovative since they also spend rather significant shares of their resources on R&D.[6] In the following, knowledge-intensive services are viewed as a subgroup of the innovative industries.

Innovative industries tend to be highly concentrated in space (Markusen et al. 1986; Bade and Nerlinger 2000; Storey and Tether 1998). A number of previous analyses of the regional distribution of innovative start-ups in Germany have shown a high concentration in larger cities and agglomerations.[7] Bade and Nerlinger (2000) and Harhoff (1999) compared the results of multivariate analyses for start-ups in innovative industries with models for new businesses in sectors that are not regarded as being particularly innovative. Both studies find that universities,

[6]Since many service firms do not have a standardized product program but provide customer-specific services, they are not innovative in the same sense as manufacturing firms. Hence, service industries that may be relevant for innovation are defined as such based on the knowledge intensity of their inputs. These knowledge-intensive service industries include, for example, "computer services," "research and development in natural sciences and engineering," and "business consultancy." For definitions of these groups of industries, see Grupp and Legler (2000) and OECD (2005). For a review of different methods of identifying innovative businesses, see Fritsch (2011).

[7]Audretsch and Lehmann (2005), Bade and Nerlinger (2000), Harhoff (1999), Hülsbeck and Pickavé (2014), Lasch et al. (2013).

non-university public research institutes, and private sector R&D have a statistically significant positive effect only for start-ups in innovative industries, not for new businesses in industries that are not classified as being innovative. Harhoff (1999) also finds a significantly positive relationship between a high qualification of the regional workforce and the emergence of innovative new businesses. Audretsch and Lehmann (2005) and Audretsch et al. (2005) showed that there is a significantly positive relationship between the number of start-ups in innovative manufacturing and the presence of a university in a region as well as the number of students.

When analyzing the determinants of the regional number of start-ups in high technology and technologically advanced manufacturing industries, Hülsbeck and Pickavé (2014) identify a positive effect of several variables that reflect the activities of universities. According to their results, the number of university patents and the number of PhD students per professor seem to be conducive to new business formation in high-technology industries; other university-related variables, however, have unexpected and statistically significant negative signs.[8]

Baptista and Mendonça (2010) investigate the geographic distribution and determinants of start-ups in innovative industries in Portugal. According to their analysis, the number of students, as well as the number of university graduates, has a significantly positive effect on the number of regional start-ups in all innovative industries, whereas the overall education level of the regional workforce is statistically significant only for the start-ups in knowledge-intensive services. Another significantly positive influence was found for the number of firms in innovative industries per 1000 inhabitants, which can be regarded as a measure of relevant private-sector knowledge. Distinguishing between students and graduates in different academic fields, Baptista and Mendonça (2010) identify a statistically significant effect for students and graduates in engineering. The number of students and graduates in social sciences has an effect only for new business in knowledge-intensive services, not for start-ups in innovative manufacturing.

In another analysis of Portuguese regions, Baptista et al. (2011) study the effect the establishment of a university has on the level of new business formation in the region. They find a positive effect on new business formation in innovative industries taken as a whole, but not for subsamples of innovative manufacturing and or knowledge-intensive services, which may be due to there being very few start-ups of these types. They conclude that setting up a university in a region contributes to that region becoming more of a knowledge-based economy.

In a study of Italian provinces, Piva et al. (2011) find a significantly positive effect of the number of patents per capita as well as a weakly significant effect of the share of people with a tertiary degree in the region on the emergence of start-ups in innovative manufacturing. For new businesses in knowledge-intensive services, the number of patents per capita continued to be statistically significant, but the share of persons with a tertiary degree was not. Remarkably, the share of

[8]The reason for these mixed results may be high correlation among the different indicators (see Sect. 2.4).

researchers in the resident population had no effect. Bonaccorsi et al. (2014) specifically investigate the effect of different types of knowledge and channels of knowledge transfer on the emergence of knowledge-intensive new businesses in Italy. The results of their analysis suggest that universities play a significant role, particularly if the university specializes in engineering or the medical sciences. Including alternative indicators for universities and regional innovation activity, the authors find positive effects for the presence of a university in the region, for the number of university graduates and university staff, for the number of publications that are listed in the ISI Web of Science, and for the number of patents. It is interesting that among these alternative indicators, the dummy variable for the mere presence of at least one university in the region leads to the highest coefficient. Other variables that have a statistically significant positive effect are the share of firms that belong to innovative industries in the regional firm population, population density, the share of unemployed persons in the regional workforce, value added per population, and the presence of a business incubator center in the region. Bonaccorsi et al. (2014) interact the different university-related indicators with dummy variables for location in either South Italy or North Italy. The results indicate that universities have an effect on the formation of innovative new businesses only in the southern part of the country, not in the economically more developed regions of northern Italy.

Summarizing the empirical evidence on the emergence of innovative new businesses in geographic space, there is a strong indication for a very important positive effect of regional knowledge, especially of HEIs. The strength and significance of this positive effect, however, varies between subsectors of innovative industries[9] as well as across regions, and the reasons behind these variations are far from clear. Moreover, it is also less than clear what specific characteristics of universities and other public research institutions are most important for the emergence of innovative start-ups. Is it their mere presence in the region, their size in terms of the number of students and professors and the amount of R&D activity, or is it the quality of research that is important for the emergence of innovative start-ups?[10] This lack of knowledge is chiefly due to data limitations, especially since what information there is usually covers only some selected aspects of what universities do. Since the data used in the analyses of this chapter provide richer information on different types of university activities, this chapter will attempt to identify which types of activity have the strongest effect on the regional formation of innovative new businesses.

[9]A study of the USA by Bania et al. (1993) shows that there may also be considerable differences in the effect of different regional knowledge sources among four-digit industries that are classified as highly innovative.

[10]An indication for different effects of size and quality-related university indicators is provided by Fritsch and Slavtchev (2007), who find that only the volume of external funds has a positive effect on regional innovation activity; no such positive effect can be found for indicators that are related to size, such as the number of professors and academic personnel or the number of students and of graduates.

2.3 Data and Descriptive Statistics

2.3.1 Data

The data on start-ups are from the Founder Panel of the Center for European Economic Research (ZEW-Mannheim) and include nearly every newly founded independent firm during the period 1995–2008 (ZEW 2011). These data are based on information from the largest German credit rating agency (Creditreform). It covers all private sectors in Germany and identifies innovative new businesses based on their affiliation with certain industries. The common classification of industries according to their presumed innovativeness is used which distinguishes among (1) high-technology manufacturing industries that devote more than 8.5 % of their input to R&D activity, (2) technologically advanced manufacturing industries with an R&D intensity between 3.5 and 8.5 %, and (3) technology-oriented services, which cover some selected service industries closely related to innovation and new technology (Grupp and Legler 2000; OECD, 2005; Gehrke et al. 2010). The technology-oriented services are a subgroup of knowledge-intensive services and include industries that are particularly related to innovation activity, such as "architectural and engineering activities," "technical consultancy," and "technical testing and analysis." In addition, all models will be also run for those industries not classified as innovative or knowledge intensive. A main problem of such a classification is that industry affiliation can be "fuzzy," seeing as there are innovative and not so innovative firms in all industries. Given the limited availability of data on innovation, however, this is often the only feasible way to identify new businesses as being innovative.[11]

Most of the information on the independent variables comes from one of two sources. Data on regional private-sector employment and R&D employment come from the German Employment Statistics, which covers all employees subject to compulsory social insurance contributions (Spengler 2008). The second data source is the University Statistics of the German Federal Statistical Office, which provides detailed information about every university in Germany (Statistisches Bundesamt, various volumes). Data on unemployment are from the German Employment Agency (*Bundesagentur für Arbeit*). The spatial framework of the analysis is based on the 402 German districts (*Kreise*). To attain functional regions, those districts that only encompass cities (*kreisfreie Stadt, urban district*) are merged with the surrounding territorial districts, resulting in 325 regions.[12]

The available data from the German University Statistics aid identification of five types of higher education institutions (HEI): regular universities (*Universitäten*), medical schools (*Universitätsklinike*n), *Fachhochschulen*, which are also called universities of applied sciences, universities of public administration

[11]See Fritsch (2011) for the classification of German industries as "innovative," "technologically advanced," or "technology-intensive services."

[12]For an official translation for the German administrative divisions, see EC-DGT (2014).

(*Verwaltungshochschulen*), and art colleges (*Kunsthochschulen*). Distinguishing among these types is important because of significant differences in both their research and their educational profiles. Medical schools at universities also have hospitals and are another type of specialized tertiary education. Due to their special characteristics, a medical school at a university is counted as a separate university. The German *Fachhochschulen* are mainly intended to provide undergraduate education, while research is predominantly the domain of the regular universities. Moreover, *Fachhochschulen* offer predominantly engineering and management courses, while the regular universities usually cover a very broad range of academic disciplines, including a number of non-technical departments, the research results of which are rarely commercialized by private-sector innovators. The main mission of the universities of public administration is to educate civil servants for higher positions in public service, with a clear focus on law and management. Art colleges engage in very little research at all, according to the conventional understanding of the term, and are characterized by quite special forms of education. The more symbolic type of knowledge that these institutions generate and possess, however, could be important for the emergence of innovative new businesses. Arts colleges and universities of public administration are categorized under "other" HEIs.

No detailed regional data are available for the non-university public research institutions. However, the number of such institutes in each region is known.[13] Information about the number of patents is from the Patent Statistics. Patents are assigned to the region where the inventor has his or her residence.[14] Tables A.1 and A.3 in the Appendix provide descriptive statistics for the variables used in the empirical analysis.

2.3.2 The Spatial Distribution of Innovative Start-Ups in Germany

Figure 2.1 shows the geographic distribution of start-ups in high technology and technologically advanced manufacturing, as well as those in technology-intensive services. As seen in the figure, the emergence of an innovative new business in manufacturing is a rare event. The median value for the yearly number of high-technology start-ups is one and it is three for technologically advanced industries. On average, regions have less than three start-ups in high-technology industries.

[13]All institutes of the four large public research organizations in Germany are accounted for, i.e., the *Fraunhofer*, the *Helmholtz*, the *Leibnitz*, and the *Max Planck Society*. Data have been collected from different sources, mainly from publications of these organizations and the Federal Ministry of Education and Research. Since a number of these institutes have several locations, the publicly available information about their budgets and number of personnel cannot be meaningfully assigned to regions.

[14]If a patent has more than one inventor, the count is divided by the number of the inventors involved and each inventor is registered with his or her share of that patent.

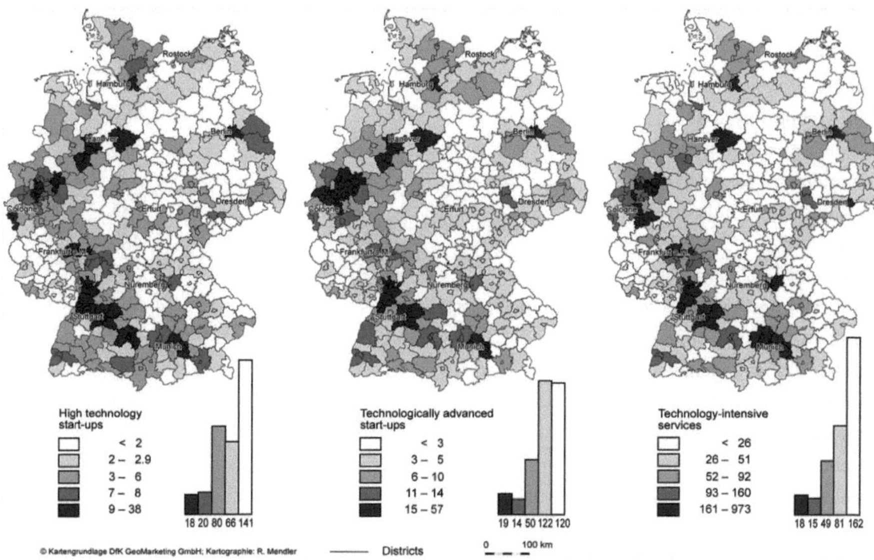

Fig. 2.1 Average yearly number of start-ups in innovative and knowledge-intensive industries, 1995–2008

The number of new businesses in technology-oriented services is considerably larger (median value of 26), but the geographic distribution is highly uneven in this sector. Regions with a relatively high number of innovative start-ups tend to be larger cities with a rich infrastructure of public research institutions, particularly universities. The basic pattern of the geographic distribution is largely the same for the start-up rate that relates the number of innovative start-ups to the labor force.

Looking at the geographic concentration of new businesses in the different industries (Table 2.1) reveals that the highest value of the Gini coefficient is for start-ups in high-technology manufacturing industries followed by those in technology-oriented services and technologically advanced industries. Compared to the concentration of start-ups in all industries and in non-innovative industries, the difference in the respective Gini coefficients is not very large. The numbers of professors, graduates, private-sector R&D employees, and regular universities show about the same degree of geographic concentration, while the concentration of the *Fachhochschulen* is much less pronounced. Remarkably, the geographic concentration of non-university institutes for public research as well as other HEIs (arts colleges and universities of public administration) is much higher than the concentration of the regular universities and the *Fachhochschulen*. Most of the HEIs (56 %) and non-university research institutes (69.5 %) are located in regions commonly classified as agglomerations[15]: 79 of the 272 non-university public

[15]This common classification of German regions by the Federal Office for Building and Regional Planning is based on a region's population density and settlement structure. For details, see Federal Office for Building and Regional Planning (2003).

Table 2.1 Gini coefficients for the geographic concentration of start-ups and related variables

Variable	Gini coefficient
Number of new businesses in:	
High-technology industries	.586
Technologically advanced industries	.529
Technology-intensive services	.545
Non-innovative industries	.481
All industries	.483
Number of R&D employees	.616
Number of higher education institutions (HEIs)	.477
Number of regular universities	.627
Number of *Fachhochschulen*	.447
Number of other HEIs	.831
Number of professors	.612
Number of graduates	.654
Number of extra-university public research institutes	.901

research institutes (29 %) are in moderately congested regions, and only 4 of these institutes (1.5 %) are located in areas that can be regarded as "rural." The share of HEIs in moderately congested and rural regions is 35.7 % and 8.4 %, respectively.[16]

2.4 Empirical Approach

2.4.1 *Estimation Strategy*

As dependent variables, the number of start-ups is used in high-technology manufacturing industries, in technologically advanced manufacturing industries, in technology-oriented services, and in those industries that are not classified as innovative or knowledge intensive. Due to the count character of these variables, a negative binomial estimation technique is employed in order to analyze the impact of different variables on the formation of innovative start-ups. Because a relatively high share of observations with no regional start-up is found in high-technology manufacturing in a year (27.78 %), the "too many zero values" problem could appear. A possible solution to this problem is to apply the zero-inflated version of the negative binomial method, which includes only a selection of "true" zero values in the estimation. In such a procedure, regions where one can never expect the event of interest, that is, the formation of an innovative start-up, are excluded from the estimation. The zero-inflated negative binomial method requires an assumption for

[16]The highest number of HEIs can be found in Berlin (34 HEIs), followed by Munich (19), Hamburg (17), and Stuttgart (10). The regions with the highest number of non-university institutions for public research are Berlin (26), Munich (20), and Dresden (17).

identifying and selecting the "true" zero values. Since the data show that all regions in Germany have at least one start-up in high-technology industries from time to time, all the zero values in the data have to be regarded as "true" and thus the zero-inflated negative binomial estimation method is inappropriate here.[17] For the technologically advanced start-ups, the share of observations without a new business in a year is 13.54 % and for technology-intensive services it is 0.07 %, suggesting that there is no "too many" zero values problem.

The analyses are conducted on the basis of a time series of yearly observations for a period of 14 years, and panel estimation techniques can be applied. Since many of the potential explanatory variables (e.g., number of universities in the region) show no or not much of variation over time, a fixed effects estimator that would account for unobserved regional characteristics is not appropriate because a considerable part of the influence of such variables is captured by the fixed effects. For this reason, a random effects estimator is used. Moreover, some examples of fixed effects estimations are presented in the Appendix. Since the standard statistical software packages do not provide spatial lag and spatial error corrections for negative binomial panel models, dummy variables for the German Federal States (*Laender*) are included in order to control for effects of the wider regional environment. Since the German Federal States are an important policy-making level, this variable may also indicate the effect of policy measures at this level.[18] Year dummies are included as controls for time-specific effects. All independent variables are lagged by 1 year.

A severe problem of the empirical analysis is the high correlation among most of the indicators for the universities (see Table A.4 in the Appendix). These pronounced correlations are to a considerable extent caused by a variation of these variables with size due to complementarity, for example, having a large number of students means a larger teaching staff and a greater amount of resources. This problem is captured as follows. In a first step, a baseline model without the indicators for universities and non-university public research institutes is estimated. In a second step, only one of these indicators at a time is added to this model. The measure for the impact of these indicators is change in the AIC (Akaike information

[17]A plausible assumption for the selection of "true" zero values could be that the emergence of an innovative start-up in a region requires the presence of at least one university or of a non-university public research institute. This assumption, however, is not unproblematic because it already implies the general hypothesis that innovative start-ups emerge from public research. Running a zero-inflated negative binomial model with the variable "presence of a university or non-university public research institute in the region" for the selection of the "true" zero values, reveals a Vuong test suggesting that doing so is not a significant improvement over a standard negative binomial model.

[18]A great deal of the financing and legal framework for universities and non-university public research institutes is the responsibility of the Federal States in Germany. Most of the Federal States also operate their own programs for promoting entrepreneurship.

criterion)[19] (see Greene 2012) compared to the baseline model. A decrease in the AIC value due to the inclusion of an additional variable indicates a better fit of the model in terms reducing the remaining "unexplained" variance. An increase in the remaining variance leads to a higher AIC value. In a final step, a factor analysis is performed for the variables that represent public research in order to aggregate this information and add a factor that represents the regional HEIs to the variables of the baseline model. Since the dependent as well as the independent variables are logged, the values of the estimated coefficients can be interpreted as elasticities that indicate the relative importance of the respective effect.

2.4.2 Independent Variables and Expected Results

In the empirical analyses of the factors that determine the emergence of innovative start-ups significant effects are expected for all those variables that reflect the presence of a regional knowledge stock as well as general conditions that may be conducive for the emergence of innovative start-ups. The number of the regional workforce is included, which represents the pool of potential entrepreneurs and also reflects economies of size and agglomeration effects. The regional workforce is divided into the number of private-sector R&D employees, the number of employed persons excluding R&D employees, and the number of persons registered as being unemployed. The number of R&D employees is an important part of the knowledge pool in the region. Since the number of R&D employees is highly correlated with the number of people with a tertiary degree, an indicator for the share of the workforce with high education levels is not included. A positive effect on the emergence of innovative start-ups is expected for the number of employed people, particularly the number of R&D employees, but the impact of the number of unemployed people is a priori unclear. On the one hand, innovative start-ups can, of course, be set up by the unemployed. On the other hand, unemployed people have a relatively low propensity for starting their own business (Fritsch and Falck 2007), and this may be particularly true when it comes to innovative ventures that primarily represent opportunity, rather than necessity, entrepreneurship and require a relatively high level of qualification. Moreover, a high number of unemployed people in a region can be viewed as an indication of bad economic conditions and, therefore, poor prospects for success, which may prevent potential founders from setting up a firm in the region (Reynolds et al. 1994; Carree 2002; Sutaria and Hicks 2004).

It is expected that founders have a strong tendency to start a business in the industry with which they were previously affiliated (Fritsch and Falck 2007) and, in

[19]The AIC is a measure of the relative goodness of fit of a statistical model that accounts for the number of independent variables included in the model. For details, see Akaike (1974) and Greene (2012).

Table 2.2 Explanatory variables and expected signs for the effect on the number of innovative start-ups

Variable	Expected sign
Number of employed persons excluding R&D employees	+
Number of R&D employees	+
Number of unemployed	+/− or n.s.
Share of employees in the respective industries	+
Share of employees in establishment with less than 50 employees	+
Number of R&D employees in adjacent regions	+
Number of patents per 1000 employees	+

Notes: "+" indicates a positive expected sign, in case of "−" the expected sign is negative. "n.s." means that any statistically significant relationship is not expected

turn, this should result in a positive effect for the employment share of these industries. Hence, the employment share in the respective group of industries (high-technology, technologically advanced, technology-oriented services, non-innovative industries) is included. This variable also reflects regional specialization in the respective group of industries as well as the available industry-specific knowledge. The share of employees in small establishments (those with fewer than 50 employees) should have a positive effect due to a generally higher propensity of small-firm employees to engage in start-up.[20] A positive effect can also be expected for the number of private R&D employees in adjacent districts, as these represent spatial knowledge spillovers over relatively short distances (Anselin et al. 1997; Asheim and Gertler 2005). A positive effect is also expected for the number of patents per 1000 employees, which is a general measure for regional knowledge and R&D activity.[21] Table 2.2 provides an overview of the definitions, sources, and expected signs for those independent variables not related to public research.

Since the presence of universities and other kinds of public research institutes in the region may be an important source of knowledge for innovative start-ups, a positive effect is expected for them. Regional proximity to these institutions may be important because a great deal of their knowledge is of a tacit nature and tends to be "sticky," that is, it is regionally bound. This stickiness of regional knowledge is reflected in the pronounced tendency of spin-offs from universities and other public research institutions to locate close to their incubator organization. The positive effect of universities and other public research institutions should be stronger for

[20]Employment in industry groups and small-firm employment are entered in the regressions as shares in overall regional employment because including these numbers would lead to double counting with the overall number of employees and cause multicollinearity.

[21]It is not distinguished between patents registered by HEIs, non-university public research institutes, or the private sector for several reasons. One reason is that universities and other public research institutes in Germany are to different degrees selective with respect to patenting inventions so the number of patents is not a meaningful indicator of innovative output. A second reason is a change in the legal framework for university patenting that led to considerable change in patenting behavior during the period of analysis (for details, see Proff et al. 2012).

new businesses in high-technology manufacturing industries than for start-ups in technologically advanced manufacturing or in technology-oriented services because many parts of high technology manufacturing can be regarded as science based. Along these lines, HEIs' presence may be insignificant for new businesses in non-innovative industries. To account for the possibility of spatial knowledge spillovers, indicators for public research and tertiary education in adjacent regions are included. If these indicators are statistically significant, their effect should be positive but less pronounced than for HEIs and other public research institutes actually located within the respective region due to the sticky character of the knowledge.

Indicators that reflect the universities and non-university public research institutes are:

- The presence of at least one HEI (yes = 1; no = 0), as well as the number of HEIs in the region and in adjacent regions. To the extent that HEIs are specialized in certain academic disciplines, the number of HEIs can be viewed as an indication of the variety of academic knowledge present in a region.
- The presence of at least one non-university public research institute (yes = 1; no = 0) and the number of such institutes in the region and in adjacent regions. As with the number of HEIs, the number of non-university research institutes may reflect the variety of research fields.
- The numbers of students, graduates, PhD students, and professors. These variables reflect different aspects of the HEI's size. The number of students and graduates indicates a contribution to workforce's education (i.e., its qualifications); the number of professors and PhD students primarily signifies the volume of research being conducted.
- The amount of internal financing as well as the amount of third-party funds (external funds). To the extent that third-party funds come from private firms, they most likely reflect contract R&D and cooperation with these firms. Because third-party funds are nearly always allocated via some kind of competitive procedure, they can also be regarded as an indication of research quality.
- The amount of internal funds and third-party funds per professor. These indicators represent the resource endowment and the quality of research largely independent of the HEI's size.

If public and private research in a region is conducive to the emergence of innovative start-ups, It may be expected that a concentration of this kind of new business takes place in larger cities and agglomerations because both public research institutes as well as private-sector R&D tend to be concentrated in such high-density areas. Other reasons for expecting a relatively high number of innovative start-ups in larger cities include agglomeration economies, such as large and diversified input markets and rich opportunities for direct face-to-face contacts, which can be assumed conducive to the transfer of knowledge. A measure for population density is not included in the standard models because of its close statistical relationship with other variables that would lead to severe multicollinearity problems. Due to its close correlation with many other factors that may be the "true" determinants of innovative start-ups, including population density could obscure the effects that these other factors have on the emergence of innovative start-ups. However, in order to analyze the influence of agglomeration effects, the models are run for groups of regions having various population densities (see Sect. 2.5.3).

2.5 Results

Section 2.5.1 first reports the results for the baseline model with and without indicators for public research. Given the close correlation between the different measures for public research, a factor analysis is performed and a factor is included that represents the overall activities of regional HEIs in the model (Sect. 2.5.2). All models are estimated for four groups of industries: high-technology manufacturing, technologically advanced manufacturing, technology-oriented services, and non-innovative or knowledge-intensive industries. Section 2.5.3 sets out the results of a number of extensions and robustness checks.

2.5.1 Results for the Baseline Model and Indicators for Regional Public Research

In the baseline model, positive and statistically significant effects are found for the number of employed persons, excluding R&D employees, as well as for the employment share for the number of start-ups in all four industry groups (Table 2.3). Matching our expectations, the coefficient for the number of R&D employees has the highest value for new businesses in high-technology manufacturing industries followed by those in technologically advanced manufacturing and in technology-oriented service; it is not statistically significant for start-ups in non-innovative industries. The fact that the number of unemployed people has an effect only on start-ups in non-innovative industries clearly indicates that new businesses set up by unemployed people tend to occur in these industries. The share of employees in establishments with fewer than 50 employees also has a statistically significant positive effect except for start-ups in technologically advanced manufacturing. This positive effect may be an indication that founders of new businesses were previously employed in small firms or that the presence of industries with low minimum efficient size is conducive to start-ups (Fritsch and Falck 2007).

The number of patents per 1000 employees has a positive effect on start-ups in high-technology manufacturing and in technology-oriented services, but it is not statistically significant for start-ups in technologically advanced manufacturing (Table 2.3). The relationship with the number of start-ups in non-innovative industries is statistically significant but with a negative sign. This clearly indicates

Table 2.3 Baseline model for explaining number of start-ups in different groups of industries

	High-technology manufacturing	Technologically advanced manufacturing	Technology-oriented services	Non-innovative industries
Number of employed persons, excluding R&D employees (ln)	.0347*** (3.26)	.0311*** (3.56)	.0304*** (7.12)	.5467*** (19.76)
Number of R&D employees (ln)	.00002*** (4.11)	7.97e-06*** (2.45)	3.54e-06** (1.92)	6.89e-07 (0.88)
Number of unemployed (ln)	.0110 (0.55)	.0095 (0.59)	.0042 (1.00)	.0067*** (7.14)
Share of employees in high-technology manufacturing industries (ln)	.0971*** (7.02)	–	–	–
Share of employees in technologically advanced manufacturing industries (ln)	–	.0199** (2.09)	–	–
Share of employees in technology-oriented service industries (ln)	–	–	.0198*** (2.76)	–
Share of employees in non-innovative industries	–	–	–	.0724*** (2.50)
Share of employees in establishments with fewer than 50 employees (ln)	.2427** (1.99)	.0625 (1.57)	.2322*** (2.92)	.2665*** (11.05)
Number of R&D employees in adjacent regions	.0194 (0.84)	−.0102 (0.56)	−.0214*** (3.69)	−.0040* (1.64)
Number of patents per 1000 employees (ln)	51.3587*** (3.38)	−.3425 (0.03)	17.5053*** (3.34)	−2.4442*** (0.94)
Constant	.7197*** (10.26)	1.3684*** (13.82)	2.6735*** (29.67)	−1.4930*** (39.38)
Wald chi^2	573.25***	479.07***	899.48***	2756.17***
Dummies for Federal States	Yes***	Yes***	Yes***	Yes***
Dummies for years	Yes***	Yes***	Yes***	Yes***
Number of observations (number of zeros)	4,550 (1,264)	4,550 (616)	4,550 (3)	4,550 (0)
Log likelihood	−8489.27	−10,252.94	−16,669.05	−20,695.38
AIC	17,042.54	20,563.87	33,402.10	41,455.08
Pseudo R^2	.6342	.5545	.7431	.6518
McFadden's R^2	.105	.106	.109	.178

Notes: The dependent variable is the number of start-ups per year in the respective group of industries. Negative binomial panel regression with random effects. Z-values in parentheses
***Statistically significant at the 1 % level; **Statistically significant at the 5 % level; *Statistically significant at the 10 % level

the importance of regional knowledge for the formation of innovative new businesses. No significantly positive effect is found for the number of R&D employees in surrounding regions, suggesting that interregional spillovers from R&D employment are irrelevant for the emergence of new businesses, even in the rather narrowly defined regions in the analyses of this chapter. Including measures for the concentration of the regional industry structure that would indicate an effect of spatial clustering does not lead to any plausible or statistically significant results.

When indicators for public research are included in these models, the highest increases of explained variance, as indicated by reduction of the AIC values, are found for the number of such institutions in a region, i.e., the number of HEIs, and the number of non-university public research institutes (Table 2.4). The effect of the "other" HEIs (arts colleges and universities of public administration) is considerably weaker than the effect of regular universities and *Fachhochschulen*. Surprisingly, indicators for the number of professors and the number of graduates, as well as for the amount and type of available financial resources, have a much smaller impact. The number of HEIs, and of non-university public research institutes in adjacent regions, is intended to indicate spatial spillover effects. The results for the HEIs in adjacent regions suggest that there are such spillover effects, but that their importance for new business formation is considerably weaker than the effect of HEIs located in the same region. There is no statistically significant effect of the presence and number of non-university research institutes in adjacent regions on start-ups in innovative industries. It is remarkable that adding measures for public research institutes to the baseline model for start-ups in non-innovative industries degrades model fit. This clearly indicates that public research is rather unimportant for new business formation in these sectors.

Since all independent variables are logged, the estimated coefficients can be interpreted as elasticities and used as indicators for the relative importance of the different variables. Comparing the estimated coefficients of the diverse measures for public research with the coefficients for private-sector R&D, such as the number of R&D employees, reveals that many of the public research indicators are much more important. In most cases, the effect of the indicators for public research institutions is strongest for start-ups in high-technology manufacturing and weakest for new businesses in technology-oriented services.

2.5.2 Aggregation of Indicators for Regional Public Research

Factor analyses are conduced in order to aggregate the information provided by the diverse indicators for HEIs. The factor analyses showed that different types of HEI activity, such as education and research, could not be meaningfully separated into different factors. Hence, only one factor is generated in order to represent regional HEIs, which is based on the number of graduates, the number of PhD students, the

Table 2.4 Effect of including indicators for public research in the baseline model

	High-technology manufacturing	Technologically advanced manufacturing	Technology-oriented services	Non-innovative industries
Institution for tertiary education (HEI) (yes = 1; no = 0)	−28.66 .3014 (5.45)***	−14.81 .1574 (4.11)***	−11.62 .0767 (3.68)***	1.99 .0010 (.12)
Number of HEIs (ln)	−83.56 .3907 (9.75)***	−105.23 .3169 (10.68)***	−28.74 .1037 (5.56)***	24.75 .0097 (1.24)
Regular university (yes = 1; no = 0)	−25.81 .3004 (5.31)***	−30.81 .2178 (5.71)***	−8.33 .0655 (3.21)***	0.57 −.0102 (1.20)
Number of regular universities (ln)	−33.63 .5633 (5.99)***	−46.19 .4410 (6.86)***	−3 .0884 (2.25)**	23.86 .0241 (1.56)
Fachhochschule (yes = 1; no = 0)	−16.11 .2216 (4.07)***	−17.33 .1652 (4.40)***	−5.31 .0557 (2.70)***	1.97 .0015 (.17)
Number of *Fachhochschulen* (ln)	−55.93 .4894 (7.85)***	−60.07 .3553 (8.03)***	−13.23 .1091 (3.93)***	26.22 .0026 (.24)
Other HEIs (yes = 1, no = 0)	−6.83 .0931 (6.68)***	−5.15 .0612 (5.76)***	−1.36 .0231 (3.71)	2.35 −.0024 (.91)
Number of other HEIS (ln)	−15.41 .1277 (7.44)***	−23.5 .0923 (7.24)***	−3.43 .0116 (1.55)	7.33 .0045 (1.52)
Number of students (ln)	−41.57 .0467 (6.61)***	−30.63 .0334 (5.80)***	−14.79 .0128 (4.09)***	26.83 −.0045 (1.71)*
Number of graduates (ln)	−36.56 .0541 (6.16)***	−29.69 .0397 (5.68)***	−26.78 .0192 (5.34)***	1.92 .0007 (0.30)
Number of PhD students (ln)	17.45 .0555 (4.53)***	−36.41 .0609 (6.26)***	−7.88 .0162 (3.14)***	356.59 −.0079 (1.87)*
Number of professors (ln)	−36.99 .0742 (6.22)***	−36.31 .0607 (6.28)***	−19.2 .0240 (4.59)***	358.87 −.0050 (1.10)
Amount of regular funds (ln)	−28.21 .0364 (6.44)***	−25.54 .0224 (5.27)***	−19.34 .0103 (4.62)***	359.58 .0009 (.71)
Amount of external funds (ln)	−32.23 .0402 (6.47)***	−29.35 .0261 (5.63)***	−16.64 .0105 (4.31)***	359.17 .0011 (.96)
Regular and external funds (ln)	−34.19 .0356 (6.62)***	−30.47 .0231 (5.73)***	−20.58 .0099 (4.75)***	359.16 .0032 (.96)
Regular funds per professor (ln)	−19.73 .0530 (4.82)***	−21.08 .0399 (4.83)***	−14.42 .0169 (4.06)***	358.39 .0033 (1.30)

(continued)

Table 2.4 (continued)

	High-technology manufacturing	Technologically advanced manufacturing	Technology-oriented services	Non-innovative industries
External funds per professor (ln)	−26.04 .0745 (5.46)***	−17.37 .0457 (4.42)***	−7.46 .0159 (3.08)***	358.8 .0026 (1.14)
Regular and external funds per professor (ln)	−29.99 .0616 (5.82)***	−21.80 .0390 (4.90)***	−13.66 .0161 (3.96)***	358.85 .0061 (1.11)
Non-university public research institute (yes = 1; no = 0)	−61.09 .7171 (7.95)***	−93.40 .8023 (9.51)***	−61.23 .6118 (8.18)***	1.67 −.0315 (.58)
Number of non-university public research institutes (ln)	−48.24*** .5337 (7.19)	−58.04*** .5385 (7.90)	−17.4*** .2870 (4.54)	360.06 .0081 (.16)
Number of HEIs in adjacent regions	−12.04*** .2197 (3.77)	−23.20*** .2662 (5.04)	−31.26*** .2924 (5.86)	1 .0194 (1.00)
Non-university public research in adjacent regions (yes = 1; no = 0)	1.21 .3161 (.91)	−0.02 .4639 (1.46)	0.37 .4007 (1.32)	1.7 −.0959 (.55)
Number of non-university public research institutes in adjacent regions	−7.87 −.0255 (.59)	−2.52 −.0296 (.75)	0.44 .0430 (1.13)	348 .0810 (3.42)***

Notes: First row: Change in the AIC value due to the inclusion of the variable. Second row: Estimated coefficient and z-value in parentheses
***Statistically significant at the 1 % level; **Statistically significant at the 5 % level; *Statistically significant at the 10 % level

number of professors, the amount of regular funds, and the amount of external funds (see Table A.5 in the Appendix). This factor for HEI activity in the region and in adjacent regions was then included in the baseline model. Since the information about the non-university public research institutes is limited, the number of such institutes in the region and in the adjacent regions is included in order to represent this part of public research.

The results of the baseline model with the aggregate indicators for public research included are displayed in Table 2.5. A main difference between these results and those from the baseline model without indicators for public research (Table 2.3) is that the number of regional private-sector R&D employees loses statistical significance, whereas both indicators for public research in the region are highly significant with the expected sign in the models for innovative and knowledge-intensive industries, but not in the estimate for non-innovative industries. However, it is problematic to conclude from this result that public R&D is more important for innovative start-ups than private-sector R&D because of the

Table 2.5 Baseline model with aggregate indicators for public research

	High-technology manufacturing	Technologically advanced manufacturing	Technology-oriented services	Non-innovative industries
Number of employed persons, excluding R&D employees (ln)	.0251** (2.39)	.0229*** (2.66)	.0277*** (6.43)	.5262*** (18.93)
Number of R&D employees (ln)	−9.86e-08 (.03)	−2.83e-06 (1.01)	1.15e-07 (.07)	4.33e-07 (.87)
Number of unemployed (ln)	−.0189 (.99)	−.0088 (.59)	−.0056 (1.28)	.0061*** (6.20)
Share of employees in high-technology manufacturing industries (ln)	.0945*** (6.97)	–	–	–
Share of employees in technologically advanced manufacturing industries (ln)	–	.0200** (2.14)	–	–
Share of employees in technology-oriented service industries (ln)	–	–	.0186*** (2.58)	–
Share of employees in non-innovative industries	–	–	–	.0727*** (2.46)
Share of employees in establishments with fewer than 50 employees (ln)	.3860*** (3.15)	.0694* (1.80)	.4036*** (4.83)	.2902*** (11.44)
Number of R&D employees in surrounding regions	.0321 (1.48)	.0021 (0.13)	−.0131** (2.26)	−.0034* (1.73)
Number of patents per 1000 employees (ln)	48.9386*** (3.30)	.8756 (0.09)	19.999*** (3.82)	−3.6376 (1.19)
Aggregate indicator of HEIs in the region	.1917*** (6.44)	.1481*** (6.21)	.0696*** (5.16)	.0031 (0.25)
Number of non-university research Institutes (ln)	.4834*** (6.74)	.4796*** (7.30)	.2777*** (4.39)	−.0011 (.02)
Aggregate indicator of HEIs in adjacent regions	.0425 (1.22)	.0439 (1.59)	−.0140 (1.04)	.0285*** (3.02)
Number of non-university research institutes in adjacent regions (ln)	.0017 (.04)	−.0102 (.29)	.0665* (1.84)	.0873*** (3.77)
Constant	.7922*** (10.33)	1.4283*** (14.43)	2.5437*** (29.93)	−1.2388*** (39.06)
Wald chi^2	737.74***	646.67***	969.70***	2835.25***
Dummies for Federal States	Yes***	Yes***	Yes***	Yes***
Dummies for years	Yes***	Yes***	Yes***	Yes***
Number of observations (number of zeros)	4550 (1264)	4550 (616)	4550 (3)	4550 (0)
Log likelihood	−8442.80	−10,201.91	−16,644.18	−20,684.20

(continued)

Table 2.5 (continued)

	High-technology manufacturing	Technologically advanced manufacturing	Technology-oriented services	Non-innovative industries
AIC (change in AIC compared to the baseline model in Table 2.3)	16,957.59 (−84.95)	20,469.81 (−94.06)	33,360.36 (−41.74)	41,412.86 (−42.22)
Pseudo R^2	.6218	.5787	.4956	.7060
McFadden's R^2	.124	.125	.139	.180

Notes: The dependent variable is the number of start-ups per year in the respective group of industries. Negative binomial panel regression with random effects. Z-values in parentheses
***Statistically significant at the 1 % level; **Statistically significant at the 5 % level; *Statistically significant at the 10 % level

considerable correlation between the indicators for the two types of activities.[22] Presumably, the main source of these correlations is that there are pronounced spatially concentrated knowledge spillovers between these two types of R&D (Fritsch and Slavtchev 2007). Such spatially bounded knowledge spillovers are one reason for the co-location of public and private-sector R&D facilities. Moreover, both types of R&D prefer the same kind of region, mainly larger cities. The relationship between public and private R&D is complex. Public institutions of education and research may provide important inputs for private-sector R&D, and R&D in both sectors may be interrelated, particularly at the regional level.

It is remarkable that the number of non-university public research institutes has a considerably stronger effect than the aggregate indicator for the regional HEIs. The relatively high coefficients for the number of non-university public research institutions in the region may, to a degree, reflect the concentration of this type of public research in high-density areas, which are also the areas where most of the innovative start-ups occur, and therefore could be an overestimation of their effect. Measures for public research in adjacent regions are not statistically significant for high-technology manufacturing or for technologically advanced industries. A weakly significant effect of the number of non-university public research institutes in adjacent regions is found for start-ups in technology-oriented services. Surprisingly, the estimates for start-ups in non-innovative industries indicate a pronounced effect of HEIs and of the number of non-university research institutes in adjacent regions, but not for public research in the same region; however, this finding could be a statistical artifact caused by correlation among explanatory variables. The inclusion of the indicators for public research leads to large reductions in the AIC value in all four models, particularly in the estimates for new businesses in high-

[22]The correlation coefficient between the aggregate indicator for the regional HEIs (the number of non-university public research institutes) and the number of private-sector R&D employees is 0.465 (0.596); see Table A.2 in the Appendix. The correlation between the regional number of private-sector R&D employees and the aggregate indicator for HEIs (the number of non-university public research institutes) in adjacent regions is 0.323 (−0.021).

technology manufacturing and in technologically advanced manufacturing industries. All in all, these results confirm the very important role of public research identified in Sect. 2.5.1.

2.5.3 *Extensions and Robustness Checks*

A number of robustness checks are performed in order to test the stability of the results.[23] First, the models are run with fixed effects. As expected, a fixed effects panel estimator does not lead to meaningful results. In these models, many of the indicators for public research are not statistically significant, which is obviously due to low levels of variation over time. Second, given the strong effect that is found for the presence of at least one HEI or non-university public research institute, the regressions are run for only those regions that have at least one such institute (about 62 % of all regions). Considerable differences in the estimates from the models for all regions could indicate that the coefficients for the number of institutes mainly reflect the presence of at least one such institute. It is found, however, that the results are similar. Excluding regions with a relatively high number of HEIs and non-university public research institutes, such as Berlin and Munich, did not produce any significantly different results either. Third, the models are run separately for East and West Germany, and again there is not much difference in the results, indicating that the commercialization of knowledge through the formation of innovative new businesses follows the same pattern in both parts of the country.

Finally, in order to further analyze the influence of agglomeration effects, the regions based on population density are sorted into three groups of equal size and the regressions separately are run for regions with relatively low, medium, and high levels of population density. It is found that the coefficient for the aggregate effect of HEIs is highest in regions with low population density, somewhat lower in regions with medium density, and relatively low in high density areas. These results suggest that HEIs may have a particularly pronounced effect in low-density regions and that their effect in high-density areas is somewhat obscured by other factors, making it difficult to identify their precise role using this type of analysis. It is also found that the number of non-university public research institutes has a statistically significant effect only in regions with relatively high population density. One main reason for this result may be the rather high concentration of these institutions in agglomerations and that there are nearly no non-university public research institutions in rural areas. Another reason could be the relatively high correlation between the aggregate indicator for HEIs and the number of non-university research institutes.[24]

---

[23]See Tables A.6–A.14 in the Appendix.

[24]The coefficient of correlation between these two indicators in the overall sample is 0.488 (see Table A.2 in the Appendix).

2.6 Summary and Conclusions

This chapter analyzed the role of the regional knowledge base for start-ups in innovative industries using a rich dataset that contained particularly detailed information about higher education institutions (HEIs)in German regions. According to the empirical analysis, there is a strong relationship between the mere presence of universities and other types of public research institutes and the emergence of new businesses in industries commonly classified as innovative. Other indicators that reflect the size of these institutions or the quality of research are also statistically significant, but have a considerably smaller impact. Some positive effects are also found for public research institutes in adjacent regions, thus indicating interregional spillovers, but these effects are modest and often not statistically significant. The impact of public research is particularly pronounced for start-ups in high-technology and technologically advanced manufacturing industries and tends to be considerably less important for new business formation in technology-oriented services. Empirical results of this chapter suggest that public research has hardly any impact on new business formation in industries that are not particularly innovative. All in all, the results are consistent with the knowledge spillover theory of entrepreneurship, which highlights the role of the regional knowledge base for the formation of innovative businesses (Acs et al. 2009, 2013).

Due to the pronounced correlations between many of the various indicators for public research, however, the empirical analyses of this chapter were not able to exactly determine which characteristics of public research institutions are the most important with regard to the emergence of innovative new businesses. In particular, even factor analysis did not reveal separate factors representing different aspects of public education and research. Moreover, it is supposed that even more sophisticated econometric methods applied to aggregate data for whole regions can overcome the problem of strong interrelation between the variables for public research. Further insights that may provide more detailed policy guidance are mainly to be expected from analyzing microdata and by means of qualitative analysis on a case-study basis. Despite such limitations, however, the main conclusion from the analysis is crystal clear: public research in a region is a main source of innovative start-ups, and the regional distribution of innovative new businesses is highly influenced by the regional distribution of public research institutions. Hence, policy aimed at increasing and/or improving public research may be crucial for long-term regional development (Carree et al. 2014). However, this in no way means that other aspects of regional conditions are unimportant. On the contrary, there are strong indications that the effect of public research on regional development may vary considerably across regions. Whether this is due to characteristics of the research institutes or to other region-specific factors (e.g., Åstebro and Bazzazian 2011; Bonaccorsi et al. 2014; Piva et al. 2011) is an important avenue for further research.

References

Acs ZJ, Braunerhjelm P, Audretsch DB, Carlsson B (2009) The knowledge spillover theory of entrepreneurship. Small Bus Econ 32:15–30
Acs ZJ, Audretsch DB, Lehmann E (2013) The knowledge spillover theory of entrepreneurship. Small Bus Econ 41:767–774
Adams JD (2002) Comparative localization of academic and industrial spillovers. J Econ Geogr 2:253–278
Akaike H (1974) A new look at the statistical model identification. IEEE Trans Autom Control 19:716–723
Anselin L, Varga A, Acs ZJ (1997) Local geographic spillovers between university research and high technology innovations. J Urban Econ 42:422–448
Asheim BT, Gertler MS (2005) The geography of innovation: regional innovation systems. In: Fagerberg J, Mowery DC, Nelson RR (eds) The Oxford handbook of innovation. Oxford University Press, Oxford, pp 291–317
Åstebro T, Bazzazian N (2011) Universities, entrepreneurship and local economic development. In: Fritsch M (ed) Handbook of research on entrepreneurship and regional development. Elgar, Cheltenham, pp 252–333
Audretsch DB, Lehmann EE (2005) Does the knowledge spillover theory of entrepreneurship hold for regions? Res Policy 34:1191–1202
Audretsch DB, Lehmann EE, Warning S (2005) University spillovers and new firm location. Res Policy 34:1113–1122
Audretsch DB, Keilbach M, Lehmann EE (2006) Entrepreneurship and economic growth. Oxford University Press, Oxford
Bade F-J, Nerlinger EA (2000) The spatial distribution of new technology-based firms: empirical results for West-Germany. Papers Region Sci 79:155–176
Bania N, Eberts RW, Fogerty MS (1993) Universities and the startup of new companies can we generalize from Route 128 and Silicon Valley? Rev Econ Stat 75:761–766
Baptista R, Mendonça J (2010) Proximity to knowledge sources and the location of knowledge-based start-ups. Ann Region Sci 45:5–29
Baptista R, Lima F, Mendonça J (2011) Establishment of higher education institutions and new firm entry. Res Policy 40:751–760
Bonaccorsi A, Colombo MG, Guerini M, Rossi-Lamastra C (2014) How universities contribute to the creation of knowledge-intensive firms: detailed evidence on the Italian case. In: Bonaccorsi A (ed) Knowledge, diversity and performance in European Higher Education—A changing landscape. Edward Elgar, Cheltenham, pp 205–230
Boschma R (2005) Proximity and innovation: a critical assessment. Region Stud 39:61–74
Bosma N, Hessels J, Schutjens V, van Praag M, Verheul I (2012) Entrepreneurship and role models. J Econ Psychol 33:410–424
Carree MA (2002) Does unemployment affect the number of establishments? A regional analysis for US states. Region Stud 36:389–398
Carree MA, Della-Malva A, Santarelli E (2014) The contribution of universities to growth: empirical evidence for Italy. J Technol Transf 39:393–414
Dahl MS, Sorenson O (2009) The embedded entrepreneur. Eur Manag Rev 6:172–181
EC-DGT: European Commission; Directorate-General for Translation (2014) Country compendium: a companion to the English style guide. EC Directorate-General for Translation, Brussels
Elfenbein DW, Hamilton BH, Zenger TR (2010) The small firm effect and the entrepreneurial spawning of scientists and engineers. Manag Sci 56:659–681
Federal Office for Building and Regional Planning (Bundesamt für Bauwesen und Raumordnung) (2003) Aktuelle Daten zur Entwicklung der Städte, Kreise und Gemeinden, vol 17. Federal Office for Building and Regional Planning, Bonn

Feldman MP (2001) The entrepreneurial event revisited: firm formation in a regional context. Indus Corp Change 10:861–891

Figueiredo O, Guimaraes P, Woodward D (2002) Home-field advantage: location decisions of Portuguese entrepreneurs. J Urban Econ 52:341–361

Fritsch M (2011) Start-ups in innovative industries—Causes and effects. In: Audretsch DB, Falck O, Heblich S, Lederer A (eds) Handbook of innovation and entrepreneurship. Elgar, Cheltenham, pp 365–381

Fritsch M (2013) New business formation and regional development—A survey and assessment of the evidence. Found Trends Entrepreneurship 9:249–364

Fritsch M, Falck O (2007) New business formation by industry over space and time: a multidimensional analysis. Region Stud 41:157–172

Fritsch M, Slavtchev V (2007) Universities and innovation in space. Industry Innov 14:201–218

Gehrke B, Schasse U, Rammer C, Frietsch R, Neuhäusler P, Leidmann M (2010) Listen wissens- und technologieintensiver Güter und Wirtschaftszweige. Studien zum deutschen Innovationssystem, 19, Frauenhofer ISI, NIW, ZEW

Greene WH (2012) Econometric analysis, 7th edn. Pearson Prentice Hall, Upper Saddle River, NJ

Grupp H, Legler H (2000) Hochtechnologie 2000: Neudefinition der Hochtechnologie für die Berichterstattung zur technologischen Leistungsfähigkeit Deutschlands. Karlsruhe and Hannover, FhG, ISI, NIW

Harhoff D (1999) Firm formation and regional spillovers – Evidence from Germany. Econ Innov New Technol 8:27–55

Hülsbeck M, Pickavé EN (2014) Regional knowledge production as determinant of high-technology entrepreneurship: empirical evidence for Germany. Int Entrepreneurship Manag J 10:121–138

Klepper S (2009) Spinoffs: a review and synthesis. Eur Manag Rev 6:159–171

Lasch F, Robert F, Le Roy F (2013) Regional determinants of ICT new firm formation. Small Bus Econ 40:671–686

Markusen A, Glasmeier A, Hall P (1986) High tech in America—The what, how, where, and why of the sunrise industries. Allen & Unwin, Boston, MA

OECD: Organisation for Economic Co-operation and Development (2005) OECD handbook on economic globalization indicators. OECD, Paris

Parker SC (2009) Why do small firms produce the entrepreneurs? J Socio-Econ 38:484–494

Piva E, Grilli L, Rossi-Lamastra C (2011) The creation of high-tech entrepreneurial ventures at the local level: the role of local competences and communication infrastructures. Industry Innov 18:563–580

Proff S v, Buenstorf G, Hummel M (2012) University patenting in Germany before and after 2002: what role did the professors' privilege play? Industry Innov 19:23–44

Reynolds PD, Storey DJ, Westhead P (1994) Cross-national comparisons of the variation in new firm formation rates. Region Stud 28:443–456

Spengler A (2008) The establishment history panel. Schmollers Jahrbuch/J Appl Social Sci Stud 128:501–509

Sternberg R (2009) Regional dimensions of entrepreneurship. Found Trends Entrepreneurship 5:211–340

Storey DJ, Tether BS (1998) New technology-based firms in the European Union: an introduction. Res Policy 26:933–946

Sutaria V, Hicks DA (2004) New firm formation: dynamics and determinants. Ann Region Sci 38:241–262

Zentrum für Europäische Wirtschaftsforschung (ZEW) (2011) Die Bereitstellung von Standardauswertungen zum Gründungsgeschehen in Deutschland für externe Datennutzer. ZEW, Mannheim

Chapter 3
Fields of Knowledge, Types of Higher Education Institutions, and Innovative Start-Ups

3.1 Introduction

There is very little doubt that higher education institutions (HEIs) and the knowledge they embody are an important source of new businesses, particularly innovative start-ups. According to the knowledge spillover theory of entrepreneurship (Acs et al. 2009, 2013), new businesses in general, and highly innovative start-ups in particular, are manifestations of knowledge spillover from extant knowledge sources. Hence, the number and type of new businesses should be influenced considerably by the size and characteristics of the respective knowledge base. In particular, the generation of new knowledge via research and development (R&D) activity should be essential to the emergence of innovative start-ups. Since HEIs play an important role in gathering, generating, and distributing knowledge, they can be expected to have a significant effect in this respect.

The regional dimension in terms of geographic proximity is important in the process of entrepreneurial knowledge spillover for at least two reasons. First, new knowledge does not flow freely across space but tends to be regionally bounded (Anselin et al. 1997; Adams 2002; Asheim and Gertler 2005; Boschma 2005). Second, founders have a pronounced tendency to locate their firm in close spatial proximity to their former workplace or near where they reside (Figueiredo et al. 2002; Dahl and Sorenson 2009). Hence, innovative entrepreneurship tends to be a "regional event" (Feldman 2001; Sternberg 2009), meaning that the regional knowledge stock, the regional workforce, and the regional conditions for entrepreneurship are important factors in the emergence of innovative new businesses.

Indeed, many studies find a significantly positive correlation between regional HEIs and the number of innovative startups[1]; however, only little is known about

[1]See, for example, Acosta et al. (2011); Audretsch et al. (2004); Audretsch and Lehmann (2005); Bade and Nerlinger (2000); Baptista and Mendonça (2010); Baptista et al. (2011); Bonaccorsi et al. (2013); Fritsch and Aamoucke (2013); Harhoff (1999) and Hülsbeck and Pickavé (2014).

R. Aamoucke, *Innovative Start-Ups and the Distribution of Human Capital*, Contributions to Economics, DOI 10.1007/978-3-319-44462-8_3

the importance of different fields of academic knowledge or different types of HEIs. In addition, little is known about what type of activity, that is, research or education, that has the strongest impact. Based on a rich data set, this chapter investigates the role played by different knowledge fields, types of HEIs, and activities in the emergence of innovative start-ups in German regions, with the expectation that not all knowledge fields, types of HEIs, or fields of activity will be equally important.

Section 3.2 provides an overview of previous research in this area. Different fields of knowledge are then characterized with regard to their assumed relevance for innovative entrepreneurship and different types of German HEIs are described (Sect. 3.3). Section 3.4 introduces the hypotheses; Sect. 3.5 describes data and variables. Based on an outline of the empirical approach (Sect. 3.6), the results are presented and discussed in Sect. 3.7. Section 3.8 concludes.

3.2 Theoretical Framework

3.2.1 Knowledge Spillovers and Innovative Start-Ups

The knowledge spillover theory of entrepreneurship (Acs et al. 2009, 2013) is based on the assumption that starting an innovative venture requires knowledge. Since a large part of the necessary knowledge resides in universities, non-university public research organizations, and incumbent firms, this approach views innovative start-ups as a form of knowledge spillover, that is, the knowledge of these institutions spills over into the newly founded business. A key assumption of the theory is that the knowledge commercialized by the innovative start-up would not otherwise be exploited. For example, incumbent firms may be unaware of the economic value of the knowledge or they may be unwilling to exploit it because they fear cannibalization of their established product portfolio. Universities and other research institutes either may have no incentive for commercializing their knowledge or not permitted to due to their status as nonprofit organizations. Hence, if someone with an idea about how to turn knowledge into a new product finds it impossible to realize this idea in his or her incumbent organization, then starting an own business may be the only feasible option for putting the idea into practice, especially since, due to the uncertainty of their economic value, new ideas in themselves cannot be traded on the open market.

3.2.2 Characteristics of Different Scientific Fields

Scientific fields vary considerably with regard to the type of knowledge they generate and its potential for commercialization. It is now common practice to classify knowledge as either codified or tacit. Codified knowledge is easily transmitted across space; tacit knowledge is bound to people and can be transmitted only by direct personal face-to-face contact (Kogut and Zander 1992; Gertler 2003). Thus, spatial proximity to a knowledge source is important for the transmission of tacit knowledge, but far less so for codified knowledge.

Classifying knowledge as either tacit or codified, however, is not always an easy task. According to Stephan (1996) and Asheim and Gertler (2005), knowledge generated by the natural sciences is generally codified knowledge due to this discipline's strict adherence to standard scientific methods, which enables the knowledge to be accessed via, for example, reading scientific publications. Moreover, knowledge in natural sciences tends to be analytic (Asheim and Gertler 2005) and abstract and thus potentially applicable in diverse contexts. In contrast, knowledge generated by the social sciences tends to be more tacit due to the lower degree of formalization in this field, and the same is true of certain applied sciences, such as engineering, that are more problem oriented than natural science and in which experience plays an important role. Asheim and Gertler (2005) characterize such problem-oriented, experience-based knowledge as "synthetic."[2]

A third type of knowledge base identified by Asheim et al. (2007) is "symbolic knowledge," which plays a significant role in fields such as cultural production, design, and marketing. Symbolic knowledge manifests as the creation of meaning, aesthetic qualities, and affect. The main sources of symbolic knowledge are creative processes, experimentation, and learning-by-doing. Like synthetic knowledge, symbolic knowledge is largely tacit and often context specific. Thus, spatial proximity will be more relevant for cooperation and spillovers in fields where knowledge is synthetic or symbolic than when it is of an analytic nature.

There is good reason to expect that knowledge generated by different scientific fields will not all be equally suited for commercialization by an innovative start-up. For example, applied research may be much easier to commercialize than knowledge generated from basic research in the natural sciences (e.g., chemistry, physics, and biology) because it is often geared toward solving concrete problems. And, most likely, it will be far easier to transition a technological invention from the natural or applied sciences into a marketable product than it will be to do so with the discoveries of the social sciences, for example, a new interpretation of an ancient philosopher or a further refinement of accounting methods.

[2]According to Asheim and Gertler (2005, 295), synthetic knowledge "is created less in a deductive process or through abstraction than through an inductive process of testing, experimentation, computer-based simulation or practical work." It is much more context specific than analytic knowledge.

3.3 Previous Research and Open Questions

There are very few empirical studies into how knowledge from different scientific fields influences the emergence of innovative start-ups. There is, however, a fair amount of work that investigates how research conducted in different scientific fields impacts industrial R&D. The majority of these studies suggest that applied sciences are the most important fields in this regard and that their impact clearly exceeds that of the natural sciences (Nelson 1986; Klevorick et al. 1995; Cohen et al. 2002). However, it is plausible that basic natural sciences have a substantial indirect impact given that they provide the input for the more applied sciences and that quite often those who work in applied sciences have had previous training in basic natural sciences. In support of this idea, work that limits itself to studying HEI activity in the natural and the applied sciences finds a positive relationship between this activity and the opening of new innovative businesses in the respective region (e.g., Acosta et al. 2011; Woodward et al. 2006; Zucker et al. 1998).[3] With regard to the relevant type of activity, Acosta et al. (2011) identify a relationship when looking at the number of graduates, but not for the number of university patents or number of publications. Woodward et al. (2006) only use R&D expenditure of HEIs engaged in significant research activity. Zucker et al. (1998) find that the number of regional start-ups in biotechnology can be explained by the number of highly productive star scientists and by the number of faculty that have obtained federal support for their research.[4] The authors suggest that the star scientists play a considerable role as founders of these new firms.

There are three studies that consider a broader spectrum of academic disciplines when assessing their impact on the emergence of innovative start-ups. The first of these, that by Audretsch et al. (2004), analyzes the regional distribution of 281 publicly listed firms in German high-technology and knowledge-intensive industries. According to this analysis, knowledge spillovers from universities had a strong effect on the location decisions of these firms, which were based not only on the output of universities but also on the nature of this output. The second study, Audretsch and Lehmann (2005), finds that if the number of publications is taken as a measure of a university's research output, it is only the number of publications generated by the natural sciences, not by the social sciences, that is statistically related to the number of innovative start-ups in the region. If the number of students and graduates is used as an output indicator, then both fields of knowledge appear to have a positive effect on the location decisions of innovative start-ups. The age of a

[3]The study by Acosta et al. (2011) is limited to HEI activity in "science and technology," but how this field is defined in detail is unclear. Woodward et al. (2006) analyze engineering, physical sciences, geosciences, mathematics and computer sciences, life sciences (including agricultural, biological, medical, and other life sciences), and science and engineering technologies. The study by Zucker et al. (1998) is limited to biotechnology.

[4]Remarkably, the number of co-authors of the star scientists has no statistically significant positive effect.

university, which may be viewed as an indication of reputation, is not statistically significant.

The third study (Baptista and Mendonça 2010) uses longitudinal data for firms, universities, and human capital in the regions of Portugal. The authors distinguish between two groups of disciplines: one group includes the basic sciences and engineering, the other is comprised of the social sciences. Three indicators for the presence of universities are included in the empirical models: the number of universities in the region, the number of students, and the number of graduates. Baptista and Mendonça (2010) find a positive and statistically significant effect for all three indicators. The number of students and graduates in basic and applied sciences has a significant positive effect on the number of new businesses in innovative manufacturing industries and knowledge-intensive services, whereas the effect of students and graduates in social sciences is limited to having a positive effect only on new business creation in knowledge-intensive services.

To summarize this rather sparse evidence, there is some indication that university activity in the fields of natural and applied sciences is somewhat more important for regional new business formation than activity in the social sciences.

Previous work on how different academic disciplines influence the emergence of innovative new business leaves many questions unanswered. The three studies that account for different fields of academic knowledge (Baptista and Mendonça 2010; Audretsch et al. 2004; Audretsch and Lehmann 2005) distinguish between only two research fields[5] and disregard others. Moreover, these studies have limited information about HEI activity in these fields. A further limitation of the work by Audretsch et al. (2004) and Audretsch and Lehmann (2005) is that the authors analyze only a selection of German universities, notably ignoring universities of applied sciences (*Fachhochschulen*), art colleges, and universities of public administration.[6] Another limitation of these works is their restricted focus on firms that are publicly listed on the German stock market. Clearly, these firms are not representative of the total population of innovative start-ups but are instead firms for which financiers had positive expectations with regard to growth and profitability. Hence, the relative importance of various disciplines to the emergence of innovative business remains an open question. Moreover, nothing is known about the possible impact of other types of HEIs, such as medical schools, universities of applied sciences, art colleges, or universities of public administration.

Another as yet unanswered question concerns the channels by which the knowledge that resides in HEIs spills over to new businesses. Who is it that transforms the academic knowledge into innovative start-ups? How many of these innovative new firms are started by former students? How many by faculty and former researchers? While Zucker et al. (1998) suggest that star scientists play an important role as

[5]Baptista and Mendonça (2010) merge engineering and basic sciences into one field and consider the social sciences as their second field. Audretsch et al. (2004) and Audretsch and Lehmann (2005) distinguish between natural sciences and the social sciences.

[6]Baptista and Mendonça (2010) provide no information about different types of HEIs in their data.

founders of new firms in the US biotech-industry, Åstebro et al. (2012) argue that the majority of founders should be former students simply because there are more of them (compared to faculty or researchers). Moreover, researchers with tenure may be unlikely to give up their secure job for something as risky as starting a firm. This may be particularly true of professors in German public universities who are civil servants and thus considerably restricted in regard to engaging in private-sector activity.

3.4 Research Design and Hypotheses

3.4.1 Classification of HEIs and Fields of Scientific Knowledge

Nearly all HEIs in Germany are public. The higher education system consists of regular universities and universities of applied sciences (*Fachhochschulen*), and the two are different in many respects, including purpose, scope and size, teaching, and research (Warning 2007). Universities of applied sciences are mainly intended to provide undergraduate education with a focus on transferring theoretical concepts and scientific methods into practical application; these universities do not grant PhDs. Courses are more structured than in regular universities and classes are smaller. Professors at the universities of applied sciences have much higher teaching loads than those at the regular universities and little or no support in terms of finance or personnel for conducting research. On average, universities of applied sciences are much smaller in terms of personnel and students than regular universities.

Regular universities usually cover a broad range of academic disciplines. They include medical schools (*Universitätskliniken*), schools of public administration (*Verwaltungshochschulen*), and arts colleges (*Kunsthochschulen*), all of which are significantly different in regard to both their research as well as their educational profiles. A special feature of the medical schools is that they have hospitals. Due to their distinct characteristics, they are counted as a separate university although nearly all of them are part of a university. The main mission of the universities of public administration is to educate civil servants for higher positions in public service with a clear focus on law and management. Art colleges engage in very little research at all, according to the conventional understanding of the term, and are characterized by quite special forms of education. The more symbolic type of knowledge that these institutions generate and possess, however, could be important for the emergence of innovative new businesses.

Germany is also home to a number of independent non-university research institutes, including those of the Max Planck Society, the Fraunhofer Society, the Helmholtz Association, and the Gottfried Wilhelm Leibniz Scientific Community. Although these institutes have in common that they are predominantly nongovernmental and nonprofit associations funded by the federal and state governments, they differ with regard to the type of research in which they engage. For example, the institutes of the Max Planck Society conduct predominantly basic research in different fields such as applied sciences, natural sciences, social sciences, and the arts and humanities, whereas the institutes of the Fraunhofer Society specialize in applied sciences research in collaboration with various industrial sectors. The Helmholtz Association of German Research Centers and the Gottfried Wilhelm Leibniz Scientific Community are networks of national laboratories and institutes that perform research in applied sciences as well as in basic natural sciences. These non-university research institutes are famous for the quality and prominence of their work. For instance, the Max Planck Institutes, which are regarded as the foremost basic research organization in Germany and Europe, have received no fewer than 17 Nobel prizes over the last 65 years.

All indicators for HEIs distinguish between five categories of academic knowledge: natural sciences, applied sciences, medical science, administrative and political sciences, and other disciplines. This typology is designed to account for the unique aspects of each field and for the common assignment of academic disciplines to specific departments or schools. Note that the non-university research institutes are assigned to these fields, too.[7] Natural sciences include fields that seek to discover the rules that govern the natural world, for example, physics, chemistry, biology, mathematics, and the like. Applied sciences cover technical fields that focus on developing more practical applications from existing scientific knowledge, for example, architecture, engineering, and spatial planning. Medical science is largely based on natural sciences with a focus on concrete problem solving. Administration and political sciences include those fields concerned with the organization of society, such as economics, law, management, political sciences, public administration, and sociology. "Other disciplines" cover a broad range of nontechnical academic fields, such as linguistics, history, arts, and theology, the research results of which are rarely commercialized by private-sector innovators. Table A.15 in the Appendix contains a list of the disciplines included in each category. With regard to the type of HEI, it will be distinguished between regular universities, universities of applied sciences, medical schools, universities of public administration, and arts colleges.

3.4.2 *Expectations*

Given the limited knowledge about the relationship between academic disciplines, type of HEI, and innovative start-ups, the investigation in this chapter is explorative

[7]The non-university research institutes that may be relevant for medical science focus on natural sciences such as pharmacy and biology. Hence, these institutes are assigned to the natural sciences and not to medicine.

in nature. The basic hypothesis is that the knowledge generated by different disciplines will not all equally create opportunities for innovative start-ups; moreover, when such knowledge does have such potential, it is hypothesized that its realization will take different forms. It also seems reasonable to expect that knowledge spillovers in each scientific field predominantly foster a certain kind of start-ups. Accordingly, research and education in basic and applied sciences (including medical science) should be particularly conducive to new business formation in high-tech manufacturing, while the activities of other disciplines may primarily generate start-ups in technology-oriented services.

It is expected that regional knowledge in natural, applied, and medical science will have a positive effect on the emergence of innovative start-ups. Since applied and medical science often generate technical knowledge from practical problem solving, this knowledge should be easier to commercialize than knowledge generated by the natural sciences. Hence, the relationship between knowledge in the applied and medical sciences and start-ups should be stronger than for knowledge in the natural sciences. Knowledge from administrative, political, and other sciences such as sociology, psychology, law, and management has only limited potential for commercialization. Thus, it is expected that HEI activity in such fields will have a weak effect, if any, on the emergence of innovative start-ups.

Because the regular universities and medical schools conduct much more research than the universities of applied sciences, it is expected that they have a stronger impact on the emergence of innovative new businesses. Similarly, because arts colleges and universities of public administration have hardly any focus on technology, their effect should be relatively weak. Another reason for expecting that universities of public administration will have no pronounced effect on the emergence of innovative start-ups is that their mission is to train personnel for the public sector, which, almost by definition, should attract individuals with a low propensity to start an own business.

HEIs' knowledge resides in their scientific staff, particularly the professors, who are key to organizing research and applying for research funds. Hence, the number of professors can be viewed as a key indicator for the knowledge stock. Another measure for the amount and quality of research is the amount of external research funds obtained. Because external funds are nearly always allocated via some kind of competitive procedure, they can be regarded as an indication of research quality. When funding is granted by private firms, it is usually for collaborative and contract research and, therefore, indicates knowledge transfer to the private sector for purposes of commercialization. A considerable part of HEIs' knowledge is transferred to students via teaching activities. Later in life, these students may attempt to commercialize this knowledge by founding an own business. Since professors in German public universities are civil servants who are subject to considerable restriction in regard to engaging in private-sector activity, their propensity for starting an own firm can be assumed to be much lower than that of former students. Moreover, sheer numbers alone make it more likely that more new businesses are set up by students, as opposed to professors or other researchers (Åstebro et al. 2012). For these reasons, it is plausible to expect a closer statistical relationship between the number of students and graduates and the number of innovative new businesses than between the number of professors and research staff and the number of new businesses.

3.5 Data, Variables, and Descriptive Statistics

3.5.1 Data

The data on start-ups are from the Founder Panel of the Center for European Economic Research (ZEW-Mannheim) and include nearly every independent firm founded during the period 1995–2008 (ZEW 2011). These data are based on information from the largest German credit rating agency (Creditreform). This agency covers all private sectors in Germany and identifies innovative new businesses based on their affiliation with certain industries. The common way of classifying industries based on their presumed innovativeness is used, which distinguishes among (1) high-technology manufacturing industries that devote more than 8.5 % of their input to R&D, (2) technologically advanced manufacturing industries with an R&D intensity between 3.5 and 8.5 %, and (3) technology-oriented services (Grupp and Legler 2000; OECD 2005; Gehrke et al. 2010). Technology-oriented services comprise a subgroup of knowledge-intensive services and include industries that are particularly related to innovation activity such as architectural and engineering activities, technical consultancy, and technical testing and analysis. In addition, all models are run for those industries not classified as innovative or knowledge intensive. A main problem of this classification system is that industry affiliation is a fuzzy criterion because there are innovative and not so innovative firms in all industries. Given the limited availability of data on innovation, however, this is often the only feasible way to identify new businesses as being innovative.[8]

Most of the information on the independent variables comes from one of two sources. Data on regional private-sector employment and R&D employment are from the German Employment Statistics, which covers all employees subject to compulsory social insurance contributions (Spengler 2008). The second data source is the University Statistics of the German Federal Statistical Office, which provides detailed information about every university in Germany (Statistisches Bundesamt, various volumes). Data on unemployment are from the German Employment Agency (*Bundesagentur für Arbeit*). The spatial framework of the analysis is based on the 402 German districts (*Kreise*). To attain functional regions those districts that only encompass cities (*kreisfreie Stadt, urban district*) are merged

[8]See Fritsch (2011) for the classification of German industries as "innovative," "technologically advanced," or "technology-intensive services."

with the surrounding territorial districts, resulting in 325 regions (Federal Office for Building and Regional Planning 2003).[9]

No detailed regional data are available for the non-university public research institutions. However, the number of such institutes in each region is known.[10] Information about the number of patents is from the Patent Statistics. Patents are assigned to the region where the inventor has his or her residence.[11]

3.5.2 Variables

As dependent variables, the number of start-ups is used in high-technology manufacturing industries, in technologically advanced manufacturing industries, in technology-oriented services, and in those industries that are not classified as innovative or knowledge intensive. In the baseline model the size of the regional workforce is included, which represents the pool of potential entrepreneurs and also reflects economies of size and agglomeration effects. The regional workforce is divided into the number of private-sector R&D employees, the number of employed persons excluding R&D employees, and the number of persons registered as being unemployed. The number of R&D employees is an important part of a region's knowledge pool. Since the number of R&D employees is highly correlated with the number of people with a tertiary degree, an indicator for the share of the workforce holding a tertiary degree is not included. A positive effect on the emergence of innovative start-ups is expected from the number of employed people, particularly the number of R&D employees, but the impact of the number of unemployed people is a priori unclear. On the one hand, innovative start-ups, of course, can be set up by the unemployed. On the other hand, unemployed people have a relatively low propensity for starting their own business (Fritsch and Falck 2007), and this may be particularly true when it comes to innovative ventures that primarily represent opportunity, rather than necessity, entrepreneurship and require a relatively high level of qualification. Moreover, a high number of unemployed people in a region can be viewed as an indication of bad economic conditions and, therefore, indicate poor prospects for success, which may prevent potential founders from setting up a firm in the region (Carree 2002; Sutaria and Hicks 2004).

---

[9]For an official translation for the German administrative divisions, see EC-DGT (2014).

[10]All institutes of the four large public research organizations in Germany are accounted for, i.e., the Fraunhofer, the Helmholtz, the Leibnitz, and the Max Planck Society. Data were collected from various sources, chiefly from publications of these organizations and the Federal Ministry of Education and Research. Since a number of these institutes have several locations, the publicly available information about their budgets and number of personnel cannot be meaningfully assigned to regions.

[11]If a patent has more than one inventor, the count is divided by the number of inventors and each inventor is assigned his or her share of that patent.

If public and private research in a region is conducive to the emergence of innovative start-ups, a concentration of this kind of new business may be expected in larger cities and agglomerations because both public research institutes as well as private-sector R&D tend to be concentrated in such high-density areas. Other reasons for expecting a relatively high number of innovative start-ups in larger cities include agglomeration economies, such as large and diversified input markets and rich opportunities for direct face-to-face contact, which can be assumed conducive to the transfer of knowledge. A measure for population density is not included in the standard models because of its close statistical relationship with other variables that would lead to severe multicollinearity problems. Due to its close correlation with many other factors that may be the "true" determinants of innovative start-ups, including population density could obscure the effects that these other factors have on the emergence of innovative start-ups. However, in order to analyze the influence of agglomeration effects, the models are run for groups of regions having various population densities.

As indicators for HEI activity the number of professors, the number of students, and the number of PhD graduates, as well as the amount of external funds is used.[12] These variables reflect different aspects of the HEI's size. The number of students and PhD graduates indicates a contribution to the workforce's education (i.e., its qualifications), particularly the number of potential founders with an academic background. The number of professors and amount of external funding obtained primarily signify the knowledge stock and the volume of research being conducted. Tables A.16–A.19 present descriptive statistics and correlations for the variables included in the analyses.

3.6 Empirical Approach

Due to the count character of the independent variable—the number of start-ups—a negative binomial estimation technique is employed. Because of a relatively high share of observations with no regional start-up in high-technology manufacturing in a year (27.78 %), a "too many zero values" problem could appear. A possible solution to this problem is to apply the zero-inflated version of the negative binomial method, which includes only a selection of "true" zero values in the estimation. Under this method, regions in which the event of interest (i.e., formation of an innovative start-up) is never expected to occur are excluded from the estimation. The zero-inflated negative binomial method requires an assumption for identifying and selecting the "true" zero values. Since the data show that all

[12]Alternative indicators of HEI activity, such as the number of graduates, amount of regular funds, etc. (see Fritsch and Aamoucke 2013), are highly correlated with the indicators reported here and do not provide additional insight. The results are not reported for such alternative indicators due to space limitations. Note that the data do not provide information about the number of PhD students but only about those who have actually earned a PhD.

regions in Germany have at least one start-up in high-technology industries from time to time, all the zero values in the data have to be regarded as "true" and thus the zero-inflated negative binomial estimation method is inappropriate. For the technologically advanced start-ups, the share of observations without a new business in a year is 13.54 % and for technology-intensive services it is 0.07 %, suggesting that there is no "too many zero values" problem.

The analyses are conducted on the basis of a time series of yearly observations for a period of 14 years and thus a panel estimation techniques can be employed. Since many of the potential explanatory variables (e.g., number of universities in the region) show little or no variation over time, a fixed effects estimator that would account for unobserved regional characteristics is not appropriate because a considerable part of the influence of such variables is captured by the fixed effects. Thus a random effects estimator is used. Since the standard statistical software packages do not provide spatial lag and spatial error corrections for negative binomial panel models, dummy variables for the German Federal States (*Laender*) are included in order to control for effects of the wider regional environment. Moreover, the number of R&D employees in adjacent regions is included as a control for interregional spillovers. Since the German Federal States are an important policy-making level, this variable may also indicate the effect of policy measures at this level. Year dummies are included as controls for time-specific effects. All independent variables are lagged by 1 year.

A severe problem of the empirical analysis is the high correlation among most of the indicators for the universities (see Table A.19 in the Appendix). To a considerable extent, these pronounced correlations are caused by a variation of these variables with size due to complementarity, for example, having a large number of students means a larger teaching staff and more resources. This problem is captured as follows. In a first step, a baseline model without the indicators for universities and non-university public research institutes is estimated. In a second step, the indicators for public research are added one at a time. The measure for the impact of these indicators is change in the AIC (Akaike information criterion) compared to the baseline model. The AIC is a measure of a statistical model's relative goodness of fit that accounts for the number of independent variables included in the model (Akaike 1974; Greene 2012). A decrease in the AIC value due to the inclusion of an additional variable indicates a better fit of the model in terms of reducing the remaining "unexplained" variance. An increase in the remaining variance leads to a higher AIC value. In a final step, factor analyses are performed in order to aggregate the information about HEIs and add the resulting factor to the variables of the baseline model. Since the dependent as well as the independent variables are logged, the values of the estimated coefficients can be interpreted as elasticities that indicate the relative importance of the respective effect.

3.7 Results

3.7.1 Results for the Baseline Model

In the baseline model positive and statistically significant effects are found for the number of regional employees, excluding R&D employees, as well as for the employment share in the respective industries for the number of start-ups in all four industry groups (Table 3.1). In line with the expectations, the coefficient for the number of R&D employees has the highest value for new businesses in high-technology manufacturing industries followed by those in technologically advanced manufacturing and in technology-oriented services; it is not statistically significant for start-ups in non-innovative industries. The fact that the number of unemployed people has an effect only on start-ups in non-innovative industries clearly indicates that new businesses set up by unemployed people tend to occur in these industries. The share of employees in establishments with fewer than 50 employees also has a statistically significant positive effect except for start-ups in technologically advanced manufacturing. This positive effect may indicate that founders of new businesses were previously employed in small firms or that the presence of industries with low minimum efficient size is conducive to start-ups (Fritsch and Falck 2007).

The number of patents per 1000 employees has a positive effect on start-ups in high-technology manufacturing and technology-oriented services but it is not statistically significant for start-ups in technologically advanced manufacturing. The relationship between number of patents and number of start-ups in non-innovative industries is statistically significant but with a negative sign. This clearly indicates the importance of regional knowledge for the formation of innovative new businesses. No significantly positive effect is found for the number of R&D employees in surrounding regions, suggesting that interregional spillovers from R&D employment are irrelevant for the emergence of new businesses, even in the rather narrowly defined regions in the analyses of this chapter. Including measures for the concentration of the regional industry structure (i.e., spatial clustering) does not lead to any plausible or statistically significant results.

3.7.2 How Does the Impact of HEIs Differ Across Various Scientific Fields and Types of HEI?

The number of professors in different scientific fields is included in the baseline model and the changes in the AIC value is computed.[13] The highest increase in

[13]Professors in arts colleges and in universities of public administration are omitted here because of the special character of these types of institutions.

Table 3.1 Baseline model for explaining number of start-ups in different groups of industries

	High-technology manufacturing	Technologically advanced manufacturing	Technology-oriented services	Non-innovative industries
Number of employed persons, excluding R&D employees	.0347*** (3.26)	.0311*** (3.56)	.0304*** (7.12)	.5467*** (19.76)
Number of R&D employees	.00002*** (4.11)	7.97e-06*** (2.45)	3.54e-06** (1.92)	6.89e-07 (.88)
Number of unemployed	.0110 (.55)	.0095 (.59)	.0042 (1.00)	.0067*** (7.14)
Share of employees in high-technology manufacturing industries	.0971*** (7.02)	–	–	–
Share of employees in technologically advanced manufacturing industries	–	.0199** (2.09)	–	–
Share of employees in technology-oriented service industries	–	–	.0198*** (2.76)	–
Share of employees in non-innovative industries	–	–	–	.0724*** (2.50)
Share of employees in establishments with fewer than 50 employees	.2427** (1.99)	.0625 (1.57)	.2322*** (2.92)	.2665*** (11.05)
Number of R&D employees in adjacent regions	.0194 (.84)	−.0102 (.56)	−.0214*** (3.69)	−.0040* (1.64)
Number of patents per 1000 employees	51.3587*** (3.38)	−.3425 (.03)	17.5053*** (3.34)	−2.4442*** (.94)
Constant	.7197*** (10.26)	1.3684*** (13.82)	2.6735*** (29.67)	−1.4930*** (39.38)
Wald chi^2	573.25***	479.07***	899.48***	2756.17***
Dummies for Federal States	Yes***	Yes***	Yes***	Yes***
Dummies for years	Yes***	Yes***	Yes***	Yes***
Number of observations (number of zeros)	4550 (1264)	4550 (616)	4550 (3)	4550 (0)
Log likelihood	−8489.27	−10,252.94	−16,669.05	−20,695.38
AIC	17,042.54	20,563.87	33,402.10	41,455.08
Pseudo R^2	.6342	.5545	.7431	.6518
McFadden's R^2	.105	.106	.109	.178

Notes: The dependent variable is the number of start-ups per year in the respective group of industries. Negative binomial panel regression with random effects. Z-values in parentheses. All independent variables except dummies are entered with their logarithmic values (ln)
***Statistically significant at the 1 % level; **Statistically significant at the 5 % level; *Statistically significant at the 10 % level

explained variance is found for the number of professors in applied sciences followed by the number of professors in natural sciences and in medical science (Table 3.2). The effect of the number of professors in administration and political sciences is considerably less pronounced, and professors in "other" scientific fields, such as linguistics, arts, and theology, appear to have the weakest effect on the number of start-ups. It is possible that the results for the applied sciences underestimate the impact of the natural sciences because the basic training in natural sciences that students in applied science receive is assigned to the applied sciences in these estimates (Nelson 1986; Klevorick et al. 1995; Cohen et al. 2002). For this reason both natural and applied sciences are included together into the model. The variable that reflects natural and applied sciences together yields the strongest increase in the explained variance as indicated by reduction of the AIC value. This finding indicates that natural and applied sciences are the most influential fields for stimulating innovative start-ups.

To compare the effect of different types of HEIs on the explained variance the indicators for regular universities and universities of applied sciences are included with regard to natural sciences and applied sciences separately (Table 3.2). Moreover, the effect of the type of institution (including art colleges and universities of public administration) is tested taking all scientific fields together. With regard to the number of professors in the natural sciences the highest increase in explained variance, as indicated by reduction of the AIC values, is found for the number of professors in regular universities followed by the number of professors in universities of applied sciences (Table 3.2). In the applied sciences, professors in both types of institutions produce about the same improvements of the AIC (with a slightly smaller impact of the professors at the regular universities).Taking all scientific fields together results in mixed findings. The effects of regular universities and medical schools are stronger than those of the universities of applied sciences with regard to entries in high-technology manufacturing, but this difference is negligible for start-ups in the other three categories (Table 3.2). This result may be due to the fact that universities of applied sciences have much higher shares of professors in the applied sciences than do other types of HEIs. Not surprisingly, the effect of the arts colleges and of universities of public administration is considerably weaker than the effect of all other types of HEIs.

3.7.3 *How Does the Impact of HEIs Differ Across Transmission Channel?*

This section analyzes different transmission channels of knowledge spillovers and compares the effects of the number of professors with those of the number of students, the number of PhD graduates, and the amount of external funding obtained. These indicators represent two types of transmission channels for knowledge spillovers: (1) the number of students, PhD graduates, and professors indicate

Table 3.2 Change in the AIC value compared to the baseline model due to the inclusion of the number of professors in different disciplines and types of HEIs

	High-technology manufacturing	Technologically advanced manufacturing	Technology-oriented services	Non-innovative industries
All professors	−36.99 .0742 (6.22)***	−36.31 .0607 (6.28)***	−19.2 .0240 (4.59)***	358.87 −.0050 (1.10)
Scientific field[a]				
Natural sciences	−111.97 .2835 (2.70)***	−135.11 .2992 (3.51)***	−124.95 .2312 (5.34)***	435.05 −.0536 (1.51)
Applied sciences	−163.11 .7482 (4.32)***	−154.43 .4486 (3.18)***	−146.92 .2955 (3.95)***	440.02 −.1262 (2.04)**
Medical science	−105.17 .7572 (3.40)***	−134.73 .6832 (2.50)***	−28.91 .0723 (.098)*	445.03 −.0040 (.59)
Natural and applied sciences	−179.31 .9575 (3.23)***	−168.12 .6081 (2.52)***	−163.45 .6010 (4.76)***	441.20 −.2060 (1.72)*
Medical science	−105.17 .7572 (3.40)***	−134.73 .6832 (2.50)***	−28.91 .0723 (.098)*	445.03 −.0040 (.59)
Administrative and political sciences	−63.80 .0982 (1.06)	−70.11 .2246 (4.79)***	−124.75 .2511 (4.09)***	108.23 .0097 (.200)
Others	−3.38 .0153 (.93)	−4.43 .0188 (1.49)	−11.30 .0222 (3.64)***	93.84 −.0047 (−.740)
Natural sciences[a]				
Regular universities	−82.42 .2481 (3.68)***	−110.24 .1711 (5.30)***	−100.88 .0099 (1.07)	436.23 .0860 (1.06)
Universities of applied sciences	−46.79 .0909 (1.66)*	−93.47 .0850 (2.11)**	−88.05 .0248 (1.22)	430.03 .0017 (.140)
Applied sciences[a]				
Regular universities	−149.64 .4232 (2.81)***	−144.38 .5928 (4.59)***	−113.95 .1532 (1.35)	447.71 −.0370 (2.05)**
Universities of applied sciences	−151.12 .4772 (4.32)***	−148.37 .5165 (4.44)***	−124.26 .3094 (3.49)***	446.92 −.1139 (1.53)
Type of HEIs				
Regular universities	−104.79 .8589 (3.56)***	−137.00 .7739 (4.96)***	−25.33 .0494 (.53)	437.00 −.0418 (2.81)***
Universities of applied sciences	−84.75 .9419 (4.20)***	−137.30 .9475 (3.77)***	−31.45 .1123 (2.06)**	443.41 −.0444 (.97)
Medical schools	−105.17 .7572 (3.40)***	−134.73 .6832 (2.50)***	−28.91 .0723 (.098)*	445.03 −.0040 (.59)

(continued)

Table 3.2 (continued)

	High-technology manufacturing	Technologically advanced manufacturing	Technology-oriented services	Non-innovative industries
Arts colleges	−10.10 .0045 (2.16)**	−15.73 .0056 (3.75)***	−8.53 .0012 (1.49)	87.55 −.0007 (1.09)
Universities of public administration	−7.29 .0017 (.65)	−7.13 .0047 (2.34)**	−30.79 .0206 (1.93)**	73.38 .0026 (3.88)***

Notes: Number of professors entered with the logarithmic value (ln). First row: Change in the AIC value due to the inclusion of the variable. Second row: Estimated coefficient and z-value in parentheses

*Statistically significant at the 10 % level; **Statistically significant at the 5 % level; ***Statistically significant at the 1 % level

[a]Professors of regular universities (including medical schools) and universities of applied sciences only

the role of these groups as potential founders of innovative new businesses and (2) the extent of research activities and the knowledge stock is represented by the number of professors, the number of PhD students and the amount of external funding obtained. This section compares these two types of transmission channels by scientific field as well as by type of HEI.[14]

A key result of these analyses is that in all scientific fields, the number of professors shows the highest decrease in the AIC value, indicating better model fit (Tables 3.3 and 3.4). This finding is valid for all types of innovative start-ups as well as for all types of HEIs. The better fit of models with the number of professors compared to models with the number of students and PhD graduates seems contrary to the idea that students and PhD graduates are the main channels through which knowledge is transformed into new innovative businesses. This result is interesting because—as mentioned earlier—due to the institutional framework in Germany, it is unlikely that professors will found an own firm. Hence, it is not so much professors as founders themselves, but more their role as knowledge sources, researchers, and fundraisers that has such an impact on the emergence of innovative businesses. Surprisingly, the amount of external funding obtained leads to the lowest decrease in the AIC value in most of the models, possibly indicating that the translation of knowledge into entrepreneurship via the education of students is quantitatively more important than via research.

[14]The analyses omit arts colleges and universities of public administration because of the special character of these types of institutions and because of their rather weak effect, as discussed in the previous section.

Table 3.3 Change in the AIC value compared to the baseline model due to the inclusion of diverse indicators of HEIs in natural sciences and engineering

	High-technology manufacturing	Technologically advanced manufacturing	Technology-oriented services	Non-innovative industries
Natural sciences				
Professors	−111.97 .2835 (2.70)***	−135.11 .2992 (3.51)***	−124.95 .2312 (5.34)***	435.05 −.0536 (1.51)
Students	−90.34 .1365 (3.46)***	−123.54 .1154 (3.70)***	−106.21 .0859 (5.47)***	437.11 −.0054 (0.46)
PhD graduates	−74.02 .0609 (4.10)***	−100.05 .0462 (3.83)***	−121.14 .0310 (4.98)***	437.01 −.0030 (0.55)
External funds	−74.15 .0194 (3.00)***	−111.03 .0098 (1.97)**	−83.97 .0071 (2.84)***	437.27 .0004 (0.23)
Applied sciences				
Professors	−163.11 .7482 (4.32)***	−154.43 .4486 (3.18)***	−146.92 .2955 (3.95)***	440.02 −.1262 (2.04)**
Students	−158.00 .2957 (3.68)***	−111.69 .1653 (2.51)***	−137.40 .1140 (3.32)***	436.57 −.0754 (2.76) ***
PhD graduates	−118.13 .0460 (2.56)***	−68.71 .0441 (3.02)***	−115.40 .0175 (2.33)**	443.69 −.0038 (0.68)
External funds	−118.64 .0181 (2.65)***	−90.45 .0111 (2.06)**	−110.67 .0054 (2.03)**	444.12 .0003 (0.17)
Natural and applied sciences				
Professors	−179.31 .9575 (3.23)***	−168.12 .6081 (2.52)***	−163.45 .6010 (4.76)***	441.20 −.2060 (1.72)*
Students	−164.38 .3114 (2.67)***	−132.90 .2620 (2.77)***	−143.38 .1936 (3.91)***	441.89 −.0639 (1.50)
PhD graduates	−118.24 .1575 (3.27)***	−120.47 .1562 (4.01)***	−118.30 .0185 (0.97)	442.11 .0158 (1.43)
External funds	−118.94 .0847 (3.37)***	−101.77 .0498 (2.47)***	−118.81 .0118 (1.20)	443.77 −.0028 (0.61)
Medical science				
Professors	−105.17 .7572 (3.40)***	−134.73 .6832 (2.50)***	−28.91 .0723 (.098)*	445.03 −.0040 (.59)
Students	−101.00 .0231 (2.73)***	−131.95 .3744 (1.88)*	−20.47 .05923 (2.22)**	445.21 .0008 (.41)
PhD graduates	−103.33 .0437 (3.13)***	−131.60 .3841 (1.78)*	−22.84 .0454 (2.71)***	444.76 −.0037 (.79)
External funds	−47.98 .0157 (2.15)**	−130.44 .1592 (1.41)	−11.15 −.0003 (.11)	424.20 −.0080 (.00)

Notes: Variables entered with their logarithmic values (ln). First row: Change in the AIC value due to the inclusion of the variable. Second row: Estimated coefficient and z-value in parentheses
***Statistically significant at the 1 % level; **Statistically significant at the 5 % level; *Statistically significant at the 10 % level

Table 3.4 Change in the AIC value compared to the baseline model due to the inclusion of diverse indicators of HEIs in regular universities, universities of applied sciences, and medical schools

	High-technology manufacturing	Technologically advanced manufacturing	Technology-oriented services	Non-innovative industries
Regular universities				
Professors	−104.79 .8589 (3.56)***	−137.00 .7739 (4.96)***	−25.33 .0494 (.53)	437.00 −.0418 (2.81)***
Students	−99.15 .5717 (3.90)***	−124.25 .5983 (4.99)***	−13.78 .0014 (0.30)	448.62 −.0298 (3.40)***
PhD graduates	−95.34 .0612 (3.76)***	−120.82 .0661 (5.01)***	−11.93 .0038 (0.628)	449.65 −.0386 (3.29)***
External funds	−85.36 .0317 (3.51)***	−105.63 .0353 (4.75)***	−9.81 .0001 (0.23)	446.15 −.0288 (3.69)***
Universities of applied sciences				
Professors	−84.75 .9419 (4.20)***	−137.30 .9475 (3.77)***	−31.45 .1123 (2.06)**	443.41 −.0444 (.97)
Students	−75.65 .5955 (3.65)***	−111.60 .4429 (3.82)***	−29.75 .0990 (1.60)	436.45 −.1425 (2.81)***
PhD graduates	−72.81 .0269 (3.25)***	−102.73 .0148 (2.37)**	−29.76 .0051 (1.60)	442.56 −.0030 (1.34)
Medical schools				
Professors	−105.17 .7572 (3.40)***	−134.73 .6832 (2.50)***	−28.91 .0723 (.098)*	445.03 −.0040 (.59)
Students	−101.00 .0231 (2.73)***	−131.95 .3744 (1.88)*	−20.47 .05923 (2.22)**	445.21 .0008 (.41)
PhD graduates	−103.33 .0437 (3.13)***	−131.60 .3841 (1.78)*	−22.84 .0454 (2.71)***	444.76 −.0037 (.79)
External funds	−47.98 .0157 (2.15)**	−130.44 .1592 (1.41)	−11.15 −.0003 (.11)	424.20 −.0080 (.00)

Notes: First row: Change in the AIC value due to the inclusion of the variable. Second row: Estimated coefficient and z-value in parentheses. Universities of applied sciences are not entitled to grant PhD degrees

***Statistically significant at the 1 % level; **Statistically significant at the 5 % level; *Statistically significant at the 10 % level

3.7.4 Aggregation of Indicators for Regional Public Research

To aggregate the information provided by the indicators for HEIs, factor analyses are conducted. These factor analyses show that different types of HEI activity, such as education and research, cannot be meaningfully separated into different factors. Hence, only one factor is generated in order to represent regional HEIs, which is based on the number of professors, the number of students, the number of graduates, the number of PhD graduates, and the amount of external funding obtained (see Table A.20 in the Appendix). In the baseline model, for each scientific field one factor is included for the activity of all HEIs within the region and one factor for HEI activity in adjacent regions. These factors are not logged because negative values would result in missing values of the logs.

The results of the baseline model with the aggregate indicators for public research are set out in Table 3.5. The results show that aggregate indicators for applied sciences are highly significant with the expected sign in the models for start-ups in high-technology manufacturing, technologically advanced manufacturing, and technology-oriented services. For natural sciences, the aggregate indicators are significant with the expected sign for both types of manufacturing start-ups. Aggregate indicators for adjacent regions are not significant for any of the scientific fields. A main difference between these results and those of the baseline model without aggregate indicators for public research (Table 3.1) is that the number of regional private-sector R&D employees loses considerable statistical significance, thus raising questions as to the relationship between and relative importance of private and public R&D. Since the relationship between public and private R&D is complex and because of the considerable correlation between the indicators for the two types of activity, it is problematic to conclude from these results that public R&D is more important for innovative start-ups than private-sector R&D.

Presumably, the main source of this correlation is that there are pronounced spatially concentrated knowledge spillovers between public and private R&D (Fritsch and Slavtchev 2007). Such spatially bounded knowledge spillovers are one reason for the co-location of public- and private-sector R&D facilities. Moreover, both types of R&D prefer the same type of location, mainly larger cities. Hence, public institutions of education and research may provide important inputs for private-sector R&D, and R&D in both sectors may be interrelated, particularly at the regional level.

3.7.5 The Impact of Non-university Research Institutes

Since the information on non-university public research institutes is limited to the type and number of such institutes, this section includes in the baseline model the number of each type of institute in the region and in adjacent regions and computes the change in the AIC value (Table 3.6). The results reveal that the number of non-university research institutes in natural and applied sciences together shows the highest decrease of the AIC value. This finding is valid for all types of innovative start-ups. If each scientific field is considered separately, the number of non-university institutes in applied sciences induces the highest decrease in the AIC value followed by the institutes working in the natural sciences.

Table 3.5 Baseline model with aggregate indicators for HEIs

	High-technology manufacturing	Technologically advanced manufacturing	Technology-oriented services	Non-innovative industries
Number of employed persons, excluding R&D employees	.0228** (2.28)	.0290*** (3.64)	.0287*** (6.91)	.5522*** (19.09)
Number of R&D employees	8.16e-06*** (2.40)	1.82e-06 (0.64)	2.97e-06* (1.82)	2.85e-07 (0.36)
Number of unemployed	−.0215 (1.12)	−.0250* (1.67)	−.0159** (2.23)	.0041*** (2.64)
Share of employees in high-technology manufacturing industries	1057*** (7.43)	–	–	–
Share of employees in technologically advanced manufacturing industries	–	.0348*** (3.30)	–	–
Share of employees in technology-oriented service industries	–	–	.0287*** (4.99)	–
Share of employees in non-innovative industries	–	–	–	.0814*** (2.80)
Share of employees in establishments with fewer than 50 employees	.2993** (2.33)	−.1328 (1.62)	.1594*** (4.19)	.2559*** (9.83)
Number of R&D employees in adjacent regions	.0500** (2.28)	.0175 (1.03)	.0007 (.08)	−.0009 (.35)
Number of patents per 1000 employees	46.832*** (3.15)	−2.726 (.27)	10.586** (2.41)	−2.249 (.85)
Aggregate indicator for HEIs in:				
Natural sciences	.0922 (.90)	.0862*** (1.10)	−.0524 (1.22)	.0102 (.55)
Applied sciences	.2901*** (2.47)	.3072*** (3.47)	.1100** (2.18)	.0194 (.89)
Medical science	.0369 (1.01)	.0542* (1.87)	.0169 (1.04)	−.0038 (.51)
Administration and political sciences	−.0389 (.93)	.0079 (.23)	.0046 (.29)	.0131 (1.53)
Other disciplines	−.0199 (.39)	.0168 (0.33)	−.0236 (1.07)	−.0075 (.65)
Aggregate indicator for HEIs (adjacent regions) in				
Natural sciences	.1075 (1.00)	−.0366 (.44)	.0104 (.49)	−.0037 (1.31)
Applied sciences	.0188 (.91)	.0164 (1.03)	−.0238 (1.16)	−.0001 (.02)
Medicine	−.0750 (1.04)	.0026 (0.05)	−.0206*** (3.76)	−.0080*** (3.09)

(continued)

Table 3.5 (continued)

	High-technology manufacturing	Technologically advanced manufacturing	Technology-oriented services	Non-innovative industries
Administration and political sciences	−.0296 (.33)	.0607 (.89)	.0024 (.39)	.0120 (1.39)
Other disciplines	.0662 (1.34)	.0438 (1.18)	−.0309 (1.13)	.0050 (.35)
Constant	.3367 * (1.86)	1.338*** (9.28)	2.604*** (25.31)	−1.756*** (5.77)
AIC change	−102.91	−96.82	−39.97	18.34

Notes: The dependent variable is the number of start-ups per year in the respective group of industries. Negative binomial panel regression with random effects. Z-values in parentheses
***Statistically significant at the 1 % level; **Statistically significant at the 5 % level; *Statistically significant at the 10 % level

Table 3.6 Change in the AIC value compared to the baseline model due to the inclusion of the number of non-university research institutes altogether and according to discipline

	High-technology manufacturing	Technologically advanced manufacturing	Technology-oriented services	Non-innovative industries
Number of all non-university research institutes (ln)	−135.90 .2907 (4.16)***	−79.10 .2235 (3.26)***	−68.60 .1752 (2.75)***	96.34 .0003 (0.994)
Scientific fields				
Natural sciences	−137.63 .4275 (4.23)***	−71.44 .0525 (5.18)***	−65.19 .0378 (4.89)***	430.90 −.0008 (0.993)
Applied sciences	−156.24 .8488 (3.69)***	−91.30 .1775 (4.81)***	−83.71 .1565 (4.83)***	429.56 .0557 (0.244)
Natural and applied sciences	−170.11 .9019 (5.21)***	−117.97 .3494 (6.17)***	−108.02 .3442 (6.95)***	431.88 −.0079 (0.939)
Administration and political sciences	−62.33 .2100 (4.12)***	−53.20 .0127 (4.88)***	−17.92 .0056 (3.12)***	10.43 .0444 (0.173)
Other disciplines	−2.09 .0744 (2.17)**	−13.10 .0075 (2.22)**	−9.55 .0116 (4.25)***	−0.75 −.0015 (0.951)

Notes: First row: Change in the AIC value due to the inclusion of the variable. Second row: Estimated coefficient and z-value in parentheses
*Statistically significant at the 10 % level; **Statistically significant at the 5 % level; ***Statistically significant at the 1 % level

When the number of institutes differentiated by scientific field is added simultaneously to the baseline model (Table 3.7), the results reveal that the number of non-university research institutes in the region is highly significant with the

Table 3.7 Baseline model with number of non-university research institutes according to discipline

	High-technology manufacturing	Technologically advanced manufacturing	Technology-oriented services	Non-innovative industries
Number of employed persons, excluding R&D employees	.0351*** (3.66)	.0259*** (3.74)	.0310*** (8.08)	.5532*** (18.75)
Number of R&D employees	−1.73e-06 (.65)	−3.13e-06 (1.50)	−3.59e-07 (.28)	−9.82e-08 (.12)
Number of unemployed	−.0055 (.35)	−.0221*** (4.63)	−.0140*** (2.53)	.0052*** (3.72)
Share of employees in high-technology manufacturing industries	.0585*** (3.18)	–	–	–
Share of employees in technologically advanced manufacturing industries	–	.0342*** (3.54)	–	–
Share of employees in technology-oriented service industries	–	–	.0177*** (2.56)	–
Share of employees in non-innovative industries	–	–	–	.0775*** (2.57)
Share of employees in establishments with fewer than 50 employees	.5561*** (3.57)	−.2848*** (3.49)	.1817*** (4.86)	.1453*** (6.06)
Number of R&D employees in adjacent regions	.01808 (1.10)	.0131 (1.39)	−.0054 (.89)	−.0036 (1.34)
Number of patents per 1000 employees	27.0327* (1.81)	21.343** (2.05)	11.782** (2.29)	−9.827*** (3.65)
Number of non-university research institutes in				
Natural sciences	.5058*** (4.47)	.3083*** (2.93)	.2704*** (3.11)	−.1579 (1.34)
Applied sciences	.6400*** (2.50)	.8732*** (3.71)	.7053*** (3.52)	.1390 (1.56)
Administrative and political sciences	.0058* (1.86)	.0115*** (4.08)	.0285 (0.14)	−.0372 (.20)
Other disciplines	.2061 (.48)	−.3625 (.97)	.4505 (1.44)	.0696 (.25)
Number of non-university research institutes in adjacent regions in				
Natural sciences	−.0274 (.29)	.1043 (1.29)	.3295* (1.86)	−.0711 (1.32)
Applied sciences	.0259 (.34)	.0428 (.74)	−.1064 (1.61)	.0392 (.94)
Administration and political sciences	.1412 (1.54)	.1168 (1.41)	.1409 (1.38)	.3242*** (5.97)
Other disciplines	.0358 (.46)	−.1060* (1.83)	.0497 (.75)	.0432 (1.04)

(continued)

Table 3.7 (continued)

	High-technology manufacturing	Technologically advanced manufacturing	Technology-oriented services	Non-innovative industries
Constant	.2704 (1.21)	1.299 (8.11)	2.5736*** (22.77)	−1.829*** (5.82)
AIC change	−104.62	−153.81	−34.00	396.32

Notes: Z-values in parentheses
***Statistically significant at the 1 % level; **Statistically significant at the 5 % level; *Statistically significant at the 10 % level

expected sign and that this effect is stronger for the institutes working in applied sciences than it is for those working in natural sciences and other disciplines. Again, the number of regional private-sector R&D employees loses statistical significance compared to the baseline model (Table 3.1), probably for the reasons discussed above.

Measures for the number on non-university research institutes in adjacent regions are not statistically significant with the expected signs for the majority of the models. Also of interest is that the number of non-university public research institutes has a considerably stronger effect than the aggregate indicators for the regional HEIs. The relatively high coefficients for the number of non-university public research institutions in the region may reflect, at least to some degree, the concentration of this type of public research in high-density areas, which are also where most of the innovative start-ups occur, and therefore could be an overestimation of their effect.

3.7.6 *Extensions and Robustness Checks*

A number of robustness checks are performed in order to test the stability of the results. First, the models are run with fixed effects. As expected, a fixed effects panel estimator does not provide meaningful results. In these models, many of the indicators for public research are not statistically significant, which is obviously due to low levels of variation over time. Second, the regressions are run for only those regions that have at least one such institute (about 62 % of all regions). Considerable differences from the estimates of the models for all regions could indicate that the coefficients for the number of institutes mainly reflect the presence of at least one such institute. It is found, however, that the results are similar. Excluding regions with a relatively high number of HEIs and non-university public research institutes, such as Berlin and Munich, did not produce any significantly different results. Third, the models are run separately for East and West Germany, and again there is not much difference in the results, indicating that the commercialization of knowledge through the formation of innovative new businesses follows the same pattern in both parts of the country.

Finally, in order to further analyze the influence of agglomeration effects, based on population density, the regions are sorted into three groups of equal size and the regressions are run separately for regions with relatively low, medium, and high levels of population density. It is found that the coefficient for the aggregate effect of HEIs is highest in regions with low population density, somewhat lower in regions with medium density, and relatively low in high-density areas. These results suggest that HEIs may have a particularly pronounced effect in low-density regions and that their effect in high-density areas is somewhat obscured by other factors, making it difficult to identify their precise role with this type of analysis. It is also found that the number of non-university public research institutes has a statistically significant effect only in regions with relatively high population density. One main reason for this result may be the high concentration of these institutions in agglomerations and their virtual absence from rural areas. Another reason could be the relatively high correlation between the aggregate indicator for HEIs and the number of non-university research institutes.

3.8 Summary and Conclusions

Knowledge embodied in HEIs may have the potential to be commercially exploited in the form of innovative start-ups. However, this effect may vary based on the type of knowledge and the type of HEI. This chapter analyzed the impact of three properties of HEIs on the formation of new businesses in innovative industries. It first looked at the impact of five different types of scientific field: applied sciences, natural sciences, medical science, administration and political sciences, and "other" disciplines. Second, it analyzed the effect of five types of HEIs: regular universities, universities of applied sciences, medical schools, arts colleges, and universities of public administration. Third, it investigated the importance of two transmission channels for knowledge spillover: (1) the number of students, PhD graduates, and professors as potential founders of innovative new businesses and (2) the extent of research activities and the knowledge stock as represented by the number of professors, the number of PhD students and the amount of external funding obtained.

The results of the analyses of this chapter reveal, first, that different scientific fields have different impact on innovative start-ups. The results suggest that the applied sciences (including medical science) are more influential for fostering innovative start-ups than are basic natural sciences. The effect of administration and political sciences is weak. No statistically significant effect could be found for other disciplines. Second, the type of HEI plays an important role, with regular universities and medical schools having the strongest effects, presumably due to their relatively high research intensity. Third, the number of professors as sources of knowledge exhibits the strongest statistical relationship with regional levels of innovative start-ups. Fourth, no indication of knowledge spillover is found from adjacent regions. This suggests that the process of transforming knowledge into innovative new businesses is highly localized. All in all, these results suggest that investing in institutions of education and research in applied sciences is an effective way of fostering innovative start-ups in a region.

However, despite these findings of a correlation between type of HEI and number of regional start-ups, the underlying causal relationships have not bee identified. What is particularly unclear is how the knowledge embodied in HEIs is transferred into new business formation in the region. It is plausible that some of the regional new businesses are set up by graduates or employees of the local HEIs. However, some of the regional founders may have received their education outside the region and a number of students or employees of local HEIs may set up their firms elsewhere. Studies have shown that the vast majority of academic founders first work as dependent employees before starting their own firm (Mueller 2010; Stuetzer et al. 2012).[15] A number of these individuals are spatially mobile during their career and so are at least partly motivated by the availability of attractive jobs (Chen and Rosenthal 2008; Dahl and Sorenson 2010). Since founders have a strong tendency to locate their businesses close to their place of residence (Figueiredo et al. 2002; Stam 2007; Dahl and Sorenson 2009), the geographical labor market mobility of potential founders as well as the attractiveness of the region for entrepreneurially-minded people are important factors.[16] Hence, the knowledge of local HEIs is not only important as input for potential founders, but may also contribute to a positive development of regional incumbent firms that provide jobs for potential entrepreneurs from outside the region. Moreover, universities can have other "atmospheric" effects on the regional "climate" that may attract potential founders. The results clearly confirm that the emergence of innovative new businesses is a regional phenomenon (Feldman 2001; Sternberg 2009). However, the channels by which regional factors such as the presence of HEIs stimulate the founding of these innovative businesses is still not clear.

References

Acosta M, Coronado D, Flores E (2011) University spillovers and new business location in high-technology sectors: Spanish evidence. Small Bus Econ 36:365–376

Acs ZJ, Braunerhjelm P, Audretsch DB, Carlsson B (2009) The knowledge spillover theory of entrepreneurship. Small Bus Econ 32:15–30

Acs ZJ, Audretsch DB, Lehmann E (2013) The knowledge spillover theory of entrepreneurship. Small Bus Econ 41:767–774

[15]The average age of an innovative founder in Germany is 41 years (Metzger et al. 2010). Assuming that an average founder has finished his or her university education by age 25, this means that he or she has worked as a dependent employee for around 15 years before starting an own firm.

[16]The importance of spatial mobility is illustrated in a study by Roberts and Eesley (2011) that attempts to assess the employment effects of new businesses set up by alumni of the Massachusetts Institute of Technology. The study finds that less than one-third of the jobs created by these firms are located in Massachusetts and that a considerable number of jobs are in California and Texas.

Adams JD (2002) Comparative localization of academic and industrial spillovers. J Econ Geogr 2:253–278
Akaike H (1974) A new look at the statistical model identification. IEEE Trans Autom Control 19:716–723
Anselin L, Varga A, Acs ZJ (1997) Local geographic spillovers between university research and high technology innovations. J Urban Econ 42:422–448
Asheim BT, Gertler MS (2005) The geography of innovation: regional innovation systems. In: Fagerberg J, Mowery DC, Nelson RR (eds) The Oxford handbook of innovation. Oxford University Press, Oxford, pp 291–317
Asheim BT, Coenen L, Moodysson J, Vang J (2007) Constructing knowledge-based regional advantage: implications for regional innovation policy. Int J Entrepreneurship Innov Manag 7:140–155
Åstebro T, Bazzazian N, Braguinsky S (2012) Startups by recent university graduates and their faculty: implications for university entrepreneurship policy. Res Policy 41:663–677
Audretsch DB, Lehmann EE (2005) Does the knowledge spillover theory of entrepreneurship hold for regions? Res Policy 34:1191–1202
Audretsch DB, Lehmann EE, Warning S (2004) University spillovers: does the kind of science matter. Industry Innov 11:193–205
Bade F-J, Nerlinger EA (2000) The spatial distribution of new technology-based firms: empirical results for West-Germany. Papers Region Sci 79:155–176
Baptista R, Mendonça J (2010) Proximity to knowledge sources and the location of knowledge-based start-ups. Ann Region Sci 45:5–29
Baptista R, Lima F, Mendonça J (2011) Establishment of higher education institutions and new firm entry. Res Policy 40:751–760
Bonaccorsi A, Colombo MG, Guerini M, Rossi-Lamastra C (2013) University specialization and new firm creation across industries. Small Bus Econ 41:837–863
Boschma R (2005) Proximity and innovation: a critical assessment. Region Stud 39:61–74
Carree MA (2002) Does unemployment affect the number of establishments? A regional analysis for US states. Region Stud 36:389–398
Chen Y, Rosenthal S (2008) Local amenities and life-cycle migration: do people move for jobs or fun? J Urban Econ 64:519–537
Cohen WM, Nelson RR, Walsh JP (2002) Links and impacts: the influence of public research on industrial R&D. Manag Sci 48:1–23
Dahl MS, Sorenson O (2009) The embedded entrepreneur. Eur Manag Rev 6:172–181
Dahl MS, Sorenson O (2010) The migration of technical workers. J Urban Econ 67:33–45
EC-DGT: European Commission; Directorate-General for Translation (2014) Country compendium: a companion to the English style guide. EC Directorate-General for Translation, Brussels
Federal Office for Building and Regional Planning (Bundesamt für Bauwesen und Raumordnung) (2003) Aktuelle Daten zur Entwicklung der Städte, Kreise und Gemeinden, vol 17. Federal Office for Building and Regional Planning, Bonn
Feldman MP (2001) The entrepreneurial event revisited: firm formation in a regional context. Indus Corp Change 10:861–891
Figueiredo O, Guimaraes P, Woodward D (2002) Home-field advantage: location decisions of Portuguese entrepreneurs. J Urban Econ 52:341–361
Fritsch M (2011) Start-ups in innovative industries—Causes and effects. In: Audretsch DB, Falck O, Heblich S, Lederer A (eds) Handbook of innovation and entrepreneurship. Elgar, Cheltenham, pp 365–381
Fritsch M, Aamoucke R (2013) Regional public research, higher education, and innovative start-ups—An empirical investigation. Small Bus Econ 41:865–885
Fritsch M, Falck O (2007) New business formation by industry over space and time: a multidimensional analysis. Region Stud 41:157–172
Fritsch M, Slavtchev V (2007) Universities and innovation in space. Industry Innov 14:201–218

Gehrke B, Schasse U, Rammer C, Frietsch R, Neuhäusler P, Leidmann M (2010) Listen wissens- und technologieintensiver Güter und Wirtschaftszweige. Studien zum deutschen Innovationssystem, 19, Frauenhofer ISI, NIW, ZEW

Gertler MS (2003) Tacit knowledge and the economic geography of context, or the undefinable tacitness of being (there). J Econ Geogr 3:75–99

Greene WH (2012) Econometric analysis, 7th edn. Pearson Prentice Hall, Upper Saddle River, NJ

Grupp H, Legler H (2000) Hochtechnologie 2000: Neudefinition der Hochtechnologie für die Berichterstattung zur technologischen Leistungsfähigkeit Deutschlands. Karlsruhe and Hannover, FhG, ISI, NIW

Harhoff D (1999) Firm formation and regional spillovers – Evidence from Germany. Econ Innov New Technol 8:27–55

Hülsbeck M, Pickavé EN (2014) Regional knowledge production as determinant of high-technology entrepreneurship: empirical evidence for Germany. Int Entrepreneurship Manag J 10:121–138

Klevorick AK, Levin RC, Nelson RR, Winter SG (1995) On the sources and significance of inter-industry differences in technological opportunities. Res Policy 24:185–205

Kogut B, Zander U (1992) Knowledge of the firm, combinative capabilities, and the replication of technology. Organ Sci 3:383–397

Metzger G, Heger D, Hoewer D, Licht G (2010) High-Tech-Gründungen in Deutschland ('High-tech start- ups in Germany'). Center for European Economic Research (ZEW), Mannheim (mimeo)

Mueller K (2010) Academic spin-off's transfer speed—Analyzing the time from leaving university to venture. Res Policy 39:189–199

Nelson RR (1986) Institutions supporting technical advance in industry. Am Econ Rev 76:186–189

OECD: Organisation for Economic Co-operation and Development (2005) OECD handbook on economic globalization indicators. OECD, Paris

Roberts EB, Eesley CE (2011) Entrepreneurial impact: the role of MIT. Found Trends Entrepreneurship 7:1–149

Spengler A (2008) The establishment history panel. Schmollers Jahrbuch/J Appl Social Sci Stud 128:501–509

Stam E (2007) Why butterflies don't leave: locational behaviour of entrepreneurial firms. Econ Geogr 83:27–50

Stephan P (1996) The economics of science. J Econ Lit 34:1199–1235

Sternberg R (2009) Regional dimensions of entrepreneurship. Found Trends Entrepreneurship 5:211–340

Stuetzer M, Goethner M, Cantner U (2012) Do balanced skills help nascent entrepreneurs to make progress in the venture creation process? Econ Lett 117:186–188

Sutaria V, Hicks DA (2004) New firm formation: dynamics and determinants. Ann Region Sci 38:241–262

Warning S (2007) The economic analysis of universities: strategic groups and positioning. Elgar, Cheltenham

Woodward D, Figueiredo O, Guimaraes P (2006) Beyond the silicon valley: University R&D and high technology location. J Urban Econ 60:15–32

Zentrum für Europäische Wirtschaftsforschung (ZEW) (2011) Die Bereitstellung von Standardauswertungen zum Gründungsgeschehen in Deutschland für externe Datennutzer. ZEW, Mannheim

Zucker LG, Darby MR, Brewer MB (1998) Intellectual human capital and the birth of US biotechnology enterprises. Am Econ Rev 88:290–306

Chapter 4
Quality of Life and the Geography of Human Capital

4.1 Introduction

There is a general consensus in the literature, rooted in the relationship between knowledge and economic growth (Nelson and Phelps 1966; Romer 1986, 1990; Lucas 1988; Benhabib and Spiegel 1994, 2005; Glaeser et al. 2004), that human capital, especially in the form of highly educated people, has a positive effect on regional development (Glaeser et al. 1995; Simon 1998; Moretti 2004a). Highly educated people not only have—by definition—more knowledge, but often are also possessed of the ability to absorb additional knowledge and even generate new knowledge (Schultz 1961; Becker 1962, 1964; Mincer 1958, 1974). These people tend to be highly productive and are disproportionately found to be involved in innovation processes. Moreover, they often have a relatively high propensity to set up high-quality new firms (Acs and Armington 2004, 2006; Lee et al. 2004, 2010; Qian and Acs 2011; Qian et al. 2013).

The geography of human capital is highly uneven (Berry and Glaeser 2005; Moretti 2004b; Wheeler 2006; Growe 2010). This chapter aims to explain this unequal geographic distribution by using the concept of quality of life. This concept is usually used to assess the well-being of individuals and societies by cataloguing different factors in various domains of life, both monetary and nonmonetary. Quality of life seems an appropriate tool for explaining the geography of highly educated people because, generally speaking, most people are interested in attaining a better life, perhaps in the form of higher levels of pleasure, enjoyment, and self-realization. Moreover, with time, quality of life becomes more important for people and the concept is also receiving increased attention in many academic fields, political circles, and from the media (Rappaport 2009; Stiglitz et al. 2009; CAE and SVR 2010).

Previous research on the determinants of the geographic distribution of human capital relies on single factors such as population density, universities, consumer services, tolerance, and community aesthetics (Glaeser et al. 1995; Florida

R. Aamoucke, *Innovative Start-Ups and the Distribution of Human Capital*, Contributions to Economics, DOI 10.1007/978-3-319-44462-8_4

et al. 2008, 2011; Mellander et al. 2011; Abel and Deitz 2012). Evidence based on a general framework that includes all relevant factors is rare. And yet, focusing on a single factor is potentially misleading because it ignores other important factors and thus can lead to endogeneity problems. Florida et al. (2008) note that universities, consumer services, and tolerance are more complementary than competitive in explaining the geography of human capital. If these factors are indeed complementary, then it is more accurate to deal with them as components of a more general concept of quality of life.

The absence of a general framework for studying quality of life is chiefly due to the absence of a standard definition of the concept, which is aggravated by the adoption of a relatively restricted definition of quality of life in economics. In psychology and related fields of studies, quality of life is usually based on fundamental human needs. These fields usually define quality of life quite broadly, including all relevant factors that make life more enjoyable (Frey and Stutzer 2002a, b; Frisch 1998). In economics the concept of quality of life is usually reduced to consumer services or region-specific amenities such as mild weather and recreation and leisure facilities (Rappaport 2007; Glaeser et al. 2001; Florida et al. 2008). The purpose of this chapter is to explore the possibilities for using quality of life as a comprehensive framework and multidimensional concept to explain the geography of human capital across West German regions. To this end, the regional share of human capital is related to a broad palette of indicators intended to reflect all the rich and various dimensions of human life.

The main take-away point from this chapter is that quality of life plays a central role in explaining the geography of human capital. This seems plausible, even obvious; however, the idea needs theoretical and empirical support. Theoretically, a standard definition and measurement of quality of life is still absent. Econometrically, several endogeneity problems pose a challenge and prevent any causal interpretation. While fully acknowledging the difficulty of completely overcoming the endogeneity with currently available techniques, this chapter mitigates these problems by applying path models and structural equations (SEM). This technique is the best available approach because it takes into account the dynamics between the variables on the basis of their variances and covariances. Moreover, relating quality of life to fundamental human needs may provide some theoretical support for the empirical results.

The rest of the chapter is organized as follows. Section 4.2 reviews, but by no means comprehensively, the vast literature on quality of life and shows the empirical implementation. Section 4.3 provides an overview of the most important elements of quality of life used in the empirical model. Section 4.4 explains the empirical approach; Sect. 4.5 sets out the empirical results. Section 4.6 summarizes and concludes.

4.2 Quality of Life

4.2.1 Quality of Life and Human Needs

Theoretically, "quality of life" is a complex concept, and one lacking both a standard definition and a standard measure (Wingo 1973; Schuessler and Fisher 1985; Wish 1986; Farquhar 1995; Pacione 2003; van Kamp et al. 2003; Marans 2012). Generally, quality of life has to do with the goodness of life and overall well-being: every definition of it revolves around the degree to which a person's life is desirable. According to Frisch (1998), quality of life refers to the extent to which a number of fundamental human needs that go beyond mere existence are satisfied by a combination of diverse factors that make the life particularly happy, enjoyable, and worthwhile. Hence, quality of life is based in the fulfillment of certain fundamental human needs.

Over the past few decades, two predominant approaches have emerged for classifying fundamental human needs. One assumes that human needs are hierarchical. Maslow (1943, 1954) proposes a hierarchy of the following five levels of human needs: physiological needs, safety, belonging, esteem, and self-actualization. Accordingly, individuals try to satisfy the most fundamental level of need before reaching for the next level. Alderfer (1972) reduces Maslow's hierarchy to just three levels: existence (i.e., material requirements), relatedness (i.e., interpersonal relationships), and growth (i.e. the intrinsic desire of people for personal development). Max-Neef (1991a, b) criticizes the hierarchical approach and suggest that human needs should be regarded as an interrelated and interactive system characterized by simultaneities, complementarities, and tradeoffs in the process of satisfaction. Accordingly, Max-Neef introduces a complex matrix of needs classified into nine categories: subsistence, protection, affection, understanding, participation, leisure, creation, identity, and freedom. Max-Neef (1991a) differentiates between human needs and satisfiers. For instance, education is a satisfier of the need for understanding and healthcare is a satisfier of the need for protection. While fundamental human needs are few, classifiable, and invariable across all cultures, their satisfiers are numerous, variable, and hardly classifiable.

Both approaches agree that quality of life involves implicitly or explicitly satisfying all human needs. According to the hierarchy approach, quality of life is primarily related to the needs at the top levels in the hierarchy. Sirgy (1986) and Sirgy et al. (1995) argue that the higher the need satisfaction of the majority in a given society, the greater the quality of life of that society. However, in order to satisfy higher levels of need, people attempt to first satisfy lower levels of need. Taormina and Gao (2013) found significant positive correlations among the different levels of need and argue that the more each lower-level need is satisfied, the more the next-higher-level need will be satisfied. Consequently, quality of life implicitly includes all levels of human need. According to Max-Neef (1991a), quality of life explicitly includes all human needs. Thus, a good quality of life is achieved when all human needs are adequately satisfied. Any inadequately satisfied human need reveals a type of poverty.

Related to the research cited above is a multi-disciplinary research strand, the so-called economics of happiness, which attempts to identify the basic factors that nurture human happiness and well-being. For instance, Richard Layard (2005) attributes happiness to seven major factors: financial situation, family relationships, work, community and friends, health, personal freedom, and personal values. Frey and Stutzer (2002a) attempt to integrate insights from different disciplines to demonstrate how factors such as income, unemployment, political participation, and democracy affect happiness.

4.2.2 *Quality of Life in Regional Economics*

The concept of quality of life appears to be of increasing importance. Arguably, one of the reasons the subject is such a "hot" topic is the belief that quality of life has a great deal of influence on the location decisions of firms and people (Gottlieb 1994a, b; Hall 1995; Rogerson 1999; Dissart and Deller 2000; Mulligan et al. 2004; Ritsilä and Ovaskainen 2001). Several academic fields, such as environmental studies and ecological economics (Haas 1999; Kahneman et al. 1999; Dasgupta 2000; Krutilla and Reuveny 2002; Dissart and Deller 2000), have made significant contributions to the research on quality of life.[1] In economics, the concept of quality of life is usually restricted to nonmonetary factors such as consumer services and amenities (Glaeser et al. 2001; Florida et al. 2008; CAE and SVR 2010). In contrast, Wingo (1973) assumes that opportunities that improve the quality of life tend to be scarce. Thus, people are willing to exchange certain aspects of quality of life for others that make them equally happy. Gillingham and Reece (1979) argue that individual well-being is a result of the physical and social characteristics of the environment, such consumption of market goods, leisure, public goods, etc.

Lambiri et al. (2007) review the relevant literature and argue that quality of life enters regional economic analysis in two ways. On the one hand, quality of life is treated indirectly as a way to analyze regional growth as a result of location decisions of people and firms, which decisions are assumed to be influenced by region-specific characteristics. For instance, some scholars explore the impact of environmental characteristics on population growth (Graves 1976, 1980, 1983; Rappaport and Sachs 2003; Cheshire and Magrini 2006; Rappaport 2007, 2008). Rappaport (2009) suggests that places with amenities for which individuals would initially pay 5 % of their income grow slightly faster than otherwise identical places. Glaeser (1999) and Glaeser et al. (2001) show the importance of "non-market forces" and positive externalities, in form of urban amenities and consumer services, for enhancing the competitiveness of regions and cities. Florida (2002a, b) highlights the importance of a palette of amenities in shaping the location decisions of highly skilled individuals. A number of other studies use quality of life to explain the rise and decline of regions and cities (Cheshire and Hay 1989; Glaeser 1998; Glaeser and Kahn 2004).

[1]For more literature, see http://www.uic.edu/orgs/qli/publications/publicationshome.htm

On the other hand, quality of life is been treated directly with the aim of linking the positive externalities associated with high levels of quality of life with house prices and real wages. The so-called hedonic price method attempts in this way to integrate regional characteristics that enhance quality of life and yet have no market price, into economic considerations. This methodology was first introduced by Rosen (1979) and has been followed by many economists who attempt to create indexes of quality of life and rank cities and regions.[2] Based on Rosen's (1979) method, Buettner and Ebertz (2009) attempt to introduce an indicator of quality of life for German regions. The authors show that differences in amenities explain a substantial part of observed land price differences, while the effect of amenities on wage differences is weak. Hence, they use differences in land prices to infer marginal willingness to pay for regional attributes.

Despite its widespread use, Rosen's (1979) approach has been criticized for several limitations. First, the approach is heavily dependent on the spatial equilibrium assumption; the existence of spatial disequilibrium limits its applicability (Lambiri et al. 2007). Second, the assumption that regional land prices reflect regional amenities is arguable: the majority of markets are imperfect to at least some degree and there is no reason to assume that housing markets are an exception. Different factors that have nothing to do with quality of life such as speculations may influence the land prices. Third, it is still not completely clear whether housing prices, land prices, or rents, or a combination of them, are the most appropriate reflection of regional amenities. For instance, Winters (2013) shows that rents are more suitable for reflecting differences in quality of life because rents reflect the current user cost of housing, whereas housing values are based on the net present value of future rental income. Fourth, this approach makes it difficult to control for individual-specific and region-specific characteristics. A strong positive correlation can exist between regional consumption amenities and unobserved characteristics of individuals (Combes et al. 2008; Lee 2010).

4.2.3 Dimensions of Quality of Life in the Literature

There is a large body of literature that attempts to identify and measure dimensions of quality of life at individual, regional, and national levels, all of which agrees on the multidimensional nature of quality of life (Alkire 2002; Pacione 2003; van Kamp et al. 2003). However, the selected dimensions, elements, and indicators vary from study to study. This variation in the selected dimensions may be influenced by different factors such as data availability, the aims of each study, the methodology, the level of analysis, and so forth. Table 4.1 provides an overview of different studies using various concepts of quality of life.

---

[2]For instance, Roback (1982), Blomquist et al. (1988), Gyourko and Tracy (1991), Stover and Leven (1992), and Giannias (1998).

Table 4.1 Quality of life in different studies

Study	Level	Description of the concept of quality of life
Felce and Perry (1995)	Individual	Physical well-being; material well-being; social well-being; development and activity; emotional well-being
Cummins (1997)	Individual	Material well-being; health; productivity; intimacy; safety; place in community; emotional well-being
Greenley et al. (1997)	Individual	Living situation; finance; leisure; family; social life; health; access to medical care
Frisch (1998)	Individual	Health; self-esteem; philosophy of life; standard of living; work; recreation; learning; creativity; social service; love; friendships; relationships with children; relationships with relatives; home; neighborhood; community
Costanza et al. (1997)	Individual, national	Subsistence; reproduction and care; security; affection; understanding; participation; leisure; spirituality; creativity and emotional expression; identity; freedom
Stiglitz et al. (2009)	National	Material living standards; health; education; personal activities; political voice and governance; social connections; environmental conditions; personal insecurity; economic insecurity
CAE and SVR (2010)	National	Material well-being; health; education; personal activities; political voice and governance; social connections and relationships; environmental conditions; personal and economic insecurity
Buettner and Ebertz (2009)	Regional	Leisure; crime; accessibility; education; labor market; alternative job opportunities; household income; sunshine; emissions; share of forest; share of water; tourism; peripherality; metropolitan area; poverty
Morais et al. (2013)	Regional	Political and social environment; economic environment; medical and health issues; schools and education; public services and transport; recreation; housing; natural environment
Graves (1976)	Regional USA	Health services (share of physicians); crime; social dimension (share of nonwhite population); weather (average temperature); pollution (average no. of suspended particulates/m^3 of air)
Rosen (1979)	Regional USA	Pollution (suspended particulates, sulfur dioxide, inversion days, water pollution); climate (number of rainy days, sunny days, and 90 °F days); crime; demographics (population density and size, central city population); market conditions (unemployment rate, population growth)
Roback (1982)	Regional USA	Crime; environment (total suspended particulates, unemployment rate); demographics (population size, growth, density); weather (heating degree days, total snowfall, cloudy days, clear days)
Herzog and Schlottmann (1986)	Regional USA	Housing; jobs; climate; recreation; arts; education; healthcare; transportation; crime

(continued)

Table 4.1 (continued)

Study	Level	Description of the concept of quality of life
Blomquist et al. (1988)	Regional USA	Weather (precipitation, % humidity, heating degree days, cooling degree days, wind speed, sunshine days); location (distance from the coast/lake); crime; education (teacher/pupil); environment (total suspended particulates mg/m^3, visibility in miles, no. of treatment storage and disposal facilities of hazardous wastes, licensed waste for landfills)
Cheshire and Hay (1989)	Regional EU	Car ownership; crime (murder/manslaughter, violence, burglary, criminal damage)
Gyourko and Tracy (1991)	Regional USA	Fiscal variables (income tax, state corporate tax rates, effective local property tax rate); government services (share of incidents of violent crime, insurance company local premium); health (share of hospital beds); education (student/teacher ratio); weather (average annual precipitation, relative humidity, average wind speed, sunshine days, heating days, cooling degree days); pollution (mean total suspended particulates); closeness to an amenity (Great Lake or Gulf of Mexico); access to alternative labor market (% of workers in a city that work in another region); non-land cost of living (without housing costs); urban size (population); community life and political participation (institutional strength of the public sector, % of local public workers in central city organized unions)
Stover and Leven (1992)	Regional USA	Weather (precipitation, % humidity, heating degree days, cooling degree days, wind speed, sunshine days); location (distance from the coast/lake); crime; education (teacher/pupil); environment (total suspended particulates, visibility, no. of treatment storage and disposal facilities of hazardous wastes)
Sufian (1993)	Regional world	Public safety (share of murders); food cost (share of income spent on food); living space (persons per room); housing standard (housing with water/electricity); communication (telephones per 100 people); education (share of children in secondary school); public health (share infant deaths); peace and quiet (noise levels); traffic flow (mph during rush hour)
Giannias (1998)	Regional Canada	Housing characteristics (no. of rooms, no. of bathrooms, age of housing); climate (mean of the annual temperature, no. of cloudy days); air pollution; population density; professional sports (no. of professional sports teams)
Glaeser et al. (2001)	Regional USA & EU	Weather (temperature, dry climate); proximity to ocean coast; urban leisure (restaurants, art museums, movie theatres, bowling alleys, live performance venues); tourism (hotel rooms per capita, tourist nights per capita)
Deller et al. (2001)	Regional USA	Market (nonwhite population, population above 65 years, population under 70 years, household with income below the poverty level, entropy index of income distribution); labor (share of persons with high school diploma, share of active nonfederal physicians, unemployment rate, share of crime); government (property tax rate, total government general expenditure); amenities (climate, recreational infrastructure, land, water, winter)

(continued)

Table 4.1 (continued)

Study	Level	Description of the concept of quality of life
Florida (2002a)	Regional USA	Cultural measures (radio broadcast time devoted to classical music, public television stations, public library book acquisitions, nonprofit art museums and galleries, performance of fine arts and musical groups, access to the culture of adjacent urban areas); recreation measures (restaurants, public golf courses, bowling lanes, zoos and aquariums, family theme parks, automobile race tracks, betting attractions, college and professional sports teams, miles of coast line, inland water area, national parks); climate measures (very hot and cold days, seasonal temperature variation, heating and cooling days, freezing days); "coolness factor" (share of population aged 22–29, bars and nightclubs per capita, art galleries and museums per capita), median house value; diversity measure (index of gay population)
Cheshire and Magrini (2006)	Regional EU	Wet day frequency; frost frequency ratio; max. temperature ratio; cloud cover ratio; min. temperatures ratio; mean temperature ratio
Shapiro (2006)	Regional USA	Restaurants per capita; serious crime per capita; high school drop-out rate; no. of days with Air Quality Index > 100
EU (1999)	Regional EU	Socioeconomic development (unemployment rate, percentage of not owned housing); services availability (share of beds in hospital, cinemas and night clubs); internal disparities (dwellings without bath, population with no qualification, workers, wage earners, unskilled); attractiveness (share of holiday residences, open-space areas, migration flow, registered nights in the hotels); technology and information society (presence of the city on the World Wide Web, share of computers shops)

Source: Lambiri et al. (2007) with own extensions

There are basically two methodologies for capturing quality of life (Wish 1986; Pacione 2003; Costanza et al. 1997; CAE and SVR 2010). The "subjective" methodology is based on self-reported subjective perceptions of well-being, not on objective indicators of well-being. Accordingly, questions about "satisfaction with life" can be asked of individuals and then the answers aggregated to create an indicator of quality of life (Diener and Suh 1997; Diener 2006). The "objective" methodology is based on quantifiable social and economic indicators that reflect the opportunities for satisfying human needs.[3] Moreover, some studies construct an index of quality of life based on different dimensions; others use a set of different indictors without amalgamating them into one index (Hagerty et al. 2001).[4]

[3]For more discussion, see CAE and SVR (2010, pp. 61–66).

[4]An example of the first type is the index generated by Buettner and Ebertz (2009) for German regions. An example of the second type is the approach of CAE and SVR (2010).

4.2.4 Empirical Implementation

Three decisions need to be made before implementing an empirical examination of quality of life. First, which methodology should be followed: the subjective or the objective methodology? Second, should one index for quality of life be created or a set of different indicators be relied upon? Third, which dimensions and elements of quality of life should be chosen?

The "objective" methodology is preferred for analyzing the impact of quality of life on the geography of human capital. Accordingly, quality of life in the framework of this chapter is based on the extent to which regions provide, tolerate, and stimulate opportunities to adequately satisfy fundamental human needs. This methodology is advantageous for the aim of this chapter because it focuses on available opportunities to satisfy the most common human needs and ignores individual-specific tastes that are beyond the scope of this chapter. Max-Neef (1991a, b) argues that quality of life depends on the possibilities that people have to adequately satisfy their fundamental human needs. The capability approach describes the ability of people to exploit opportunities and transform them to valuable outcome taking into account environmental and individual characteristics as well as materialistic and non-materialistic factors in assessment of well-being (Sen 1987, 1993, 1999). The sixth recommendation of the "Stiglitz-Sen-Fitoussi"-report states that "quality of life depends on people's objective conditions and capabilities" (p. 15). Moreover, the objective methodology is based on a range of objective indicators that develop a more accurate picture of social welfare than does the subjective methodology, which suffers from a number of limitations such as misjudgment and strategic misrepresentation. Moreover, ensuring comparability across regions using the subjective methodology could be difficult (CAE and SVR 2010, pp. 61–64).

Moreover, one example of the subjective methodology is a large survey called "Perspektive Deutschland" (Perspective Germany) which is conducted by the consulting firm McKinsey & Company includes more than half a million German households. These households were asked about the key reasons for their choice for the current place. For highly educated people, a number of key reasons could be identified, such as labor market, personal relationships, natural amenities, leisure, social environment, housing, transport, education, shopping, positive attitude to children and families, low crime, openness to migrants (Buettner and Janeba 2013, p. 17).

As to the second decision, reporting a set of different indicators is preferred over amalgamating them into a single index. Amalgamation of different indicators into one index is difficult. Sen (1999) acknowledges the difficulty of amalgamating different elements of well-being into a single index. Moreover, an index that contains information on different aspects of human experience might be hard to interpret. The joint report of CAE and SVR considered amalgamation of different indicators as inappropriate for several reasons, including problems with interpersonal and intergenerational comparability; measurement and misperception errors, possibly on a large scale, and the manipulability of such a measure. In contrast, a well-chosen dashboard of different indicators can inform better about the society and the diverse aspects of its members' lives (CAE and SVR 2010).

Explaining the geography of human capital by using the concept of the quality of life faces the challenge of choosing the dimensions of quality of life, their elements, and how to measure them. On one hand, satisfiers of human needs are infinite, numerous, variable, and hardly classifiable. The set of satisfiers includes, in addition to physical products, different forms of organization, political structures, values, and the like. Furthermore, no one-to-one correspondence can be assumed between needs and satisfiers. A satisfier may contribute simultaneously to the satisfaction of different needs (Max-Neef 1991b). On the other hand, identifying a finite number of satisfiers and organizing them in a limited number of dimensions is crucial for the empirical analysis. Stiglitz-Sen-Fitoussi (2009, p. 15) argue that specification of the dimensions, elements, and indicators of quality of life is a value judgment, rather than a technical exercise. CAE and SVR (2010, p. 61) suggest that the set of indicators used should strike an appropriate balance between providing sufficiently rich information and preventing its recipients from becoming overwhelmed by its complexity.

There are basically two solutions to this challenge. First, one study or one concept can be selected from the literature and followed strictly and solely. Second, several studies can be explored and the most common variables can be used, to the extent appropriate data are available. Since no one concept is easily identified as "standard," the second solution is taken and a number of the most common dimensions and elements are selected to reflect quality of life. Table 4.2 provides a brief overview of the dimensions, elements, and indicators of quality of life proposed for the empirical framework of this chapter.

4.3 Elements of Quality of Life

Quality of life in the framework of this chapter consists of six dimensions: material well-being, protection, education and arts, sociopolitical dimension, amenities, and tolerance. Each dimension includes several elements. In total, there are 27 indicators of quality of life.

4.3.1 Material Well-Being

The first dimension concerns itself with the material requirements for a good life. Regions with a strong economic base are expected to influence the geography of human capital positively because they reward qualifications better and provide better public goods, suitable employment opportunities, better infrastructure, and so forth. Seven indicators are used to measure material well-being. Disposable income is the amount of money available for consumption and saving after taxes.

Table 4.2 Dimensions of quality of life and proposed indicators

Dimensions and elements	Indicators
I. Material well-being	
Income	Disposable income per capita in 1000 €
Public spending	Public spending per capita in 1000 €
Labor market	Growth in jobs that require a tertiary degree
Infrastructure	Share of area devoted to streets, highways, squares, etc.
Housing	Available space per capita to live (in m^2)
Internet	Number of .dedomains per capita
Unemployment	Share of unemployed people
II. Protection	
Healthcare	Number of beds in hospitals per capita
Psychotherapy	Number of beds in facilities of mental health per capita
Hazardous waste	Per capita amount of all dangerous materials produced or stored in the region (in tons)
Coal energy	Share of produced energy by coal burning relative to total energy produced in the region
Renewable energy	Share of produced energy by renewable resources relative to total energy produced in the region
Crime	Number of criminal acts per capita that are the subject of a complaint handled by the police
Accidents	Number of accidents with at least one fatality per capita
III. Education and arts	
Schools	Share of secondary school students
Universities	Share of students in universities and other HEIs
Arts	Share of artists
IV. Sociopolitical dimension	
Political participation	Share of actual voters relative to number of people permitted to vote
Political preferences	Herfindahl-Hirschman Index for the share of voters for the parties in the Federal German Parliament (Bundestag)
Kindergarten	Share of available places in kindergarten
Youth facilities	Share of available places in facilities for youth care
V. Amenities	
Consumer services	Herfindahl-Hirschman Index for the diversity of available services in the region that could be attractive to consumers
Recreation	Share of area devoted to recreation facilities such as public parks
Water areas	Share of water area such as lakes, rivers, and coasts
Sunshine	Average yearly duration of sunshine
VI. Tolerance	
Foreigners	Share of foreigners relative to the domestic population
Foreigners' diversity	Herfindahl-Hirschman Index for the share of foreigners according to their country of origin

Borjas et al. (1992) argue that regions that reward human capital better attract more of it. Disposable income is used instead of wages so as to capture regional wealth. Florida et al. (2008) suggest that human capital defined as educational attainment outperforms the concept of the creative class, as defined by occupational skill, in accounting for regional income, whereas creative class does better in accounting for wages.

Public spending is used to capture the role of the state in increasing regional quality of life and explaining the geography of human capital. Tiebout (1956) argues that people compare the taxes they must pay in a particular region with the level of public service they receive in return. When they feel that they are paying for more than they receive, they "vote with their feet" and move to another region (Douglas 1997; Wall 2001). Scully (2001) finds evidence of a positive association between government consumption expenditures and quality of life. On the other hand, Tanzi and Schuknecht (1995) argue that social progress is not necessarily associated with big government.

Labor market is a variable that takes into consideration the regional labor market's demand for human capital. Berry and Glaeser (2005) show that human capital levels increase more in regions with a high labor demand for qualifications. Accordingly, highly educated people are more likely to start up a new venture and undertake innovative activity that generates more jobs for other highly educated people. The correlation between qualifications of the managers and the employees in the USA increased from 0.38 in 1970 to 0.51 in 2000. Simon (2004) argues that the presence of industries that have a high demand for human capital explains to some degree the concentration of human capital in the region. McHenry (2014) argues that labor market size plays a decisive role in shaping the geography of human capital.

The number of .dedomains is used to discover the Internet's role. Different studies attribute agglomeration economies to the close proximity of people and the opportunity for face-to-face contact. Progress in information technology, however, may show these findings to be outdated; for example, perhaps there are no longer any advantages related to face-to-face contact when people can "virtually" see each other no matter where they are (Toffler 1980; Naisbitt 1995; Negroponte 1995; Knoke 1996). On the other hand, Gaspar and Glaeser (1998) argue that telecommunications may be a complement to face-to-face interaction and thus improvements in telecommunications technology can lead to more face-to-face interaction, enhancing the relevance of agglomerations. Sinai and Waldfogel (2004) suggest that the Internet is more attractive in dense regions, indicating that Internet is complement to agglomerations.

While high unemployment rates may refer to hard economic and social situation in the region, strong infrastructure is indispensable for vital economic activities (Aschauer 1990; Rives and Heaney 1995; Cain 1997). Housing is one of the important factors contributing to the individual well-being and quality of life (García-Mira et al. 2005).

4.3.2 Protection

According to Max-Neef (1991b), the need for protection is satisfied by various life-saving and health-protective factors, such as, for example, availability of decent healthcare. People attempt to protect themselves from endangerment. Protection against disease, illness, and risks that endanger life, health, and security is one the most important aspects of human life. Living a healthy life in a healthy physical and social environment not only affects the viability of the body but also affects feelings of security, the possibility of getting a job, and the opportunity to participate in a broad range of social and economic activities (OECD 2011).

Empirical research finds a strong association between health and education (Kenkel 1991; Sander 1995; Elo and Preston 1996; Lleras-Muney 2006; Silles 2009). People's health, as well as the quality of the environment, is influenced by substances used to generate energy and hazardous waste produced or stored in the region. Due to a number of adverse health and environmental effects of coal burning, the share of produced energy by coal burning is included in the model; in addition, the share of renewable energy comes from natural resources such sunlight, wind, and the like is also included. Moreover, life-endangering risks in the region, such as criminality and accidents, have an impact on quality of life. Security is indicated by the number of criminal acts per capita that are the subject of a complaint handled by the police, such as drug offenses, robbery, murder, damage to property, and so forth. The number of accidents per capita in the region with at least one fatality measures the riskiness of the traffic system.

4.3.3 Education and Arts

Education and arts satisfy a number of human needs, such as the need for understanding, esteem, social relations, and imagination (Max-Neef 1991b). This dimension is represented by the number of universities and schools and the share of artists in the population. Arts are imaginative, creative, and nonscientific branches of knowledge. In his work, Richard Florida (Florida 2002a, b; Florida and Mellander 2010) argues that the presence of creative people such as artists makes regions more attractive for human capital and innovative industries. Falck et al. (2011) find that proximity to a baroque opera house is a strong predictor for the regional share of human capital. A number of economists find that growth and schooling are highly correlated (Barro 1991; Bils and Klenow 2000). Berry and Glaeser (2005) show that the share of people with a tertiary degree increases more in regions with higher initial schooling levels.

Universities enhance the quality of life in a region by increasing knowledge, tolerance, and social cohesion (Florida 2005; Florida et al. 2006; Drucker and Goldstein 2006, 2007; McHenry 2014).Abel and Deitz (2012) show that both the number of graduates and the extent of academic R&D activity have a positive effect on regional levels of human capital. Qian et al. (2013) and Huffman and Quigley (2002) suggest a strong association between universities and human capital. Generally, universities and other HEIs can influence the geography of human capital in several ways. First, universities facilitate the regional population's access to higher education (Card 1995; Alm and Winters 2009). Second, universities attract students from other regions who may stay in the region after completing their studies (Winters 2011a, b; Blackwell et al. 2002; Groen 2004; Hickman 2009). Third, regions with universities tend to provide rich selection of consumption opportunities (Gumprecht 2003).

On the other hand, empirical investigation shows that the match between the distribution of universities and the distribution of human capital is not perfect. Some scholars argue that concentration of human capital takes place in regions with "great" universities (Florida 2005; Florida et al. 2006). Abel and Deitz (2012) show that the effect of graduates is relatively smaller than the effect of R&D activity because migration plays an important role in distributing human capital across regions. Faggian and McCann (2009) demonstrate that most graduates in the UK do not enter the labor market of the region where they attend university. Venhorst et al. (2011) show that the presence of a large labor market is the most important factor for high retention of Dutch graduates.

4.3.4 Sociopolitical Dimension

The sociopolitical dimension is comprised of four variables. Kindergarten and youth facilities reflect public services related to the basic unit of social life—the family. Political participation refers to the political engagement of the regional population. Political preferences reflect whether a heterogeneous political orientation dominates. Frey and Stutzer (2002a, b) suggest that the extent to which political structures are developed affects the perceived satisfaction people have with their lives. For instance, institutions that facilitate more individual involvement in politics such as referendums have a substantial effect. Dee (2004) finds strong effects of educational attainment on voter participation, support for free speech, and quality of civic knowledge. Milligan et al. (2004) find a significant association between education and several measures of political and civic involvement such as voting. Slottje (1991) uses a concept of quality of life that includes political and civil rights, and freedom of the press.

4.3.5 Amenities

Amenities have become increasingly important for people. In general, amenities are things that make life more pleasant and enjoyable, such as consumer services, recreation areas, parks, mild weather, lakes, and the like (Blomquist et al. 1988;

Florida 2011). Some studies argue that regional amenities can compensate for lower income levels or higher housing prices (Rosen 1979; Roback 1982). Clark et al. (2002) and Florida et al. (2011) show that factors related to quality of life in form of amenities explain more of the desire to stay in a region or the decision of where to live than do community economic conditions. Clark et al. (2002) suggest that the role of amenities such as leisure, arts, and other aesthetic considerations in shaping modern economies is increasing due to more individualization and volatility of taste.

Empirical studies show that differences in consumption amenities explain a considerable portion of regional growth. Glaeser (2000) shows that high-amenity cities grow faster than low-amenity cities. Rappaport (2008) suggests that moderate differences in consumption amenities across regions can cause extremely large differences in population density. Glaeser et al. (2001) argue that consumption services create comparative advantages for regions because services require spatial proximity between suppliers and consumers. Moreover, the authors find that population growth is positively correlated with several measures of consumption amenities. Similarly, Shapiro (2006) attributes about 40 % of the growth effects of human capital to amenities. Shapiro argues that "consumer city" amenities such as bars and restaurants are more important than features such as crime rate, schools, and pollution. Adamson et al. (2004) suggest a key role for urban amenities in influencing human capital. Moretti (2004a) suggests that only employees with high human capital value local amenities.

The literature shows a positive correlation of several measures of exogenous amenities, such as weather and water areas, with economic development. Rappaport and Sachs (2003) argue that quality of life provides a good explanation for the concentration of US economic activity at its ocean and Great Lakes coasts. Weather's possible contribution to quality of life has garnered a certain degree of interest (Roback 1982). Deschênes and Moretti (2009) found that extreme weather result in immediate increases in mortality.[5] Graves (1976, 1980, 1983) argues that climate differences are important in the migration decision. Rappaport (2007) argues that places with nice weather have been the destination for a large number of US residents in the twentieth century. Rappaport argues that a large portion of weather-related movement appears to be driven by an increased propensity to view nice weather as a consumption amenity. In Europe, Cheshire and Magrini (2006) acknowledge that climate explains a significant portion of different population growth rates at the national level but not at the European level. Across EU countries, population growth tends to be uncorrelated with weather. Thus, weather matters but only nationally.

[5]For a survey on the empirical literature on the relationship between health outcomes and weather, see Deschênes (2012).

4.3.6 Tolerance

Tolerance is necessary for people to feel comfortable enough to express themselves and fully reveal their capabilities and peculiarities (Florida 2002b). Tolerance is one of the most important positive emotions and it contributes to individual and social well-being by broadening people's thought–action repertoires, building psychological resilience, and triggering upward spirals toward enhanced emotional well-being (Fredrickson 2001). Other psychological studies show the positive impact of tolerance on creativity and innovation (Amabile 1996; Sternberg 1999). Another line of research finds a relationship between tolerance and several economic indicators, including foreign direct investment, and GDP growth (Andersson 1985a, b; Inglehart and Norris; 2003; Inglehart and Welzel 2005; Noland 2005; Ager and Brückner 2013). Moreover, there is a strong association between tolerance and entrepreneurship and innovation because tolerance attracts human capital and thus provides the labor market with different skills that make more likely the discovery and exploitation of entrepreneurial opportunities and the production of more patents (Lee et al. 2004, 2010; Qian et al. 2013). Ottaviano and Peri (2005) show that diversity in the form of the presence of immigrants has a positive effect on regional productivity. Foreigners tend to enhance the stock of knowledge and increase the variety of services available for consumption (O'Reilly et al. 1998; Lazear 1999; Olfert and Partridge 2011).

Tolerance is argued to be one of the drivers behind the uneven geography of human capital. Florida (2002b, 2011) suggests that human capital is concentrated in regions with a high degree of tolerance. A similar result is found by Florida et al. (2008), who use a combination of the number of gay and lesbian households and the share of individuals employed in arts, design, and related fields as an indicator for tolerance. In empirical research, tolerance is reflected by three major indicators that measure the presence of three fundamentally different types of people: foreigners, artists, and homosexuals (Florida and Gates 2001). Using the share of homosexuals is difficult due to lack of data. The share of artists is already employed as an element of education and arts dimension. Thus, in this chapter, tolerance is indicated by the share of foreigners. The presence of foreigners in a region could have the potential to cause conflict due to differences in communication, prejudice, and fear of other groups (Alesina et al. 1999, 2004). However, a tolerant attitude can decrease the risk of conflict. Dill (2013) shows a negative relationship between the share of foreigners and right-wing voting in Germany. In contrast, Eriksson et al. (2014) find that variables such as diversity, share of foreigners, cultural supply tend to have far less impact on regional development in Sweden as suggested in the literature. Eriksson et al. (2014) argue that the missed positive association between diversity and regional development may be attributed to problems facing immigrants to establish themselves on the labor market (see for example, Rydgren 2004).

The share of foreigners should be supplemented by a diversity variable that controls for the heterogeneity among different groups of foreigners based on country of origin. This variable is intended to overcome the problem of there being a large number of foreigners from some certain countries. In the 1960s and 1970s, West Germany instituted the so-called worker program (*Gastarbeiterprogramm*) that facilitated the immigration of people seeking work from a few countries such as Italy, Greece, Portugal, and Turkey (Bade 1994, 2000, 2001). Without testing for heterogeneity, using the share of foreigners as a measure of tolerance may be less than valid.

4.3.7 Population Density

A large body of literature shows that wages and productivity are higher in densely populated regions.[6] Due to the physical proximity of individuals and firms, agglomerations have several advantages. The costs of transportation are lower (Krugman 1991); the volume of public goods is higher (Scotchmer 2002); the costs of knowledge production and sharing are lower (Jovanovic and Rob 1989; Duranton and Puga 2004; Rosenthal and Strange 2001, 2004; Glaeser and Resseger 2010), the rate of invention is higher (Carlino et al. 2007); the costs of worker–firm matching are lower (Wheeler 2001); incentive problems are smaller due to the high number of face-to-face contacts (Storper and Venables 2004); the process of the division of labor is faster (Becker and Murphy 1992); and the degree of diversity, which facilitates creativity and innovation, is higher (Jacobs 1961, 1969; Florida 2011).

Indeed, several positive elements of quality of life are correlated with population density (Gabriel and Rosenthal 2004). On the other hand, a negative correlation between population density and quality of life is found by Gyourko and Tracy (1991), Davis and Ortalo-Magne (2007), and Chen and Rosenthal (2008). According to Sperling and Sander (2004) and Savageau (2000), population density is positively correlated with quality of life, except in the matters of healthcare and crime. Henderson (1988) argues that people show a tendency to live in cities and highly populated regions because of consumption externalities and productivity. Cities provide a rich palette of amenities and higher wages. In contrast, there are certain aspects of cities that drive people away from then, for example, higher crime rates, less friendly neighborhoods, and higher costs of living.

The correlation between human capital and agglomerations is so high that scholars find it difficult to separate between their effects (Ciccone and Hall 1996; Ciccone 2002; Combes et al. 2008, 2011; Abel et al. 2012). Agglomeration economies and the positive externalities associated with human capital are two basic determinants of the regional level of human capital as output of a self-enforcing process over time (Moretti 2004b; Glaeser et al. 1995; Berry and Glaeser

[6]For instance, Weber (1899), Beeson and Eberts (1989), Glaeser and Maré (2001), Moeller and Haas (2003), Yankow (2006), Rosenthal and Strange (2008), Kim et al. (2009), Chung et al. (2009).

2005; Bacolod et al. 2009, 2010; Growe 2010). Elvery (2010) and Glaeser and Resseger (2010) suggest that there is more human capital in highly populated regions, whereas agglomeration economies are much stronger for regions with more human capital. Various studies argue that highly populated regions have more human capital because they facilitate knowledge sharing and reduce the costs of acquiring human capital (Rauch 1993; Glaeser 1999; Glaeser and Maré 2001). Similarly, Wheeler (2006) finds that population growth and human capital growth are positively associated with education. Moreover, Costa and Kahn (2000) suggest that highly populated regions facilitate the process of job search and reduce the occupational co-location problems sometimes faced by highly educated couples.

4.4 Empirical Approach

4.4.1 Data Sources and Descriptive Statistics

The empirical investigation in this chapter is based on relatively long time-series data from 1992 to 2008. Information on the dependent and independent variables is derived from different sources. Data on human capital, regional private-sector employment, foreigners, and artists is provided by German Employment Statistics, which covers all employees subject to compulsory social insurance contributions (Spengler 2008). University statistics are provided by the German Federal Statistical Office, which, in addition, provides a set of various regional datasets containing detailed information on regional endowment with different dimensions of quality of life. Data on criminality come from the Federal Criminal Police Office. Data on weather are from the German Weather Bureau. The spatial framework of the analysis is based on the 326 West German districts (*Kreise*). To attain functional regions, those districts that only encompass cities (*kreisfreie Stadt*, *urban districts*) are merged with the surrounding territorial districts, resulting in 238 regions.[7]

The dependent variable is the share of employees with a tertiary degree, which is used as an indicator for human capital. Different variables that represent the six dimensions of quality of life are used as independent variables. Table A.21 in the Appendix provides a summary of descriptive statistics for the variables and Table A.22 shows the correlation matrix. Figure A.1 in the Appendix shows the uneven geography of human capital in West Germany. Aside from Hamburg, Bremen, Nuremberg, and a set of other smaller cities, regions with a relatively high share of highly educated employees tend to be distributed along two major axes. The first axis stretches from Hanover in the Northeast to Rhine-Ruhr metropolitan area. The second axis stretches from Munich to Rhine-Neckar and the Rhine-Main area. Agglomeration regions tend to have higher levels of human

[7]For an official translation for the German administrative divisions, see EC-DGT (2014).

capital than moderately congested regions and rural regions. For the period 1992–2008, the share of employees with a tertiary degree was about 8 % of the total regional workforce in agglomeration regions, 6 % in moderately congested regions, and 4.6 % in rural regions.

The average Gini coefficient for the number of employees with a tertiary degree in the period 2005–2008 is 0.66. This is considerably higher than the Gini coefficient for all employees and population, which are 49.6 and 42.5, respectively (see Fig. A.2 in the Appendix). Other works suggest that the geography of human capital becomes more uneven in the USA over time (Berry and Glaeser 2005; Moretti 2004b; Wheeler 2006).[8] In Germany, there is some weak empirical evidence of an increasing concentration of human capital (Suedekum 2008; Schlitte 2012). Suedekum (2008) argues that concentration forces in Germany are not strong enough to trigger a self-reinforcing process of human capital concentration. The differences in the geographic development of human capital between the US and Germany may be attributed to lower education costs and lower labor mobility in Germany compared to the USA.

4.4.2 Empirical Difficulties

Investigating the relationship between human capital and different dimensions of quality of life is not an easy task (Moretti 2004b, p. 2246–2247). For one thing, the empirical framework is fraught with endogeneity problems. Unlike natural sciences research, this investigation involves people, which means that, basically, everything is related to everything; moreover, performing experiments under the ceteris paribus assumption is not possible (Antonakis et al. 2014). There is never any guarantee that all relevant aspects have been included in the empirical model, no matter how many variables are employed. Moreover, it is not guaranteed that there are no measurement errors of different dimensions and elements of quality of life, no interdependence and complex relations among all variables, and no reverse causalities. Hence, the empirical analysis in this chapter does not claim to be free from various biases that may result in rejecting true hypotheses or confirming false ones.

Several studies show the reverse side of causality. In work on the social returns of education, Moretti shows different effects of human capital on different aspects of life such as income, security, and political engagement (Moretti 2004a, b). Highly educated people can improve quality of life in various ways. They may be more likely to support regional public goods and to facilitate the density and the diversity of consumer services (Glaeser et al. 2001; Shapiro 2006; Waldfogel

[8]Mulligan and Sala-i-Martin (2000) find that the dispersion of the stock human capital across US increased during the 1980s, while the dispersion of the average years of schooling decreased for the same period.

2008); be more politically active (Moretti 2004b; Milligan et al. 2004); less likely to engage in crime (Lochner and Moretti 2004); and more tolerant (Florida 2002b). Winters (2011c) suggests that quality of life is positively affected by human capital and universities. However, Winters considers human capital exogenous and acknowledges that highly educated people could be endogenous to quality of life. Hence, the author recommends caution in interpreting his results.[9]

In his work, Richard Florida claims that the presence of a cultural milieu improves the competitive advantages of cities and regions as such milieus tend to attract human capital and innovation (Florida 2002b, 2011; Stolarick and Florida 2006). Although these ideas received an extraordinary amount of attention from policymakers and the media, they were fiercely criticized in academic circles for methodological problems such as endogeneity.[10] For instance, Boualam (2014) shows that when pursuing simple correlations, regions well-endowed with cultural occupations have higher housing prices, used as an indicator for quality of life. Pursing estimations based on time-series data and econometric techniques that control for city characteristics, however, reveals a negligible impact of culture.

What is the solution to these endogeneity problems? Strong theoretical background is needed definitely. Therefore, this chapter attempted to link quality of life to fundamental human needs which are the most basic drivers of human behavior. Empirically, a number of researchers rely on historical data and instrumental variables.[11] For instance, Boualam (2014) attempts to consider the endogenous determination of cultural supply by using the annual amount of federal grants to artists and art organizations as an instrument for cultural activities. Abel and Deitz (2012) use the presence of three types of universities as instrumental variables in analyzing the impact of universities on the geography of human capital.[12] Falck et al. (2011) rely on a quasi-natural experiment in German history and argue that using proximity to baroque opera houses can provide an exogenous explanation for the geography of human capital because baroque opera houses were built for the sole purpose of reflecting a ruler's prestige. However, finding good instrumental variables is difficult. Moreover, the instrumental variables approach provides a good solution for cases in which there is limited number of "problematic" exogenous variables. In the case of human capital and different aspects of quality of life, all variables are related to each other. Alternatively, path models and structural equations can be applied to estimate the impact of different elements of quality of life on the geography of human capital.

[9]"We hope to minimize concerns about endogeneity by including a large number of important amenities, but the results should still be interpreted with some caution" (Winters 2011c, pp. 451–452).

[10]For instance, Marcuse (2003), Sawicki (2003), Glaeser (2005), Montgomery (2005), Peck (2005), Markusen (2006), McGranhan and Woja (2007), and Hoyman and Faricy (2009).

[11]See, for instance, Wooldridge (2009, pp. 506–545).

[12]These universities are public universities, land-grant universities, and Research I universities. Their location of these types of HEIs is believed not to be influenced by current levels of human capital and to be outside of the control of local population.

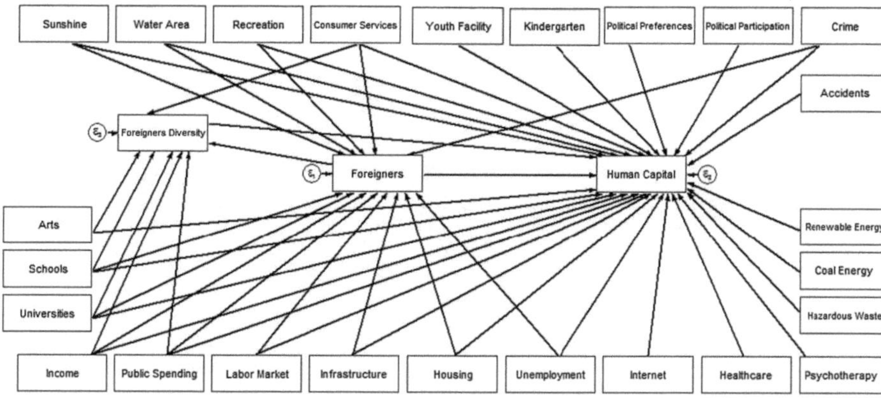

Fig. 4.1 Path model for the effect of different dimensions of quality of life on human capital (Model I)

4.4.3 Path Model and Structural Equations

Path models and structural equation modeling (SEM) are usually considered as extensions of regression analysis, factor analysis, canonical correlation, and discriminant analysis. This technique is the best available choice for the subject of this chapter because it attempts to examine the dynamics between the variables on the basis of variances and covariances.[13] Alternatively, seemingly unrelated regression (SUR) and ordinary least square (OLS) can be used. However, SUR does not work due to the large number of relationships and OLS cannot consider the indirect relationships among the variables.

To perform the analyses, two model versions are adopted. One model (Model I) includes all variables; Model II includes the strongest variables. Figure **4.1** shows the big model and Fig. **4.2** shows the small model with the limited number of variables. This strategy is applied to check the stability of the results as well as to obtain an overview of the most important variables and the relationships among them.[14] In both versions of the path model, there are three types of variables: exogenous, endogenous outcome, and endogenous mediator. There are 25 exogenous variables in Model I and 5 in Model II. Exogenous variables can be correlated with each other without having to be dependent on any other variable. Any explanation for these variables is not specified and external to the model. Moreover, these variables are lagged by 1 year to avoid simultaneity problems. The only endogenous outcome in both model versions is the regional share of human capital that is dependent on all other variables.

[13]For more details, see Jöreskog (1973) and Acock (2013).

[14]Model I is very complex and so to achieve a clear view of the structure of the relationships among the variables, the covariances are not shown in Fig. 1.1. See Fig. A.3 in the Appendix for an illustration of Model I showing the covariances.

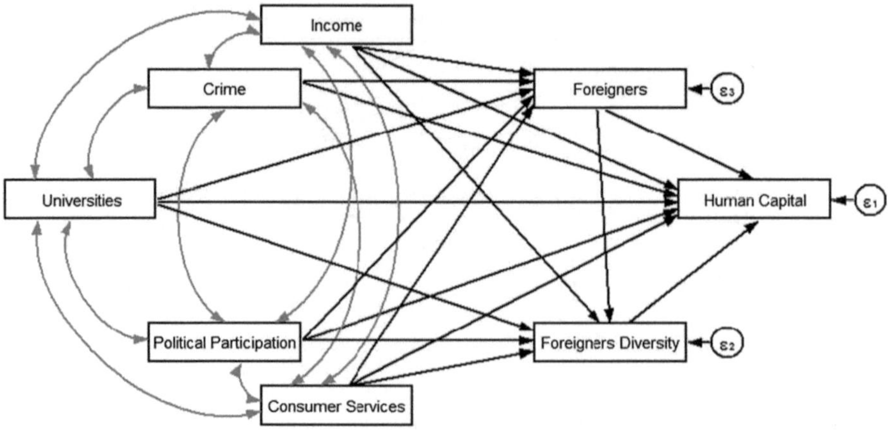

Fig. 4.2 Path model for the effect of different dimensions of quality of life on human capital, showing only the strongest exogenous variables (Model II)

The share of foreigners and their diversity are endogenous mediator variables. They are dependent on some independent variables and, at the same time, independent with respect to the endogenous outcome variable. Both variables are of great theoretical importance because they influence human capital directly and permit other exogenous variables to influence human capital indirectly. Thus, the total effect of an exogenous variable on the endogenous outcome variable is the sum of the direct and indirect effects. For instance, income influences human capital directly as well as indirectly by influencing the share of foreigners and their diversity. The exogenous variables selected to influence both of the foreigners variables are the most likely variables to influence the presence of foreigners. It is most likely that material well-being, education, and amenities influence the geography of foreigners rather than variables such as political participation, renewable energy, and the like. Moreover, allowing all exogenous variables to influence both the foreigners variables does not yield any significant result but penalizes the model by increasing the value of RMSEA over the recommended value of 0.05 due to unnecessarily increasing model complexity.

The path coefficients are estimated by the maximum likelihood method. This is the most common method when using structural models. The standardized path coefficients express the relative importance of the parameters. However, the difference between the standardized parameters should not be misunderstood. If a variable shows a higher standardized parameter than another variable, this does not automatically mean that the difference between their parameters is significant as well. The difference between the parameters should be tested. There are a number of measures that can be used to prove how well the model fits the data in addition to the well-known R-squared. Chi-squared compares the model to a saturated model with no degrees of freedom. A significant chi-squared means that the model fails to account for the covariance among the variables. The root mean squared error of approximation (RMSEA) explains the error amount for each degree of freedom. This measure reveals whether the model is unnecessarily complex. The recommended value for RMSEA is less than 0.05. The comparative fit index (CFI) compares the model with a baseline model that assumes no relationship among the variables. The frequently used cutoff value for the CFI is more than 0.95.

4.5 Results

4.5.1 Basic Results

Table 4.3 shows the standardized path coefficients for the first model, which includes direct effects (coefficients), indirect effects, and total effects of the variables. Table 4.4 shows the results of the second model. The results of the first model are discussed first, followed by those of the second model. The first model has a chi-squared of 355.825 with 394 degrees of freedom and the p-value equals 0.917. The model has a small chi-squared relative to the degrees of freedom and is not statistically significant. This implies that the model does not significantly fail to reproduce the covariance matrix. RMSEA is 0.001, much smaller than the threshold of 0.05. CFI is 0.999, far above the threshold of 0.95. This means that the model does 99.9 % better than a null model in which all variables are assumed to be unrelated to each other.

Income, public spending, labor market growth, and housing have a positive and significant direct effect on the regional share of human capital. This means that the geography of human capital is directly influenced by regions with higher income, more public spending, faster human capital growth, and more living space. The number of .dedomains per capita has no significant effect; the unemployment rate has a negative significant effect. The highest direct effect is that of housing. This means that increasing the availability of housing space per capita enhances quality of life in the region, which positively influences the geography of human capital. Housing is followed by income and public spending in regard to size of the direct effect. This does not mean that the difference between the coefficients is significant. A Wald chi-squared test can be used to check the significance of the differences between the standardized parameters. Table A.23 in the Appendix shows the test results for the direct effects of the variables measuring material well-being. The difference between the coefficients is significant for all but the following pairs: income and public spending; income and housing; public spending and housing; labor market and infrastructure; and infrastructure and Internet. Income shows strong positive indirect effect on human capital because it has strong positive effect on the regional share of foreigners. The total effect of income is the largest compared to the total effect of all other variables of material well-being.

There are three remarkable results in respect to the effects of the material well-being variables. First, unemployment shows a higher indirect effect than direct

Table 4.3 Standardized SEM results (Model I)

	Human capital			Foreigners			Foreigner diversity		
	Coef.	Indirect effects	Total effects	Coef.	Indirect effects	Total effects	Coef.	Indirect effects	Total effects
I. Material well-being									
Income	.2061***	.1026***	.3087***	.3059***	–	.3059***	–.0397	–.0014	.0411
Public spending	.2038***	.0532***	.2570***	.1459***	–	.1459***	–.0952***	–.0007	.0959***
Labor market	.0558***	–.0010	.0548**	–.0031	–	–.0031	–	.0000	.0000
Infrastructure	.0261	.0988***	.1249**	.3012***	–	.3012***	–	–.0014	–.0014
Housing	.2540***	–.1112***	.1428***	–.3391***	–	–.3391***	–	.0015	.0015
Internet	–.0384	–	–.0384	–	–	–	–	–	–
Unemployment	–.1158***	–.1377***	–.2535***	–.4199***	–	–.4199***	–	.0019	.0019
II. Protection									
Healthcare	–.0222	–	–.0222	–	–	–	–	–	–
Psychotherapy	.0044	–	.0044	–	–	–	–	–	–
Hazardous waste	–.0272	–	–.0272	–	–	–	–	–	–
Coal energy	–.0049	–	–.0049	–	–	–	–	–	–
Renewable energy	–.0124	–	–.0124	–	–	–	–	–	–
Crime	–.1765***	–.0450***	–.2215***	–.1373***	–	–.1373***	–	.0006	.0006
Accidents	–.0761***	–	–.0761***	–	–	–	–	–	–
III. Education and arts									
Schools	.2025***	.0100	.2125***	–.0172	–	–.0172	–.2748***	.0001	–.2747***
Universities	.3098***	.0083	.3181***	.0290*	–	.0290*	.0210	–.0001	.0209
Arts	.0112	.0035**	.0147	–	–	–	–.0618***	–	–.0618***
IV. Sociopolitical dimension									
Political participation	.3829***	–	.3829***	–	–	–	–	–	–

Political preferences	.3565***	–	.3565***	–	–	–	–	–	–
Kindergarten	.0001	–	.0001	–	–	–	–	–	–
Youth facilities	–.0192	–	–.0192	–	–	–	–	–	–
V. Amenities									
Consumer services	.2309***	.0533***	.2842***	.1158***	–	.1158***	–.2699***	–.0005	–.2704***
Recreation	.2110***	.0507***	.2617***	.1545***	–	.1545***	–	–.0007	–.0007
Water area	.1291***	.0016	.1307***	.0049	–	.0049	–	.0000	.0000
Sunshine	.0680***	.0091**	.0771***	.0277**	–	.0277**	–	–.0001	–.0001
VI. Tolerance									
Foreigners	.3277***	.0003	.3280***	–	–	–	–.0045	–	–.0045
Diversity of foreigners	–.0567***	–	–.0567***	–	–	–	–	–	–
Constant	–7.7721***	–	–	4.8182***	–	–	5.0175***	–	–

Notes: $chi^2(394) = 355.825$ ($p = .917$); RMSEA = .001; CFI = .999; $R^2 = .7862$; $R^2 = .5710$; $R^2 = .2434$; Number of observations = 4998
***Statistically significant at the 1 % level; **Statistically significant at the 5 % level; *Statistically significant at the 10 % level

Table 4.4 Standardized SEM results (Model II)

	Human capital			Foreigners			Foreigner diversity		
	Coef.	Indirect effects	Total effects	Coef.	Indirect effects	Total effects	Coef.	Indirect effects	Total effects
Income	.1291***	.1403***	.2694***	.3800***	–	.3800***	−.0645	.0020***	−.0625
Crime	−.1528***	−.1215***	−.2743***	−.3424***	–	−.3424***	–	−.0018	−.0018
Universities	.3621***	.0790	.4411***	.2027***	–	.2027***	−.0844***	.0011	−.0832***
Political participation	.0414*	−.0150	.0264	.0754**	–	.0754**	−.1408***	−.0004	−.1412***
Consumer services	.3140***	.0255***	.3395***	−.0129	–	−.0129	−.3596***	−.0001	−.3597***
Foreigners	.3553***	−.0004	.3549	–	–	–	.0052	–	.0052
Diversity of foreigners	−.0837***	–	−.0837***	–	–	–	–	–	–
Constant	.5994	–	–	2.2562***	–	–	6.2653	–	–

Notes: $chi^2(38) = .000$ ($p = .917$); RMSEA = .000; CFI = 1.000; R^2 (human capital) = .6649; R^2 (foreigners) = .3040; R^2 (foreigner diversity) = .1626; Number of observations = 4998

***Statistically significant at the 1 % level; **Statistically significant at the 5 % level; *Statistically significant at the 10 % level

effect. The total effect of unemployment is about −0.2535. The indirect effect is −0.1377, which represents roughly 54 % of the total effect. Unemployment exerts a strong negative effect on the regional share of foreigners, leading to a negative indirect effect of unemployment on human capital. Second, regions well-endowed with infrastructure influence the geography of human capital rather indirectly. Infrastructure shows no significant direct effect on human capital, but it has a strong indirect effect and thus a positive and significant total effect. Infrastructure has the second strongest positive effect on the regional share of foreigners. This strong effect is transformed into an indirect effect on human capital. Third, while housing shows the strongest positive direct effect on human capital, it has a negative indirect effect because of its strong negative effect on the share of foreigners. However, the positive direct effect outweighs the negative indirect effect, resulting in a positive and significant total effect.

Remarkably, healthcare and psychotherapy have no significant effect on the regional share of human capital. In addition, indicators that refer to a healthy environment, such as hazardous waste, the share of produced energy by coal burning, and the share of renewable energy, have no significant effect on the geography of human capital. In contrast, the results demonstrate an important role for security in explaining the geography of human capital. High crime rates reduce the regional share of human capital directly as well as indirectly. Increasing crime rates diminish the feeling of security and, consequently, the quality of life, which results in decreasing the share of human capital. Moreover, increasing crime rates reduce the share of foreigners, inducing a negative indirect effect of crime on human capital. The risk of accidents seems to reduce regional shares of human capital as well.

The variables of education and the intellectual dimension of quality of life show a considerably high effect. The share of students in universities exhibits the fourth highest total effect on human capital after political participation, political preferences, and foreigners. A Wald chi-squared test, however, does not report a significant difference among the coefficients of these variables.[15] Moreover, while schools show a positive and significant effect on human capital, the share of artists tends to have a weak effect on human capital. This effect is exclusively indirect, mediated by increasing the diversity of foreigners. In his work, Florida (see, e.g., 2002b, 2011) argues that tolerance can be indicated by the share of artists. If this is indeed true, then tolerance has no direct effect on human capital.

It appears that regions with high political participation and diversity tend to influence the geography of human capital positively. No effect can be found for social services such as the available places in kindergarten and youth facilities. The majority of the indicators that refer to amenities affect human capital both directly

[15] $Chi^2 = 1.75$ ($p = 0.1864$) for universities and political participation; $chi^2 = 0.79$ (0.3734) for universities and political preferences; $chi^2 = 0.42$ (0.5151) for universities and foreigners; $chi^2 = 1.09$ (0.2968) for political participation and political preferences; $chi^2 = 0.93$ (0.3344) for political participation and foreigners; $chi^2 = 0.29$ (0.5889) for political preferences and foreigners.

and indirectly. Diversity of consumer services has the highest total effect among the variables of this dimension followed by recreation. Moreover, fine weather and the presence of water areas such as lakes and shores exert a positive influence on the geography of human capital. A Wald chi-squared test shows significant differences, except for the following pairs: consumer services and recreation; and recreation and water areas.[16]

Tolerance is reflected by the share of foreigners. To control for country of origin, a Herfindahl-Hirschman Index of the diversity of foreigners is included in the model. Both of the foreigners variables act as endogenous mediator variables in the model. They intervene between the exogenous variables and the endogenous outcome variable, indirectly mediating the effect of some exogenous variables on human capital. The share of foreigners affects the geography of human capital positively and shows the third highest total effect among all variables. The Herfindahl-Hirschman Index for the diversity of foreigners has a negative and significant effect on human capital. This means that the share of human capital decreases with increasing homogeneity of foreigners according to country of origin. The most important variables that influence the share of foreigners are income and infrastructure. Unemployment has the strongest negative effect on the share of foreigners followed by housing and crime. The most important indicators that increase the diversity of foreigners are schools, consumer services, public spending, and arts. In brief, tolerance as indicated by the presence of foreigners is associated positively with human capital.

The first model included 27 indicators of quality of life. To reduce model complexity, a second model that only includes the most important variables is created. From each dimension, the variable that had the highest total effect on human capital in the first model is selected. Thus, the following variables are selected: income, crime, universities, political participation, consumer services, and foreigners. Moreover, due to its role as mediator, the diversity of foreigners is included in the second model. The explained variance of human capital in the second model equals 0.6649. This represents 85 % of the explained variance in the first model. This model (Model II) has a chi-squared of 0.00 with 38 degrees of freedom and a p-value of 0.917. Thus, this model does not significantly fail to reproduce the covariance matrix. Both RMSEA and CFI show the recommended values. Table A.24 shows the results of a Wald chi-square test for the significance of the difference among the standardized coefficients. The test shows a significant difference between the parameters of the variables with the exception of the pair universities and foreigners.

Income has lost some of its direct effect in this model, whereas its indirect effect has increased slightly. The total effect of income decreased about 13 %. Similarly,

---

[16] $Chi^2 = 0.08$ ($p = 0.7757$) for consumer services and recreation; $chi^2 = 6.12$ (0.0134) for consumer services and water areas; $chi^2 = 25.83$ (0.0000) for consumer services and sunshine; $chi^2 = 1.23$ (0.2680) for recreation and water areas; $chi^2 = 4.42$ (0.0354) for recreation and sunshine; $chi^2 = 3.44$ (0.0635) for water areas and sunshine.

the direct effect of crime declined slightly, whereas the indirect effect and total effect increased slightly. Political participation nearly lost its statistical significance. In contrast, the effect of other variables increased, especially the direct effect of universities, foreigners, and diversity of foreigners. The total effect of universities increased dramatically from 0.3181 to 0.4411 and is now the strongest total effect on human capital. Both the direct and total effect of consumer services increased, while the indirect effect decreased.

4.5.2 Checks

To show the stability of the results, two changes are made. The role of population density is analyzed as well as the influence of quality of life on people without a tertiary degree. Model II is chosen for these changes due to its less complicated structure.

To a large degree, population density is a "catch-all" variable that is statistically closely related to the majority of the variables of quality of life. On the one hand, highly populated regions are characterized by a number of benefits due to the spatial proximity of people. On the other hand, population density can obscure the effects of the variables that may be the "true" determinants of the geography of human capital. Thus, two strategies are engaged in to examine the role of population density in the geography of human capital.

First, population density is added to the second model in form that it influences all other variables. Table A.25 in the Appendix reports the results for this model and Fig. A.4 in the Appendix illustrates this path model. The variable that reflects population density exerts a strong positive and significant effect on human capital. The indirect effect of population density is larger than the direct effect. Moreover, when population density is included in the model, the effect of most variables decreases, with the exception of total effect of political participation and foreigner diversity. In addition, population density influences income, universities, consumer services, and foreigners positively, while its effect on crime, political participation and diversity of foreigners is negative.

Second, the second model is applied separately for three groups of regions, which are sorted based on population density: regions with a relatively low, medium, and high level of population density. Table A.26 reports the standardized coefficients for these three groups of regions. The effect of each variable may change dependent on population density in four ways. First, the effect of variables can increase with increasing population density such as the total effect of income and universities. Second, the effect of variables can decrease with increasing population density such as the total effect of political participation. Third, the effect of variables can increase then decrease with population density such as the total effect of foreigners and the direct effect of universities and political participation. Fourth, the effect of variables can decrease then increase with population density such as the total effect of consumer services.

The second change made to check the robustness of the results is to use the share of medium-educated as well as low-educated employees as the dependent variable. Medium-educated employees have either a high school certificate or occupational training; low-educated employees have neither. Tables A.27 and A.28 in the Appendix show the standardized path coefficients for both groups of employees. The results show that, in contrast to human capital, some variables of quality of life have a weaker or reverse effect on the geography of medium-educated and low-educated employees. For medium-educated employees, income, consumer services, and foreigners show negative effects directly and indirectly, while crime rate and political participation have positive effects. Universities exert a positive direct effect and a negative indirect effect; the total effect is statistically insignificant. For low-educated employees, political participation and consumer services show negative effects directly and indirectly, while the share of foreigners and foreigner diversity has positive effects. Income has a negative direct effect and a positive indirect effect. Crime has a positive direct effect and a negative indirect effect.

4.6 Summary and Conclusion

This chapter added new insights to the body of knowledge on the role of quality of life as a multidimensional concept and comprehensive framework for explaining the geography of human capital across West German regions. Quality of life includes six dimensions: material well-being; protection; education and arts; a sociopolitical dimension; amenities; and tolerance. Path models and structural equations are employed to link the 27 quality of life variables to the regional share of human capital. The empirical results suggest that regional endowment with various facilities that enhance the quality of life is associated with high levels of human capital. No causal relationships are claimed due to the presumed endogeneity problems.

A policy strategy based on increasing regional levels of human capital in order to drive economic progress is promising (Mathur 1999; Glaeser et al. 2004). However, the empirical literature on the determinants of the geographic distribution of human capital and quality of life is still young. Given the small number of studies on this issue, it is still too early to draw definitive policy recommendations. This chapter's main point of interest for policymakers is that it could be worthwhile to create regional environments that are attractive to human capital. Policies encouraging nondiscrimination, infrastructure, and recreation areas could be useful in this endeavor (Gottlieb 1994a, b; Glaeser et al. 2001; Adamson et al. 2004). There is a great deal of scope for improving study of this issue. For instance, the majority of the variables are not exogenously determined and there very well could be feedback loops between the independent variables and the dependent variable, better solutions for both seems a worth pursuit for future research. In addition, other dimensions and elements of quality of life could be taken into consideration. Moreover, using educational attainment as an indicator for human capital may be too broad. Additional research might attempt to capture differences within the group of people with a tertiary degree in respect to, for example, age, sex, scientific background, income, and the like (Growe 2010).

A discussion concerning the definition and measurement of quality of life is generally missing in economics. More precise definitions and measures are necessary. Also, the subject of fundamental human needs and the role they play in economic reality could use more work. Mainstream theory is intensely concerned with the economics of nations, firms, people such as entrepreneurs, and human capital. It may be time to introduce human needs as the nano-units of economic analysis into mainstream economic theory.

References

Abel JR, Deitz R (2012) Do colleges and universities increase their region's human capital? J Econ Geogr 12:667–691

Abel JR, Dey I, Gabe TM (2012) Productivity and the density of human capital. J Reg Sci 52: 562–586

Acock AC (2013) Discovering structural equation modeling using Stata. Stata Press, College Station, TX

Acs ZJ, Armington C (2004) The impact of geographic differences in human capital on service firm formation rates. J Urban Econ 56:244–278

Acs ZJ, Armington C (2006) Entrepreneurship, geography, and American economic growth. Cambridge University Press, New York, NY

Adamson DW, Clark DE, Partridge MD (2004) Do agglomeration effects and household amenities have a skill bias? J Region Sci 44:201–223

Ager P, Brückner M (2013) Cultural diversity and economic growth: evidence from the US during the age of mass migration. Eur Econ Rev 64:76–97

Alderfer CP (1972) Existence, relatedness, and growth: human needs in organizational settings. Free Press, New York, NY

Alesina A, Baqir R, Easterly W (1999) Public goods and ethnic divisions. Quart J Econ 114: 1243–1284

Alesina A, Baqir R, Hoxby C (2004) Political jurisdictions in heterogeneous communities. J Polit Econ 112:349–396

Alkire S (2002) Dimensions of human development. World Dev 30:181–205

Alm J, Winters JV (2009) Distance and intrastate college student migration. Econ Educ Rev 28: 728–738

Amabile T (1996) Creativity in context. Westview Press, Boulder, CO

Andersson ÅE (1985a) Creativity and regional development. Papers Region Sci Assoc 56:5–20

Andersson ÅE (1985b) Creativity – The future of metropolitan regions. Prisma, Stockholm

Antonakis J, Bendahan S, Jacquart P, Lalive R (2014) Causality and endogeneity: problems and solutions. In: Day DV (ed) The Oxford handbook of leadership and organizations. Oxford University Press, Oxford, pp 93–116

Aschauer DA (1990) Why is infrastructure important? Federal Reserve Bank of Boston (mimeo)

Bacolod M, Blum BS, Strange WC (2009) Skills in the city. J Urban Econ 65:136–153

Bacolod M, Blum BS, Strange WC (2010) Elements of skill: traits, intelligences, education, and agglomeration. J Region Sci 50:245–280

Bade KJ (1994) Das Manifest der 60. Deutschland und die Einwanderung. C. H. Beck, München, English: The manifesto of the 60th Germany and immigration
Bade KJ (2000) Europa in Bewegung: Migration vom späten 18. Jahrhundert bis zur Gegenwart. C. H. Beck, München, English: Europe on the move: migration from the late 18th century to the present
Bade KJ (2001) Migration und Asyl im geteilten Deutschland. Blätter für deutsche und internationale Politik 2:230–240, English: Migration and asylum in divided Germany
Barro RJ (1991) Economic growth in a cross section of countries. Quart J Econ 106:407–443
Becker GS (1962) Investment in human capital: a theoretical analysis. J Polit Econ 70:9–49
Becker GS (1964) Human capital, 1st edn. Columbia University Press, New York, NY
Becker GS, Murphy KM (1992) The division of labor, coordination costs, and knowledge. Quart J Econ 107:1137–1160
Beeson PE, Eberts RW (1989) Identifying productivity and amenity effects in interurban wage differentials. Rev Econ Stat 71:443–452
Benhabib J, Spiegel MM (1994) The role of human capital in economic development: evidence from aggregate cross-country data. J Monet Econ 34:143–173
Benhabib J, Spiegel MM (2005) Human capital and technology diffusion. In: Aghion P, Durlauf SN (eds) Handbook of economic growth, vol 1A. Elsevier, Amsterdam, pp 935–966
Berry C, Glaeser EL (2005) The divergence of human capital levels across cities. Papers Region Sci 84:407–444
Bils M, Klenow PJ (2000) Does schooling cause growth? Am Econ Rev 90:1160–1183
Blackwell M, Cobb S, Weinberg D (2002) The economic impact of educational institutions: issues and methodology. Econ Dev Quart 16:88–95
Blomquist GC, Berger MC, Hoehn JP (1988) New estimates of quality of life in urban areas. Am Econ Rev 78:89–107
Borjas G, Bronars SG, Trejo SJ (1992) Self-selection and internal migration in the United States. J Urban Econ 32:159–185
Boualam B (2014) Does culture affect local productivity and urban amenities? Reg Sci Urban Econ 46:12–17
Buettner T, Ebertz A (2009) Quality of life in the regions: results for German counties. Ann Region Sci 43:89–112
Buettner T, Janeba E (2013) City competition for the creative class. CESifo Working Paper No. 4417. Ifo Institute, Munich
CAE (Conseil d'Analyse Économique), SVR (Sachverständigenrat zur Begutachtung der gesamtwirtschaftlichen Entwicklung) (2010) Monitoring economic performance, quality of life and sustainability. http://www.sachverstaendigenratwirtschaft.de/expertisen.html?&no_cache=1
Cain LP (1997) Historical perspective on infrastructure and US economic development. Reg Sci Urban Econ 27:117–138
Card D (1995) Using geographic variation in college proximity to estimate the return to schooling. In: Christofides L, Swideinsky R, Grant EK (eds) Aspects of labour market behaviour: essays in honor of John Vanderkamp. University of Toronto Press, Toronto, pp 201–222
Carlino GA, Chatterjee S, Hunt RM (2007) Urban density and the rate of invention. J Urban Econ 61:389–419
Chen Y, Rosenthal S (2008) Local amenities and life-cycle migration: do people move for jobs or fun? J Urban Econ 64:519–537
Cheshire PC, Hay DG (1989) Urban problems in Western Europe: an economic analysis. Unwin Hyman, London
Cheshire PC, Magrini S (2006) Population growth in European cities: weather matters but only nationally. Region Stud 40:23–37
Chung C, Clark J, Kim B (2009) Is the growing skill premium a purely metropolitan issue? Econ Lett 102:73–75
Ciccone A (2002) Agglomeration effects in Europe. Eur Econ Rev 46:213–227

Ciccone A, Hall RE (1996) Productivity and the density of economic activity. Am Econ Rev 86: 54–70
Clark TN, Lloyd R, Wong KK, Jain P (2002) Amenities drive urban growth. J Urban Aff 24: 493–515
Combes PP, Duranton G, Gobillon L (2008) Spatial wage disparities: sorting matters! J Urban Econ 63:723–742
Combes PP, Duranton G, Gobillon L (2011) The identification of agglomeration economies. J Econ Geogr 11:253–266
Costa DL, Kahn ME (2000) Power couples: changes in the locational choice of the college educated, 1940–1990. Quart J Econ 115:1287–1315
Costanza R, Fisher B, Ali S, Beer C et al (1997) Quality of life: an approach integrating opportunities, human needs, and subjective wellbeing. Ecol Econ 61:267–276
Cummins RA (1997) Comprehensive Quality of Life Scale for Adults (ComQol-A5). Deakin University, School of Psychology, Melbourne
Dasgupta P (2000) Population and resources: an exploration of reproductive and environmental externalities. Popul Dev Rev 26:643–689
Davis MA, Ortalo-Magne F (2007) Wages, rents, quality of life. Department of Real Estate and Urban Land Economics, University of Wisconsin (mimeo)
Dee TS (2004) Are there civic returns to education? J Publ Econ 88:1697–1720
Deller SC, Tsai T-H, Marcouiller DW, English DB-K (2001) The role of amenities and quality of life in rural economic growth. Am J Agric Econ 83:352–365
Deschênes O (2012) Temperature, human health, and adaptation: a review of the empirical literature. NBER Working Paper No. 18345
Deschênes O, Moretti E (2009) Extreme weather events, mortality and migration. Rev Econ Stat 91:659–681
Diener E (2006) Guidelines for national indicators of subjective well-being and ill-being. Appl Res Qual Life 1:151–157
Diener E, Suh E (1997) Measuring quality of life: economic, social, and subjective indicators. Social Indicators Res 40:189–216
Dill V (2013) Ethnic concentration and extreme right-wing voting behavior in West Germany. SOEP Papers on Multidisciplinary Panel Data Research. DIW, Berlin
Dissart J-C, Deller SC (2000) Quality of life in the planning literature. J Plann Lit 1:36–61
Douglas S (1997) Estimating relative standard of living in the United States using cross-migration data. J Region Sci 37:411–436
Drucker J, Goldstein H (2006) The economic development impacts of universities on regions: do size and distance matter? Econ Dev Quart 20:22–43
Drucker J, Goldstein H (2007) Assessing the regional economic development impacts of universities: a review of current approaches. Int Region Sci Rev 30:20–46
Duranton G, Puga D (2004) Micro-foundations of urban agglomeration economies. In: Henderson JV, Thisse JF (eds) Handbook of regional and urban economics, vol 4. Elsevier, Amsterdam, pp 2063–2115
EC-DGT: European Commission; Directorate-General for Translation (2014) Country compendium: a companion to the English style guide. EC Directorate-General for Translation, Brussels
Elo IT, Preston SH (1996) Educational differentials in mortality: United States, 1979–85. Soc Sci Med 42:47–57
Elvery J (2010) City size and skill intensity. Reg Sci Urban Econ 40:367–379
Eriksson RH, Hansen HK, Lindgren U (2014) The importance of business climate and people climate on regional performance. Region Stud 48:1135–1155
EU Committee of the Regions (1999) Evaluation quality of life in European regions. Commission of the European Communities, Brussels
Faggian A, McCann P (2009) Universities, agglomerations and graduate human capital mobility. Tijdschrift voor economische en sociale geografie 100:210–223

Falck O, Fritsch M, Heblich S (2011) The phantom of the opera: cultural amenities, human capital, and regional economic growth. Labor Econ 18:755–766
Farquhar M (1995) Definitions of quality of life: a taxonomy. J Adv Nursing 22:502–508
Felce D, Perry J (1995) Quality of life: its definition and measurement. Res Dev Disabil 16:51–74
Florida R (2002a) The economic geography of talent. Ann Assoc Am Geographer 92:743–755
Florida R (2002b) Bohemia and economic geography. J Econ Geogr 2:55–71
Florida R (2005) Cities and the creative class. Routledge, New York, NY
Florida R (2011) The rise of the creative class, revisted. Basic Books, New York, NY
Florida R, Gates G (2001) Technology and tolerance – The importance of diversity to high-technology growth. Brookings Institute, Washington, DC
Florida R, Mellander C (2010) There goes the metro: how and why Bohemians, artists and gays affect regional housing values. J Econ Geogr 10:167–188
Florida R, Gates G, Knudsen B, Stolarick K (2006) The university and the creative economy. http://creativeclass.com/rfcgdb/articles/University_andthe_Creative_Economy.pdf
Florida R, Mellander C, Stolarick K (2008) Inside the black box of regional development – Human capital, the creative class and tolerance. J Econ Geogr 8:615–649
Florida R, Mellander C, Stolarick K (2011) Beautiful places: the role of perceived aesthetic beauty in community satisfaction. Region Stud 45:33–48
Fredrickson BL (2001) The role of positive emotions in positive psychology: the broaden-and-build theory of positive emotions. Am Psychologist 56:218–226
Frey BS, Stutzer A (2002a) Happiness and economics: how the economy and institutions affect human well-being. Princeton University Press, Princeton, NJ
Frey BS, Stutzer A (2002b) What can economists learns from happiness research? J Econ Lit 40: 402–435
Frisch MB (1998) Quality of life therapy and assessment in healthcare. Clin Psychol Sci Pract 5:19–40
Gabriel SA, Rosenthal SS (2004) Quality of the business environment versus quality of life: do firms and households like the same cities? Rev Econ Stat 86:438–444
García-Mira R, Uzzell DL, Eulogio-Real J, Romay J (2005) Housing, space and quality of life. Ashgate, Farnham
Gaspar J, Glaeser EL (1998) Information technology and the future of cities. J Urban Econ 43: 136–156
Giannias D (1998) A quality of life based ranking of Canadian cities. Urban Stud 35:2241–2251
Gillingham R, Reece WS (1979) A new approach to quality of life measurement. Urban Stud 16: 329–332
Glaeser EL (1998) Are cities dying? J Econ Perspect 12:139–160
Glaeser EL (1999) Learning in cities. J Urban Econ 46:254–277
Glaeser EL (2000) The new economics of urban and regional growth. In: Clark GL, Feldman MP, Gertler MS (eds) The Oxford handbook of economic geography. Oxford University Press, Oxford, pp 83–98
Glaeser EL (2005) Review of Richard Florida's the rise of the creative class. Reg Sci Urban Econ 35:593–596
Glaeser EL, Kahn ME (2004) Sprawl and urban growth. In: Henderson JV, Thisse JE (eds) Handbook of regional and urban economics, vol 4. Elsevier, Amsterdam, pp 2482–2527
Glaeser EL, Maré DC (2001) Cities and skills. J Labor Econ 19:316–342
Glaeser EL, Resseger MG (2010) The complementarity between cities and skills. J Region Sci 50: 221–244
Glaeser EL, Scheinkman JA, Shleifer A (1995) Economic growth in a cross-section of cities. J Monet Econ 36:117–143
Glaeser EL, Kolko J, Saiz A (2001) Consumer city. J Econ Geogr 1:27–50
Glaeser EL, La Porta R, Shleifer A (2004) Do institutions cause growth? J Econ Growth 9: 271–303

Gottlieb PD (1994a) Amenities as an economic development tool: is there enough evidence? Econ Dev Quart 8:270–285
Gottlieb PD (1994b) Residential amenities, firm location and economic development. Urban Stud 32:1413–1436
Graves PE (1976) A re-examination of migration, economic opportunity, and the quality of life. J Region Sci 12:107–112
Graves PE (1980) Migration and climate. J Region Sci 20:227–237
Graves PE (1983) Migration with a composite amenity: the role of rents. J Region Sci 23:541–546
Greenley JR, Greenberg JS, Brown R (1997) Measuring quality of life: a new and practical survey instrument. Social Work 42:244–254
Groen JA (2004) The effect of college location on migration of college-educated labor. J Economet 121:125–142
Growe A (2010) Human capital in the German urban system: patterns of concentration and specialization. Eur J Spatial Dev, Article no. 40
Gumprecht B (2003) The American college town. Geographic Rev 93:51–80
Gyourko J, Tracy J (1991) The structure of local public finance and the quality of life. J Polit Econ 99:774–806
Haas BK (1999) A multidisciplinary concept analysis of quality of life. West J Nursing Res 21: 728–742
Hagerty MR, Cummins RA, Ferriss AL, Land K et al (2001) Quality of life indexes for national policy: review and agenda for research. Social Indicators Res 55:1–96
Hall P (1995) Towards a general urban theory. In: Brotchie J, Batty M, Blakley E, Hall P, Newton P (eds) Cities in competition: productive and sustainable cities for the 21st century. Longman, Melbourne
Henderson JV (1988) Urban development: theory, fact, and illusion. Oxford University Press, Oxford
Herzog H, Schlottmann A (1986) The metro rating game: what can be learned from recent migrants? Growth Change 17:37–50
Hickman DC (2009) The effects of higher education policy on the location decision of individuals: evidence from Florida's Bright Futures Scholarship Program. Reg Sci Urban Econ 39:553–562
Hoyman M, Faricy C (2009) It takes a village: a test of the creative class, social capital, and human capital theories. Urban Aff Rev 44:311–333
Huffman D, Quigley JM (2002) The role of the university in attracting high tech entrepreneurship: a Silicon Valley tale. Ann Region Sci 36:403–419
Inglehart R, Norris P (2003) Rising tide. Cambridge University Press, New York, NY
Inglehart R, Welzel C (2005) Modernization, cultural change and democracy. Cambridge University Press, New York, NY
Jacobs J (1961) The death and life of great American cities. Random House, New York, NY
Jacobs J (1969) The economy of cities. Vintage, New York, NY
Jöreskog KG (1973) Analysis of covariance structures. In: Krishnaiah PR (ed) Multivariate analysis III. Academic Press, New York, NY
Jovanovic B, Rob R (1989) The growth and diffusion of knowledge. Rev Econ Stud 56:569–582
Kahneman D, Diener E, Schwarz R (1999) Well-being: the foundations of hedonic psychology. Russell Sage Foundation, New York, NY
Kenkel DS (1991) Health behavior, health knowledge and schooling. J Polit Econ 99:287–305
Kim D, Liu F, Yezer A (2009) Do inter-city differences in intra-city wage differentials have any interesting implications? J Urban Econ 66:203–209
Knoke K (1996) Bold new world: the essential road map to the twenty-first century. Kodansha, New York, NY
Krugman P (1991) Geography and trade. MIT Press, Cambridge, MA
Krutilla K, Reuveny R (2002) The quality of life in the dynamics of economic development. Environ Dev Econ 7:23–45

Lambiri D, Biagi B, Royuela V (2007) Quality of life in the economic and urban economic literature. Social Indicators Res 84:1–25
Layard P (2005) Happiness: lessons from a new science. Penguin Press, New York, NY
Lazear E (1999) Culture and language. J Polit Econ Suppl:95–125
Lee S (2010) Ability sorting and consumer city. J Urban Econ 68:20–33
Lee SY, Florida R, Acs ZJ (2004) Creativity and entrepreneurship: a regional analysis of new firm formation. Region Stud 38:879–891
Lee SY, Florida R, Gates G (2010) Innovation, human capital, and creativity. Int Rev Publ Admin 14:13–24
Lleras-Muney A (2006) The relationship between education and adult mortality in the US. Rev Econ Stud 72:189–221
Lochner L, Moretti E (2004) The effect of education on crime: evidence from prison inmates, arrests, and self-reports. Am Econ Rev 94:155–189
Lucas RE Jr (1988) On the mechanics of economic development. J Monet Econ 22:3–42
Marans RW (2012) Quality of urban life studies: an overview and implications for environment-behaviour research. Proc Social Behav Sci 35:9–22
Marcuse P (2003) Review of the rise of the creative class, by Richard Florida. Urban Land 62: 40–41
Markusen A (2006) Urban development and the politics of a creative class: evidence from a study of artists. Environ Plann A 38:1921–1940
Maslow AH (1943) A theory of human motivation. Psychol Rev 50:370–396
Maslow AH (1954) Motivation and personality. Harper, New York, NY
Mathur VK (1999) Human capital-based strategy for regional economic development. Econ Dev Quart 13:203–216
Max-Neef M (1991a) Development and human needs. In: Ekins P, Max-Neef M (eds) Real life economics: understanding wealth creation. Routledge, London, pp 197–213
Max-Neef M (1991b) Human scale development. Apex Press, New York, NY
McGranhan D, Woja T (2007) Recasting the creative class to examine growth processes in rural and urban counties. Region Stud 41:197–216
McHenry P (2014) The geographic distribution of human capital: measurement of contributing mechanisms. J Region Sci 54:215–248
Mellander C, Florida R, Stolarick K (2011) Here to stay—The effects of community satisfaction on the decision to stay. Spatial Econ Anal 6:5–24
Milligan K, Moretti E, Oreopoulos P (2004) Does education improve citizenship? Evidence from the United States and the United Kingdom. J Publ Econ 88:1667–1695
Mincer J (1958) Investment in human capital and personal income distribution. J Polit Econ 66: 281–302
Mincer J (1974) Schooling, earnings, and experience. Columbia University Press, New York, NY
Moeller J, Haas A (2003) The agglomeration wage differential reconsidered—An investigation using German micro data 1984–1997. In: Broecker J, Dohse D, Soltwedel R (eds) Innovation clusters and interregional competition. Springer, Berlin, pp 182–217
Montgomery J (2005) Beware "the Creative Class". Creativity and wealth creation revisited. Local Econ 20:337–343
Morais P, Miguéis VL, Camanho AS (2013) Quality of life experienced by human capital: an assessment of European cities. Social Indicators Res 110:187–206
Moretti E (2004a) Estimating the social returns to higher education: evidence from longitudinal and repeated cross-section data. J Economet 121:175–212
Moretti E (2004b) Human capital externalities in cities. In: Henderson JV, Thisse JF (eds) Handbook of urban and regional economics, vol 4. Elsevier, Amsterdam, pp 2244–2291
Mulligan CB, Sala-i-Martin X (2000) Measuring aggregate human capital. J Econ Growth 5: 215–252

Mulligan G, Carruthers J, Cahill M (2004) Urban quality of life and public policy: a survey. In: Capello R, Nijkamp P (eds) Urban dynamics and growth, vol 266. Elsevier, Amsterdam, pp 729–802
Naisbitt R (1995) The global paradox. Avon Books, New York, NY
Negroponte N (1995) Being digital. Vintage Books, New York, NY
Nelson RR, Phelps ES (1966) Investment in humans, technological diffusion, and economic growth. Am Econ Rev 56:69–75
Noland M (2005) Popular attitudes, globalization and risk. Int Finance 8:199–229
O'Reilly CH, Williams KY, Barsade SG (1998) Group demography and innovation: does diversity help? In: Neale MA, Mannix EA, Gruenfeld D (eds) Research on managing groups and teams. JAI Press, Greenwich, pp 183–207
OECD: Organisation for Economic Co-operation and Development (2011) How's life? Measuring well-being. OECD, Paris
Olfert MR, Partridge M (2011) Creating the cultural community: ethnic diversity vs. agglomeration. Spatial Econ Anal 6:25–55
Ottaviano GIP, Peri G (2005) Cities and culture. J Urban Econ 58:304–337
Pacione M (2003) Urban environmental quality and human wellbeing—A social geographical perspective. Landsc Urban Plann 65:19–30
Peck J (2005) Struggling with the creative class. Int J Urban Region Res 29:740–770
Qian H, Acs ZJ (2011) An absorptive capacity theory of knowledge spillover entrepreneurship. Small Bus Econ 40:185–197
Qian H, Acs ZJ, Stough RR (2013) Regional systems of entrepreneurship: the nexus of human capital, knowledge and new firm formation. J Econ Geogr 13:559–587
Rappaport J (2007) Moving to nice weather. Reg Sci Urban Econ 37:375–398
Rappaport J (2008) Consumption amenities and city population density. Reg Sci Urban Econ 38: 533–552
Rappaport J (2009) The increasing importance of quality of life. J Econ Geogr 9:779–804
Rappaport J, Sachs J (2003) The United States as a coastal nation. J Econ Growth 8:5–46
Rauch JE (1993) Productivity gains from geographic concentration of human capital: evidence from the Cities. J Urban Econ 34:380–400
Ritsilä J, Ovaskainen M (2001) Migration and regional centralization of human capital. Appl Econ 33:317–325
Rives JM, Heaney MT (1995) Infrastructure and local economic development. Region Sci Perspect 25:58–73
Roback J (1982) Wages, rents, and the quality of life. J Polit Econ 90:1257–1278
Rogerson RJ (1999) Quality of life and city competitiveness. Urban Stud 36:969–985
Romer P (1986) Increasing returns and long-run growth. J Polit Econ 94:1002–1037
Romer P (1990) Human capital and growth: theory and evidence. Carnegie-Rochester Conf Ser Publ Policy 32:251–286
Rosen S (1979) Wage-based indexes of urban quality of Life. In: Mieszkowski P, Straszheim P (eds) Current issues in urban economics. Johns Hopkins University Press, Baltimore, MD, pp 74–104
Rosenthal SS, Strange WC (2001) The determinants of agglomeration. J Urban Econ 50:191–229
Rosenthal SS, Strange WC (2004) Evidence on the nature and sources of agglomeration economies. In: Henderson JV, Thisse JF (eds) Handbook of regional and urban economics, vol 4. Elsevier, Amsterdam, pp 2119–2171
Rosenthal SS, Strange WC (2008) The attenuation of human capital spillovers. J Urban Econ 64: 373–389
Rydgren J (2004) Mechanisms of exclusion: ethnic discrimination in the Swedish labour market. J Ethnic Migration Stud 30:697–716
Sander W (1995) Schooling and quitting smoking. Rev Econ Stat 77:191–199
Savageau D (2000) Places rated almanac. IDG Books, Foster City, CA

Sawicki D (2003) Review of the rise of the creative class: and how it's transforming work, leisure, community and everyday life, by Richard Florida. J Am Plann Assoc 69:90–91
Schlitte F (2012) Local human capital, segregation by skill, and skill-specific employment growth. Papers Region Sci 91:85–106
Schuessler KF, Fisher GA (1985) Quality of life research and sociology. Annu Rev Sociol 11: 129–149
Schultz TW (1961) Investment in human capital. Am Econ Rev 51:1–17
Scotchmer S (2002) Local public goods and clubs. In: Auerbach A, Feldstein M (eds) Handbook of public economics, vol 4. North-Holland, Amsterdam, pp 1997–2042
Scully GW (2001) Government expenditure and quality of life. Publ Choice 108:123–145
Sen A (1987) The standard of living. Cambridge University Press, Cambridge
Sen A (1993) Capability and well being. In: Nussbaum MC, Sen A (eds) The quality of life. Clarendon Press, Oxford, pp 30–53
Sen A (1999) Commodities and capabilities. Oxford University Press, Oxford
Shapiro JM (2006) Smart cities: quality of life, productivity, and the growth effects of human capital. Rev Econ Stat 88:324–335
Silles MA (2009) The causal effect of education on health: evidence from the United Kingdom. Econ Educ Rev 28:122–128
Simon CJ (1998) Human capital and metropolitan employment growth. J Urban Econ 43:223–243
Simon CJ (2004) Industrial reallocation across US cities, 1977–1997. J Urban Econ 56:119–143
Sinai T, Waldfogel J (2004) Geography and the Internet: is the Internet a substitute or a complement for cities? J Urban Econ 56:1–24
Sirgy MJ (1986) A quality of life theory derived from Maslow's developmental perspective. Am J Econ Sociol 45:329–342
Sirgy MJ, Cole D, Kosenko R, Meadow HL, Rahtz D, Cicic M, Jin GX, Yarsuvat D, Blenkhorn DL, Nagpal N (1995) Developing a life satisfaction measure based on need hierarchy theory. In: Sirgy MJ, Samli AC (eds) New dimensions of marketing and quality of life. Greenwood Press, Westport, CT, pp 3–26
Slottje D (1991) Measuring the quality of life across countries. Rev Econ Stat 73:684–693
Spengler A (2008) The establishment history panel. Schmollers Jahrbuch/J Appl Social Sci Stud 128:501–509
Sperling B, Sander P (2004) Cities ranked and rated. Wiley, Hoboken, NJ
Sternberg RJ (ed) (1999) Handbook of creativity. Cambridge University Press, New York, NY
Stiglitz JE, Sen A, Fitoussi J (2009) Report by the commission on the measurement of economic performance and social progress. http://www.stiglitz-sen-fitoussi.fr/en/index.htm
Stolarick K, Florida R (2006) Creativity, connections and innovation: a study of linkages in the Montréal region. Environ Plann A 38:1799–1817
Storper M, Venables AJ (2004) Buzz: face-to-face contact and the urban economy. J Econ Geogr 4:351–370
Stover ME, Leven CL (1992) Methodological issues in the determination of the quality of life in urban areas. Urban Stud 29:737–754
Suedekum J (2008) Convergence of the skill composition across German regions. Reg Sci Urban Econ 38:148–159
Sufian AJM (1993) A multivariate analysis of the determinants of urban quality of life in the world's largest metropolitan areas. Urban Stud 30:1319–1329
Tanzi V, Schuknecht L (1995) The growth of government and the reform of the state in industrial countries. IMF Working Paper. International Monetary Fund, Washington, DC
Taormina RJ, Gao JH (2013) Maslow and the motivation hierarchy: measuring satisfaction of the needs. Am J Psychol 126:155–177
Tiebout C (1956) The pure theory of local expenditures. J Polit Econ 64:416–424
Toffler A (1980) The third wave. Bantam Books, New York, NY

van Kamp I, Leidelmeijer K, Marsman G, de Hollander A (2003) Urban environmental quality and human well-being: towards a conceptual framework and demarcation of concepts; a literature study. Landsc Urban Plann 65:5–18

Venhorst V, van Dijk J, van Wissen L (2011) An analysis of trends in spatial mobility of Dutch graduates. Spatial Econ Anal 6:57–82

Waldfogel J (2008) The median voter and the median consumer: local private goods and population composition. J Urban Econ 63:567–582

Wall HJ (2001) Voting with your feet in the United Kingdom: using cross-migration rates to estimate relative living standards. J Region Sci 80:123

Weber AF (1899) The growth of cities in the nineteenth century. Macmillan, New York, NY

Wheeler C (2001) Search, sorting, and urban agglomeration. J Labor Econ 19:879–899

Wheeler C (2006) Human capital growth in a cross section of US metropolitan areas. Federal Reserve Bank of St Louis Review 88:113–132

Wingo L (1973) The quality of life: toward a microeconomic definition. Urban Stud 10:3–18

Winters JV (2011a) Why are smart cities growing? Who moves and who stays. J Region Sci 51: 253–270

Winters JV (2011b) Human capital and population growth in nonmetropolitan US counties: the importance of college. Econ Dev Quart 25:353–365

Winters JV (2011c) Human capital, higher education institutions, and quality of life. Reg Sci Urban Econ 41:446–454

Winters JV (2013) Differences in quality of life estimates using rents and home values. Ann Region Sci 51:377–409

Wish NB (1986) Are we really measuring the quality of life? Well-being has subjective dimensions as well as objective ones. Am J Econ Sociol 45:93–99

Wooldridge JM (2009) Introductory econometrics: a modern approach, 4th edn. South-Western, Masson

Yankow JJ (2006) Why do cities pay more? An empirical examination of some competing theories of the urban wage premium. J Urban Econ 60:139–161

Chapter 5
Conclusions

This thesis contributes to understanding the reasons for the uneven geographic distribution of innovative start-ups and human capital across German regions. Section 5.1 summarizes the results of Chaps. 2 and 3 and explains how my research fills certain gaps in the relevant literature. Section 5.2 summarizes the results of Chap. 4 on the role quality of life plays in explaining the geography of human capital and points out this chapter's contribution to the field. Section 5.3 discusses the limitations of my work and makes a few suggestions for future research.

5.1 Higher Education and the Geography of Innovative Start-Ups

Innovative start-ups are rare but nevertheless an important source of economic growth, chiefly because they pose great competitive threat to established firms by introducing innovations (Fritsch 2013). In the second and third chapters of this thesis, I analyzed the regional factors behind the geographic distribution of innovative start-ups with a special focus on the regional knowledge base. I was particularly interested in explaining the role of academic knowledge as reflected by HEIs and other non-university public research institutes. The theoretical framework of my empirical study was the "knowledge spillover theory of entrepreneurship" (Acs et al. 2009, 2013). This theory posits that start-ups are shaped considerably by the regional knowledge base because they require the type of knowledge largely found in academic institutions and incumbents. Hence, innovative start-ups are viewed as a form of knowledge spillover from these institutions and can be expected in regions with larger numbers of them.

Previous research shows strong indications for positive effects of regional academic knowledge on innovative start-ups (Audretsch and Lehmann 2005; Audretsch et al. 2005; Baptista and Mendonça 2010; Hülsbeck and Pickavé

R. Aamoucke, *Innovative Start-Ups and the Distribution of Human Capital*,
Contributions to Economics, DOI 10.1007/978-3-319-44462-8_5

2014). However, the strength and significance of these positive effects varies by industry and across regions and the reasons for this variation are still unclear. I concerned myself with the specific characteristics of HEIs that might explain this variation in the emergence of innovative start-ups across different innovative industries and regions. The question I intended to answer was: What are the most important characteristics of HEIs for the emergence and distribution of innovative start-ups—is it their mere presence in the region, their size, or their quality?

Previous attempts by other researchers to answer this question ran into problems involving data limitations. In contrast, my empirical investigation was based on a rich dataset that covers German regions for 14 years (1995–2008). This dataset contains detailed information on region-specific characteristics as well as about universities and other types of HEIs. This dataset allowed me to differentiate among the following four types of start-ups based on their affiliation with industries classified as innovative in terms of R&D intensity (Grupp and Legler 2000; OECD 2005; Gehrke et al. 2010): high-technology manufacturing industries, technologically-advanced manufacturing, technology-oriented services, and non-innovative industries.

Using this dataset, I was able to analyze the impact on innovative business foundation of five types of HEIs: regular universities, medical schools, universities of applied sciences, universities of public administration, and art colleges. In addition, I was able to account for the presence of the following non-university public research institutions; Max-Planck Institutes, the Frauenhofer Society, the Leibniz Association, and the Helmholtz Association of German Research Centers. Moreover, the dataset allowed me to analyze the impact of five categories of academic knowledge: applied sciences, natural sciences, medical science, administrative and political sciences, and other disciplines. I was also able to investigate the impact of the following four transmission channels of knowledge spillover: professors, students, PhD graduates, and external funds.

The empirical results derived in Chap. 2 show a strong relationship between the mere presence of HEIs and the emergence of innovative start-ups. Specifically, I found that the influence of HEIs increases with increasing innovativeness of the respective start-ups. In my empirical framework, start-ups in high-technology and technologically-advanced manufacturing industries were the start-ups most influenced by the presence of HEIs. Start-ups in technology-oriented services were influenced to a lesser degree and start-ups in "non-innovative" industries were influenced very little, if at all, by the presence of HEIs. Moreover, I found that indicators reflecting the quality of HEIs have a considerably smaller, but still statistically significant, impact. As to the question of whether knowledge spillovers have an interregional character, my results show weak and statistically insignificant effects of HEIs in adjacent regions.

In the third chapter of this thesis, I went beyond merely looking at the presence of HEIs and explored the role played by different fields of academic knowledge, different types of HEIs, and different transmission channels in the emergence of innovative start-ups across German regions, in the course of which I addressed certain shortcomings of the extant literature (Audretsch et al. 2004; Audretsch and

Lehmann 2005; Baptista and Mendonça 2010). For instance, previous research only distinguishes between two research fields and ignores others. Furthermore, previous work does not consider all types of HEIs. I also looked for an answer to the until now open question of how exactly (i.e., which channels) knowledge that resides in HEIs spills over to new businesses (Zucker et al. 1998; Åstebro et al. 2012). Who is it that transforms academic knowledge into an innovative start-up—former students, faculty, or former researchers?

My empirical results show that different fields of knowledge have different effects on innovative start-ups. The applied sciences and medical science are more influential in fostering innovative start-ups than are basic natural sciences. Administration and political sciences have very little influence. In regard to the influence of various types of HEI, the strongest effects are found for regular universities and medical schools. When it comes to transmission channels, the number of professors as sources of knowledge has the strongest statistical relationship with regional levels of innovative start-ups.

5.2 Quality and Geography of Human Capital

After analyzing the determinants of emergence and distribution of innovative start-ups, in Chap. 4 I looked at the geography of human capital across West German regions. My motivation for analyzing the geography of human capital was based in the importance of human capital for regional development (Glaeser et al. 1995; Moretti 2004a, b). I defined human capital by educational attainment. Thus, regional human capital is represented by the share of employees with a tertiary degree. I used the concept of quality of life to explain the geography of human capital.

Although previous research provides important insight into the forces that shape the geography of human capital, it suffers two major shortcomings. First, previous research relies on single factors such as the presence of universities, availability of consumer services, or tolerance (Florida et al. 2008; Abel and Deitz 2012). Moreover, some of this work relies on population density and initial levels of human capital (Glaeser et al. 1995; Berry and Glaeser 2005; Moretti 2004b). Evidence derived from a general framework that includes all relevant factors is rare, even though focusing on single factors may be inappropriate and result in misleading findings. Along these lines, Florida et al. (2008) notes that universities, consumer services, and tolerance are more complementary than competitive in explaining the geography of human capital. If these factors are indeed complementary, then it is more accurate to use them jointly when as components of quality of life. Second, for many years, economists related well-being to purely monetary factors. This approach is gradually evolving to include other factors that enhance the quality of life (Stiglitz et al. 2009; Rappaport 2007, 2009), but the process is slow. Currently, the concept of quality of life in economics is restricted to some nonmonetary factors or to consumer services and amenities (CAE and SVR 2010). In contrast, scholars in psychology and related fields employ a broad concept of quality of life that includes all relevant factors that make life more enjoyable.

In Chap. 4, I addressed both of these shortcomings and also discussed the concept of quality of life from several different perspectives. I then went on to employ quality of life as a multidimensional concept for explaining the geography of human capital. My quality of life concept included 27 elements covering six major dimensions of human life. Analyzing the impact of all these elements simultaneously was plagued by endogeneity problems that prevented causal interpretation of the empirical results. I took two approaches to overcome these problems. First, I attempted to relate the concept of quality of life to fundamental human needs with the intent of establishing a theoretical basis for the concept. Second, I used path models and structural equations, which are the best currently available techniques for analyzing the impact of different elements of quality of life on the geography of human capital. Moreover, I used two models. The first model included all 27 variables; the second model included the most important variable from each dimension, with the selection being based on standardized path coefficients. In both models, tolerance—as indicated by the share of foreigners and their diversity of origin—played an important role as mediator variables.

My results show a strong association of human capital with different indicators of quality of life. The geography of human capital was found to be positively associated with higher income, more public spending, faster human capital growth, more living space, the presence of schools and universities, more political participation, diverse political orientation, diverse consumer services, availability of recreation and water areas, and tolerance as indicated by the share of foreigners. Unemployment and the crime rate were found to be negatively associated with the geography of human capital. A number of other indicators had no significant effect, including the number of .dedomains per capita, healthcare, psychotherapy, hazardous waste, the share of energy produced by coal burning, and the share of renewable energy. Some variables, such as income, affected the geography of human capital both directly and indirectly. Other variables, such as unemployment, had a stronger indirect effect than a direct effect, while others, such as infrastructure, affected human capital only indirectly. Housing exhibited a strong positive direct effect, but its indirect effect was negative. I applied my empirical framework to people without a tertiary degree and found somewhat opposite results compared to those where human capital was measured by higher education. Moreover, I investigated the role of population density and found that it plays an important part in explaining the geography of human capital as well as in determining the influence of other variables.

5.3 Limitations and Implications for Further Research

The high correlations among the indicators for higher education and public research prevented me from exactly determining the most important characteristics of the higher education institutions for the emergence of innovative start-ups. Even factor analysis could not identify separate factors representing different aspects of higher education. At the aggregate level of analysis, I do not believe that even more sophisticated econometric methods would be able to overcome the problem of strong interrelation among the variables for public research and higher education. Further research based on microdata analysis and case studies may allow more insight into this issue, and thus be helpful for policy making.

A further limitation of my work was the failure to identify underlying causal relationships in Chaps. 2 and 3. Specifically, it is still unclear how the knowledge embodied in HEIs is translated into new business formation in the region. On the one hand, it is plausible that graduates and employees of the regional HEIs set up some of the regional start-ups. On the other hand, founders may have received their higher education outside the region. Furthermore, students, graduates, and researchers of HEIs may move and set up their firms in other regions. The empirical evidence on this issue remains ambiguous. For instance, a number of studies show that individuals are mobile during their careers (Chen and Rosenthal 2008; Dahl and Sorenson 2010), while other studies show that founders set up their firms close to their place of residence (Figueiredo et al. 2002; Stam 2007; Dahl and Sorenson 2009). Yet other studies show that the vast majority of academic founders first work as dependent employees before starting their own firm (Mueller 2010; Stuetzer et al. 2012).

My results in Chaps. 2 and 3 are consistent with the "knowledge spillover theory of entrepreneurship" (Acs et al. 2009, 2013) as well as with the view that emergence of innovative new businesses is a regional phenomenon (Feldman 2001; Sternberg 2009). Institutes of higher education and public research in a region are a main source of innovative start-ups, and the regional distribution of innovative new businesses is highly influenced by the regional distribution of public research institutions. Hence, policy aimed at increasing and improving public research may be crucial for long-term regional development (Carree et al. 2014). However, more research is needed to specify the mechanism by which regional factors and HEIs influence the emergence of innovative start-ups. For instance, more research is needed to explore the extent to which HEIs have other "atmospheric" effects on the regional "climate" that may attract potential founders. Moreover, more research is needed to analyze the interaction between HEIs and other regional conditions. There are strong indications that HEIs' impact on regional development may vary considerably across regions. Whether this is due to characteristics of the research institutes or to other region-specific factors (e.g., Åstebro and Bazzazian 2011; Bonaccorsi et al. 2013; Piva et al. 2011) is an important avenue for further research.

In regard to the role played by quality of life in explaining the geography of human capital, several aspects are still unclear. First, overcoming endogeneity problems should receive priority in order to provide clear guidance for policymakers; it is recommended that future research focus on this issue. Moreover, using educational attainment as indicator of human capital may too broad. Further research might attempt to capture differences within the group of people with a tertiary degree, for example age, sex, scientific background, and income. Indeed, some empirical studies of the USA show significant differences in respect to different criteria. For instance, Peri (2002) suggest that young highly educated individuals are more likely than their older counterparts to concentrate in highly populated regions. Gottlieb and Joseph (2006) show that PhD graduates in the USA pay greater attention to amenities, whereas technology graduates prefer places with high-quality education. Chen and Rosenthal (2008) suggest that young highly educated tend to move to regions with higher quality business environment, while the elderly are attracted to regions with higher consumer amenities. Whisler et al. (2008) find that while the out-migration rate of young workers with a tertiary degree decreases with the abundance of cultural and recreational amenities, older workers with a tertiary degree show stronger preferences for safety and a milder climate. Moreover, and perhaps most important of all, a standard definition of and measure for quality of life are essential for this concept to gain its proper place in the economic literature.

In summary, my thesis shows the importance of universities and other types of HEIs for innovative start-ups. In addition, these institutions provide society and the economy with highly educated people who influence economic progress. Moreover, HEIs enhance the quality of life in their regions and increase the attractiveness of the region to highly educated people and firms. Thus, I conclude that institutions of higher education and public research are sources of progress and development for any society. Any effort to estimate the contribution of HEIs to growth will necessarily be underestimated because they benefit nearly every aspect of society. If economic progress is argued to be attributed to knowledge, then improving the higher education and public research system is indispensable for progress and development.

References

Abel JR, Deitz R (2012) Do colleges and universities increase their region's human capital? J Econ Geogr 12:667–691

Acs ZJ, Braunerhjelm P, Audretsch DB, Carlsson B (2009) The knowledge spillover theory of entrepreneurship. Small Bus Econ 32:15–30

Acs ZJ, Audretsch DB, Lehmann E (2013) The knowledge spillover theory of entrepreneurship. Small Bus Econ 41:767–774

Åstebro T, Bazzazian N (2011) Universities, entrepreneurship and local economic development. In: Fritsch M (ed) Handbook of research on entrepreneurship and regional development. Elgar, Cheltenham, pp 252–333

Åstebro T, Bazzazian N, Braguinsky S (2012) Startups by recent university graduates and their faculty: implications for university entrepreneurship policy. Res Policy 41:663–677

Audretsch DB, Lehmann EE (2005) Does the knowledge spillover theory of entrepreneurship hold for regions? Res Policy 34:1191–1202
Audretsch DB, Lehmann EE, Warning S (2004) University spillovers: does the kind of science matter. Industry Innov 11:193–205
Audretsch DB, Lehmann EE, Warning S (2005) University spillovers and new firm location. Res Policy 34:1113–1122
Baptista R, Mendonça J (2010) Proximity to knowledge sources and the location of knowledge-based start-ups. Ann Region Sci 45:5–29
Berry C, Glaeser EL (2005) The divergence of human capital levels across cities. Papers Region Sci 84:407–444
Bonaccorsi A, Colombo MG, Guerini M, Rossi-Lamastra C (2013) University specialization and new firm creation across industries. Small Bus Econ 41:837–863
CAE (Conseil d'Analyse Économique), SVR (Sachverständigenrat zur Begutachtung der gesamtwirtschaftlichen Entwicklung) (2010) Monitoring economic performance, quality of life and sustainability. http://www.sachverstaendigenratwirtschaft.de/expertisen.html?&no_cache=1
Carree MA, Della-Malva A, Santarelli E (2014) The contribution of universities to growth: empirical evidence for Italy. J Technol Transf 39:393–414
Chen Y, Rosenthal S (2008) Local amenities and life-cycle migration: do people move for jobs or fun? J Urban Econ 64:519–537
Dahl MS, Sorenson O (2009) The embedded entrepreneur. Eur Manag Rev 6:172–181
Dahl MS, Sorenson O (2010) The migration of technical workers. J Urban Econ 67:33–45
Feldman MP (2001) The entrepreneurial event revisited: firm formation in a regional context. Indus Corp Change 10:861–891
Figueiredo O, Guimaraes P, Woodward D (2002) Home-field advantage: location decisions of Portuguese entrepreneurs. J Urban Econ 52:341–361
Florida R, Mellander C, Stolarick K (2008) Inside the black box of regional development – Human capital, the creative class and tolerance. J Econ Geogr 8:615–649
Fritsch M (2013) New business formation and regional development—A survey and assessment of the evidence. Found Trends Entrepreneurship 9:249–364
Gehrke B, Schasse U, Rammer C, Frietsch R, Neuhäusler P, Leidmann M (2010) Listen wissens- und technologieintensiver Güter und Wirtschaftszweige. Studien zum deutschen Innovationssystem, 19, Frauenhofer ISI, NIW, ZEW
Glaeser EL, Scheinkman JA, Shleifer A (1995) Economic growth in a cross-section of cities. J Monet Econ 36:117–143
Gottlieb PD, Joseph G (2006) College-to-work migration of technology graduates and holder of doctorates within the United States. J Region Sci 46:627–659
Grupp H, Legler H (2000) Hochtechnologie 2000: Neudefinition der Hochtechnologie für die Berichterstattung zur technologischen Leistungsfähigkeit Deutschlands. Karlsruhe and Hannover, FhG, ISI, NIW
Hülsbeck M, Pickavé EN (2014) Regional knowledge production as determinant of high-technology entrepreneurship: empirical evidence for Germany. Int Entrepreneurship Manag J 10:121–138
Moretti E (2004a) Estimating the social returns to higher education: evidence from longitudinal and repeated cross-section data. J Economet 121:175–212
Moretti E (2004b) Human capital externalities in cities. In: Henderson JV, Thisse JF (eds) Handbook of urban and regional economics, vol 4. Elsevier, Amsterdam, pp 2244–2291
Mueller K (2010) Academic spin-off's transfer speed—Analyzing the time from leaving university to venture. Res Policy 39:189–199
OECD: Organisation for Economic Co-operation and Development (2005) OECD handbook on economic globalization indicators. OECD, Paris
Peri G (2002) Young workers, learning and agglomerations. J Urban Econ 52:582–607

Piva E, Grilli L, Rossi-Lamastra C (2011) The creation of high-tech entrepreneurial ventures at the local level: the role of local competences and communication infrastructures. Industry Innov 18:563–580

Rappaport J (2007) Moving to nice weather. Reg Sci Urban Econ 37:375–398

Rappaport J (2009) The increasing importance of quality of life. J Econ Geogr 9:779–804

Stam E (2007) Why butterflies don't leave: locational behaviour of entrepreneurial firms. Econ Geogr 83:27–50

Sternberg R (2009) Regional dimensions of entrepreneurship. Found Trends Entrepreneurship 5:211–340

Stiglitz JE, Sen A, Fitoussi J (2009) Report by the commission on the measurement of economic performance and social progress. http://www.stiglitz-sen-fitoussi.fr/en/index.htm

Stuetzer M, Goethner M, Cantner U (2012) Do balanced skills help nascent entrepreneurs to make progress in the venture creation process? Econ Lett 117:186–188

Whisler RL, Waldorf BS, Mulligan GF, Plane DA (2008) Quality of life and the migration of the college-educated: a life-course approach. Growth Change 39:58–94

Zucker LG, Darby MR, Brewer MB (1998) Intellectual human capital and the birth of US biotechnology enterprises. Am Econ Rev 88:290–306

Appendix A

Table A.1 Descriptive statistics for relevant variables

	Mean	Min	Max	Std. dev.
Number of start-ups in high-technology manufacturing industries	3	0	58	4.82
Number of start-ups in technologically advanced manufacturing industries	5	0	85	7.07
Number of start-ups in technology-intensive service industries	50	0	1386	95.30
Number of start-ups in non-innovative industries	700	75	13,904	1065
Number of start-ups in all private industries	758	78	14,992	1165
Number of employed persons, excluding R&D employees	63,110	7090	982,295	91,112
Number of unemployed persons	12,652	1323	310,661	18,839
Number of R&D employees	2331	60	62,469	5315
Number of R&D employees in neighboring regions	12,205	126	245,205	18,882
Share of employees in high-technology manufacturing industries	.010	0	.221	.024
Share of employees in technologically advanced manufacturing industries	.037	0	.692	.069
Share of employees in technology-oriented service industries	.035	0	.200	.048
Share of employees in non-innovative industries	.915	.245	1	.120
Number of patents per 1000 employees	1.94	.01	16.72	1.57
Share of employees in establishments with fewer than 50 employees	.51	.13	.77	.09

R. Aamoucke, *Innovative Start-Ups and the Distribution of Human Capital*,
Contributions to Economics, DOI 10.1007/978-3-319-44462-8

Table A.2 Correlations for variables in the baseline model

		1	2	3	4	5	6	7	8	9	10	11	12	13
1	Number of start-ups in high-technology industries	1.00												
2	Number of start-ups in technologically advanced industries	**.755**	1.00											
3	Number of start-ups in technology-intensive service industries	**.786**	**.834**	1.00										
4	Number of employed persons, excluding R&D employees	**.160**	**.174**	**.179**	1.00									
5	Number of R&D employees	**.645**	**.693**	**.807**	**.286**	1.00								
6	Number of unemployed persons	**.119**	**.053**	**.127**	**.392**	**.174**	1.00							
7	Share of employees in high-technology manufacturing industries	**.108**	−.013	*.032*	**−.295**	**−.055**	**.063**	1.00						
8	Share of employees in technologically advanced manufacturing industries	**.088**	*−.034*	.009	**−.292**	**−.065**	**.053**	**.917**	1.00					
9	Share of employees in technology-oriented service industries	**.096**	−.025	*.030*	**−.308**	**−.065**	**.069**	**.947**	**.908**	1.00				
10	Share of employees in establishment with fewer than 50 employees	**−.088**	**−.182**	**−.106**	**.180**	**−.094**	**.625**	**.266**	**.245**	**.287**	1.00			
11	Number of R&D employees in neighboring regions	**.112**	**.111**	**.133**	**.595**	**.257**	**.672**	**−.184**	**−.187**	**−.204**	**.358**	1.00		
12	Number of patents per 1000 employees	**.160**	**.084**	**.109**	**.274**	**.133**	**.163**	**.190**	**.193**	**.175**	**.209**	**.149**	1.00	
13	Aggregate indicator of HEIs in the region	**.413**	**.421**	**.448**	**.305**	**.465**	**.303**	**−.039**	**−.073**	*−.033*	**−.042**	**.323**	*.033*	1.00
14	Number of non-university public research institutes in the region	**.594**	**.596**	**.744**	**.073**	**.596**	**.097**	.022	−.023	*.036*	**−.109**	**.071**	.011	**.488**

Notes: Coefficients statistically significant at the 1 % level in bold. Coefficients statistically significant at the 5 % level in italic

Table A.3 Descriptive statistics for the indicators for universities and other public research institutes

	Mean	Min	Max	Std. dev.
Number of (HEIs)	1.811	0	34	3.285
Number of regular universities	.425	0	7	.907
Number of *Fachhochschulen*	.856	0	27	1.599
Number of other HEIs	.422	0	6	.927
Number of students	10,512	9	143,540	18,088
Number of graduates	1331	1	20,562	2189
Number of PhD students	305	1	3038	368.432
Number of professors	222.851	1	2975	333.115
Amount of regular funds[a]	90,738	1	1,146,295	172,158
Amount of regular funds per professor[a]	200.73	.091	3782.73	293.53
Amount of external funds[a]	24,701	3.07	314,651	40,883
Amount of external funds per professor[a]	57.08	.111	980.49	61.13
Number of non-university public research institutes	.837	0	26	2.675
Number of HEIs in adjacent regions	48.96	2	15	24.372
Number of non-university public research institutes in adjacent regions	20.923	0	92	13.010

Source: German University Statistics
[a]Amount in 1000 €

Table A.4 Correlations between indicators for universities and other pubic research institutes in the region

		1	2	3	4	5	6	7	8	9	10	11	12	13	14	15	16	17	18	19
1	University (yes=1; no=0)	1.00																		
2	Number of HEIs (ln)	**.490**	1.00																	
3	Regular university (yes=1; no=0)	**.553**	**.629**	1.00																
4	Number of regular universities (ln)	**.216**	**.699**	**.391**	1.00															
5	*Fachhochschule* (yes=1; no=0)	**.817**	**.514**	**.431**	**.236**	1.00														
6	Number of *Fachhochschulen* (ln)	**.327**	**.813**	**.391**	**.648**	**.401**	1.00													
7	Number of other HEIs	**.252**	**.731**	**.361**	**.707**	**.221**	**.625**	1.00												
8	Number of students (ln)	**.728**	**.621**	**.542**	**.347**	**.638**	**.439**	**.366**	1.00											
9	Number of graduates (ln)	**.687**	**.656**	**.557**	**.377**	**.605**	**.462**	**.393**	**.973**	1.00										
10	Number of PhD students (ln)	**.351**	**.710**	**.671**	**.546**	**.288**	**.505**	**.511**	**.667**	**.705**	1.00									
11	Number of professors (ln)	**.652**	**.673**	**.586**	**.409**	**.613**	**.486**	**.403**	**.956**	**.954**	**.741**	1.00								
12	Amount of regular funds (ln)	**.579**	**.745**	**.632**	**.446**	**.467**	**.502**	**.455**	**.776**	**.792**	**.759**	**.817**	1.00							
13	Amount of external funds (ln)	**.527**	**.744**	**.657**	**.467**	**.459**	**.513**	**.464**	**.766**	**.783**	**.793**	**.832**	**.946**	1.00						
14	Amount of regular and of external funds (ln)	**.532**	**.743**	**.646**	**.459**	**.461**	**.512**	**.461**	**.764**	**.780**	**.782**	**.828**	**.954**	**.994**	1.00					

15	Amount of regular funds per professor (ln)	**.540**	**.709**	**.618**	**.420**	**.426**	**.465**	**.436**	**.741**	**.751**	**.759**	**.781**	**.961**	**.908**	**.913**	1.00				
16	Amount of external funds per professor (ln)	**.494**	**.700**	**.656**	**.440**	**.408**	**.468**	**.436**	**.725**	**.739**	**.808**	**.785**	**.916**	**.975**	**.960**	**.911**	1.00			
17	Amount of regular and of external funds per professor (ln)	**.514**	**.723**	**.647**	**.438**	**.436**	**.484**	**.444**	**.745**	**.758**	**.793**	**.804**	**.940**	**.981**	**.983**	**.936**	**.913**	1.00		
18	Number of non-university public research institutes (ln)	**.079**	**.395**	**.171**	**.474**	**.125**	**.451**	**.451**	**.181**	**.196**	**.325**	**.222**	**.207**	**.228**	**.221**	**.206**	**.211**	**.216**	1.00	
19	Number of HEIs in adjacent regions	**.142**	**.232**	**.010**	**.172**	**.159**	**.220**	**.191**	**.187**	**.183**	**.147**	**.181**	**.103**	**.093**	**.092**	**.108**	**.081**	**.090**	**.042**	1.00
20	Number of non-university public research institutes in adjacent regions (ln)	.021	−.001	−.015	−.026	−.001	−.003	**.025**	−.003	−.008	**−.074**	*−.029*	**−.043**	**−.055**	**−.054**	−0.036	**−.054**	**−.053**	**−0.059**	**.609**

Notes: Coefficients statistically significant at the 1 % level in bold. Coefficients statistically significant at the 5 % level in italic

Table A.5 Factor loadings and unique variances after varimax rotation of variables for regional universities

Variable	Factor loading	Uniqueness
Number of professors	.9611	.0762
Number of students	.9358	.1242
Number of graduates	.9465	.1041
Number of PhD students	.7909	.3745
Amount of regular funds (1000 €)	.9116	.1689
Amount of external funds (1000 €)	.9190	.1554
Variance	.9330	
Cronbach's alpha	.9436	

Notes: All variables are logged

Table A.6 Fixed effects estimates of baseline model for explaining start-ups in different industries

	High technology manufacturing	Technologically advanced manufacturing	Technology-oriented services	Non-innovative industries
Number of employed persons excluding R&D employees (ln)	.0022 (0.06)	−.0241 (0.81)	.0610*** (4.78)	1.0654*** (10.12)
Number of R&D employees (ln)	.0280* (1.80)	.0157 (1.21)	.0110 (1.53)	−.0088** (1.96)
Number of unemployed (ln)	.0421* (1.73)	−.0493*** (3.23)	.0259*** (3.31)	.0267*** (6.81)
Share of employees in high technology manufacturing industries (ln)	.1766*** (10.46)	–	–	–
Share of employees in technologically advanced manufacturing industries (ln)	–	−.0255** (2.24)	–	–
Share of employees in technology oriented service industries (ln)	–	–	.0268*** (5.30)	–
Share of employees in non-innovative industries	–	–	–	−.0288*** (11.14)
Share of employees in establishments with less than 50 employees (ln)	.0416* (1.71)	.0070 (0.17)	.0368*** (4.86)	.0581*** (14.28)
Number of R&D employees in surrounding districts	−.0990*** (3.34)	−.0457** (2.11)	−.1061*** (11.32)	−.0394*** (5.31)
Number of patents per 1000 employees (ln)	.0013 (0.06)	−.0418*** (2.60)	.0058 (0.83)	.0047 (1.32)
Constant	1.5721*** (21.59)	2.1709*** (27.42)	3.2570*** (75.54)	3.7257*** (61.81)

(continued)

Table A.6 (continued)

	High technology manufacturing	Technologically advanced manufacturing	Technology-oriented services	Non-innovative industries
Wald chi^2	236.37***	172.02***	347.76***	829.47***
Dummies for Federal States	No	No	No	No
Dummies for years	No	No	No	No
Number of observations (Number of zeros)	4550 (1264)	4550 (616)	4550 (3)	4550 (0)
Log likelihood	−7120.0603	−8720.9183	−14,524.375	−18,509.265
AIC	14,256.12	17,457.84	29,064.75	37,034.53
Pseudo R^2	0.7725	0.7385	0.7431	0.5593
McFadden's R^2	0.069	0.051	0.075	0.156

Notes: Negative binomial panel regression with fixed effects. Z-values in parentheses. ***Statistically significant at the 1 % level; **Statistically significant at the 5 % level; *Statistically significant at the 10 % level

Table A.7 Fixed effects estimates of total model for explaining start-ups in different industries

	High technology manufacturing	Technologically advanced manufacturing	Technology-oriented services	Non-innovative industries
Number of employed persons excluding R&D employees (ln)	−.0001 (0.00)	−.0347 (1.16)	.0559*** (4.12)	1.1684*** (10.21)
Number of R&D employees (ln)	.0007 (0.05)	−.0116 (1.11)	.0090 (1.19)	−.0106** (2.10)
Number of unemployed (ln)	.0357 (1.48)	−.0579*** (3.92)	.0252*** (3.23)	.0310*** (7.60)
Share of employees in high technology manufacturing industries (ln)	.1748*** (10.46)	–	–	–
Share of employees in technologically advanced manufacturing industries (ln)	–	.0242** (2.19)	–	–
Share of employees in technology oriented service industries (ln)	–	–	.0273*** (5.37)	–
Share of employees in non-innovative industries	–	–	–	.0310*** (11.80)
Share of employees in establishments with less than 50 employees (ln)	.0488** (2.00)	−.0001 (0.00)	.0375*** (4.91)	.0575 (14.10)
Number of R&D employees in surrounding districts	−.0957*** (3.47)	−.0493*** (2.48)	−.1069*** (11.52)	−.04120*** (5.74)

(continued)

Table A.7 (continued)

	High technology manufacturing	Technologically advanced manufacturing	Technology-oriented services	Non-innovative industries
Number of patents per 1000 employees (ln)	−.0011 (0.05)	−.0439*** (2.78)	.0061 (0.86)	.0038 (1.08)
Aggregate indicator for HEIs in the region	.0209 (0.60)	.0677*** (2.52)	.0112 (0.83)	−.0439*** (2.96)
Number of non-university research institutes (ln)	.5618*** (5.27)	.6874*** (6.03)	.0156 (0.21)	−.1584** (2.40)
Aggregate indicator for HEIs in adjacent regions	.0203 (0.52)	.0054 (0.19)	−.0027 (0.20)	−.01134 (1.11)
Number of non-university research institutes in adjacent regions (ln)	.0993 (1.53)	.2474*** (3.99)	.1268*** (3.00)	.1791*** (6.21)
Constant	1.5314*** (21.31)	2.1449*** (27.51)	3.2491*** (74.02)	3.7167*** (57.87)
Wald chi^2	275.30	237.78***	362.19***	904.34***
Dummies for Federal States	No	No	No	No
Dummies for years	No	No	No	No
Number of observations (Number of zeros)	4550 (1264)	4550 (616)	4550 (3)	4550 (0)
Log likelihood	−7105.5174	−8693.7738	−14,519.572	−18,480.773
AIC	14,235.03	17,411.55	29,063.14	36,985.55
Pseudo R^2	.5493	.4547	.3743	.6166
McFadden's R^2	.094	.085	.113	0.159

Notes: Negative binomial panel regression with fixed effects. Z-values in parentheses. ***Statistically significant at the 1 % level; **Statistically significant at the 5 % level; *Statistically significant at the 10 % level

Table A.8 Total model explaining innovative start-ups in different industries (West Germany only)

	High technology manufacturing	Technologically advanced manufacturing	Technology-oriented services	Non-innovative industries
Number of employed persons excluding R&D employees (ln)	−.2771 (1.54)	.0235 (0.16)	.0206 (0.27)	1.4875*** (9.20)
Number of R&D employees (ln)	.0148 (1.01)	.0014 (0.12)	.0050 (0.73)	−.0011 (0.37)
Number of unemployed (ln)	.0579** (1.96)	−.0634*** (3.60)	.0151* (1.78)	.0281*** (7.36)
Share of employees in high technology manufacturing industries (ln)	.1703*** (8.89)	–	–	–

(continued)

Table A.8 (continued)

	High technology manufacturing	Technologically advanced manufacturing	Technology-oriented services	Non-innovative industries
Share of employees in technologically advanced manufacturing industries (ln)	–	.0451*** (2.78)	–	–
Share of employees in technology oriented service industries (ln)	–	–	.0400*** (5.90)	–
Share of employees in non-innovative industries	–	–	–	.0171*** (3.78)
Share of employees in establishments with less than 50 employees (ln)	−.0027 (0.09)	−.0471** (2.26)	.0116 (1.27)	.0151*** (2.50)
Number of R&D employees in surrounding districts	.0458 (0.37)	−.0658 (0.64)	−.0632 (1.15)	.3434*** (5.68)
Number of patents per 1000 employees (ln)	.0301 (1.36)	.0080 (0.48)	.0330*** (4.62)	.0095** (2.34)
Aggregate indicator for HEIs in the region	.1565 (4.29)	.1432 (4.82)	.0601*** (3.93)	.0033 (0.25)
Number of non-university research Institutes (ln)	.4214*** (4.81)	.4081*** (5.05)	.1043 (1.33)	.0033 (0.06)
Aggregate indicator for HEIs in adjacent regions	.0463 (1.00)	.0807** (2.17)	−.0027 (0.15)	.0186* (1.78)
Number of non-university research institutes in adjacent regions (ln)	.0349 (0.79)	−.0074 (0.18)	.0774* (1.87)	.0652** (2.35)
Constant	1.3157*** (5.09)	1.3892*** (5.81)	3.4744*** (14.31)	3.9429*** (21.64)
Wald chi^2	452.32***	509.58***	575.48***	1999.34***
Dummies for Federal States	Yes***	Yes***	Yes***	Yes***
Dummies for years	Yes***	Yes***	Yes***	Yes***
Number of observations (Number of zeros)	4550 (814)	4550 (409)	4550 (1)	4550 (0)
Log likelihood	−6555.7594	−7798.9865	−12,490.898	−17,493.34
AIC	13,161.52	15,655.97	25,039.8	35,052.68
Pseudo R^2	.6181	.6534	.5891	.8468
McFadden's R^2	.106	.111	.125	0.175

Notes: Negative binomial panel regression with fixed effects. Z-values in parentheses. ***Statistically significant at the 1 % level; **Statistically significant at the 5 % level; *Statistically significant at the 10 % level

Table A.9 Total model explaining innovative start-ups in different industries (East Germany only)

	High technology manufacturing	Technologically advanced manufacturing	Technology-oriented services	Non-innovative industries
Number of employed persons excluding R&D employees (ln)	.0044 (0.06)	.1364** (2.83)	−.0250 (1.04)	2.8709*** (11.82)
Number of R&D employees (ln)	.8480** (2.41)	−.3767 (1.37)	.3185*** (2.53)	−.0713 (1.13)
Number of unemployed (ln)	−.0634 (1.12)	−.0168 (0.53)	.0301* (1.87)	.0106 (1.47)
Share of employees in high technology manufacturing industries (ln)	.1765*** (4.14)	–	–	–
Share of employees in technologically advanced manufacturing industries (ln)	–	.0241 (0.87)	–	–
Share of employees in technology oriented service industries (ln)	–	–	.0389** (2.31)	–
Share of employees in non-innovative industries	–	–	–	.0797*** (6.41)
Share of employees in establishments with less than 50 employees (ln)	.0893* (1.78)	−.0491* (1.79)	.0731*** (5.40)	.0897*** (12.47)
Number of R&D employees in surrounding districts	−.0743 (1.54)	−.0491 (1.61)	−.1359*** (9.16)	.0118 (1.33)
Number of patents per 1000 employees (ln)	−.0249 (0.24)	.0701 (0.72)	.0813* (1.90)	.0313* (1.81)
Aggregate indicator for HEIs in the region	.2415*** (3.60)	.1547*** (3.34)	−.0033 (0.14)	.0713*** (2.80)
Number of non-university research Institutes (ln)	.2345 (1.59)	.2792*** (2.31)	.5095*** (3.93)	−.0290 (0.41)
Aggregate indicator for HEIs in adjacent regions	.1803*** (2.69)	.1053** (2.16)	.0509** (2.08)	.0227 (1.20)
Number of non-university research institutes in adjacent regions (ln)	−.1793** (1.95)	−.0593 (0.85)	−.0673 (0.82)	.0781** (2.27)
Constant	1.5335*** (7.77)	2.0116*** (9.90)	2.9656*** (24.27)	3.7085*** (25.20)
Wald chi^2	84.92***	95.59***	433.78***	1779.44***
Dummies for Federal States	Yes***	Yes***	Yes***	Yes***
Dummies for years	Yes***	Yes***	Yes***	Yes***
Number of observations (Number of zeros)	4550 (450)	4550 (207)	4550 (2)	4550 (0)
Log likelihood	−1885.5092	−2323.6813	−4008.5288	−2879.1863

(continued)

Table A.9 (continued)

	High technology manufacturing	Technologically advanced manufacturing	Technology-oriented services	Non-innovative industries
AIC	3809.018	4693.363	8063.058	5800.373
Pseudo R^2	.5149	.4467	.3897	.8191
McFadden's R^2	.081	0.061	.103	.191

Notes: Negative binomial panel regression with fixed effects. Z-values in parentheses. ***Statistically significant at the 1 % level; **Statistically significant at the 5 % level; *Statistically significant at the 10 % level

Table A.10 Baseline model explaining innovative start-ups in different industries in regions with at least one university or one research institute

	High technology manufacturing	Technologically advanced manufacturing	Technology-oriented services	Non-innovative industries
Number of employed persons excluding R&D employees (ln)	.1702*** (3.28)	.1892*** (4.37)	.1282*** (6.12)	2.9300*** (24.14)
Number of R&D employees (ln)	.0533*** (3.72)	.0335*** (2.80)	.0148** (2.20)	.0009 (0.30)
Number of unemployed (ln)	.0314 (0.37)	.0025 (0.13)	.0035 (0.20)	.0315*** (7.32)
Share of employees in high technology manufacturing industries (ln)	.2259*** (7.37)	–	–	
Share of employees in technologically advanced manufacturing industries (ln)	–	.0691*** (3.31)	–	
Share of employees in technology oriented service industries (ln)	–		.0404*** (4.82)	
Share of employees in non-innovative industries	–	–	–	.0124** (2.31)
Share of employees in establishments with less than 50 employees (ln)	.0616* (1.85)	.0429* (1.79)	.0857*** (3.78)	.0496*** (6.97)
Number of R&D employees in surrounding districts	.0279 (0.39)	−.0058 (0.18)	−.0480*** (2.69)	−.0050 (0.63)
Number of patents per 1000 employees (ln)	.0501* (1.65)	−.0023 (0.10)	.0116 (1.08)	−.0040 (0.70)
Constant	1.4236*** (9.44)	1.8871*** (13.82)	3.0324*** (26.17)	−2.7779*** (29.36)
Wald chi^2	516.40***	378.91***	741.08***	2349.09***
Dummies for Federal States	Yes***	Yes***	Yes***	Yes***
Dummies for years	Yes***	Yes***	Yes***	Yes***

(continued)

Table A.10 (continued)

	High technology manufacturing	Technologically advanced manufacturing	Technology-oriented services	Non-innovative industries
Number of observations (Number of zeros)	2819 (602)	2819 (259)	2819 (1)	2819 (0)
Log likelihood	−5830.6721	−6882.9348	−11,010.222	−13,537.14
AIC	11,725.34	13,827.87	22,084.44	27,136.28
Pseudo R^2	0.7927	0.6368	0.5372	0.6633
McFadden's R^2	0.109	0.107	0.111	0.170

Notes: Negative binomial panel regression with fixed effects. Z-values in parentheses. ***Statistically significant at the 1 % level; **Statistically significant at the 5 % level; *Statistically significant at the 10 % level

Table A.11 Effect of including indicators for public research in the baseline model (only regions with at least one university or one non-university public research institute)

	High technology manufacturing	Technologically advanced manufacturing	Technology-oriented services	Non-innovative industries
Number of HEIs (ln)	−39.49 .2300 (6.95) ***	−64.14 .2154 (8.33)***	−7.76 .0498 (3.14) ***	1.61 .0045 (0.62)
Number of regular universities (ln)	−27.04 .1374 (4.97) ***	−40.15 .0898 (4.75)***	−18.03 .0532 (3.34) ***	1.6 .0029 (0.63)
Number of Fachhochschulen (ln)	−24.33 .1587 (5.48) ***	−33.43 .1288 (5.99)***	−18.87 .0817 (4.06) ***	1.77 −.0026 (0.47)
Number of students (ln)	−34.52 .2661 (6.02) ***	−52.19 .2491 (7.27)***	−6.56 .1068 (5.36) ***	1.98 .0017 (0.14)
Number of graduates (ln)	−19.77 .2101 (5.42) ***	−44.01 .1989 (6.67)***	−13.95 .0924 (6.01) ***	−49.33 .0125 (1.36)
Number of PhD students (ln)	−14.45 .1384 (4.99) ***	−45.62 .1124 (4.68)***	13.76 .0363 (3.09) ***	−2.07 −.0184 (2.02)**
Number of professors (ln)	−18.26 .2240 (5.69) ***	−60.19 .2076 (6.07)***	−32.28 .1056 (6.04) ***	1.37 .0099 (0.79)
Amount of regular funds (ln)	−10.51 .1411 (4.32) ***	−12.09 .0912 (3.56)***	−12.38 .0495 (3.91) ***	−.5 .0129 (1.58)
Amount of external funds (ln)	−13.28 .1429 (4.65) ***	−15.58 .0962 (4.02)***	−11.28 .0447 (3.76) ***	−57.4 .0099 (1.35)
Amount of regular and external funds (ln)	−14.56 .1467 (4.78) ***	−16.86 .0998 (4.18)***	−14.44 .0489 (4.16) ***	0.28 .0097 (1.31)

(continued)

Table A.11 (continued)

	High technology manufacturing	Technologically advanced manufacturing	Technology-oriented services	Non-innovative industries
Amount of regular funds per professor (ln)	−2.91 .0764 (2.63) ***	−8.98 .0694 (3.09)***	−8.52 .0366 (3.39) ***	−56.94 .0079 (1.17)
Amount of external funds per professor (ln)	−9.6 .1002 (3.71) ***	−6.28 .0550 (2.62)***	−3.62 .0259 (2.56) ***	1.69 .0001 (0.56)
Amount of regular and external funds per professor (ln)	−11.43 .1139 (3.96) ***	−9.48 .0707 (3.17)***	13.76 .0356 (3.28) ***	−0.52 .0108 (1.59)
Number of Fraunhofer Institutes (ln)	−48.96 .2262 (6.36) ***	−62.83 .2910 (7.54)***	−24.38 .1551 (5.33) ***	−16.06 .0876 (4.34)***
Number of Max Planck Institutes (ln)	−56.42 .2352 (6.81) ***	−88.22 .3141 (8.95)***	−13.68 .1102 (4.21) ***	1.86 .0070 (0.37)
Number of HEIs in adjacent regions (ln)	12.44 .2481 (3.85) ***	−9.15 .1958 (3.34)***	−12.62 .2212 (3.89) ***	1.24 .0160 (0.87)
Number of Fraunhofer Institutes in adjacent regions	53.83 .1531 (2.76) ***	−0.23 .1634 (3.07)***	−3.02 .1139 (2.25) **	−1.36 −.0822 (1.83)*
Number of Max Planck Institutes in adjacent regions	−10.49 .1862 (3.57) ***	−0.23 .1424 (2.85)***	−13.68 .1819 (3.99) ***	1.99 .0029 (0.07)

Notes: First row: Change of the AIC value due to the inclusion of the variable. Second row: Estimated coefficient and z-value in parentheses. ***Statistically significant at the 1 % level; **Statistically significant at the 5 % level; *Statistically significant at the 10 % level

Table A.12 Total model for explaining innovative start-ups in different industries in regions with the lowest third of population density

	High technology manufacturing	Technologically advanced manufacturing	Technology-oriented services	Non-innovative industries
Number of employed persons excluding R&D employees (ln)	.0409 (0.56)	.0339 (0.49)	.0624* (1.76)	1.8228*** (7.04)
Number of R&D employees (ln)	1.3264*** (2.50)	−.1610 (0.36)	.9368*** (4.31)	−.0217 (0.17)
Number of unemployed (ln)	−.1925* (1.71)	−.2280** (2.43)	−.0297 (0.82)	.0302*** (3.76)
Share of employees in high technology manufacturing industries (ln)	.0904* (1.77)	–	–	–

(continued)

Table A.12 (continued)

	High technology manufacturing	Technologically advanced manufacturing	Technology-oriented services	Non-innovative industries
Share of employees in technologically advanced manufacturing industries (ln)	–	−.0153 (0.47)	–	–
Share of employees in technology oriented service industries (ln)	–	–	.0437*** (2.47)	–
Share of employees in non-innovative industries	–	–	–	.0125* (1.62)
Share of employees in establishments with less than 50 employees (ln)	.1243** (2.14)	.0766 (0.71)	.0936*** (2.58)	.0794*** (8.63)
Number of R&D employees in surrounding districts	.3089*** (2.83)	.1941** (2.08)	.0052 (0.14)	−.0305** (2.00)
Number of patents per 1000 employees (ln)	.1852*** (4.44)	.0665** (1.99)	.0045 (0.29)	−.0020 (0.29)
Aggregate indicator for HEIs in the region	.1872* (1.80)	.1395 (1.60)	.0807 (1.52)	−.0243 (0.77)
Number non-university research Institutes (ln)	−.1411 (0.59)	−.1402 (0.71)	−.0656 (0.33)	−.2054 (1.22)
Aggregate indicator for HEIs in adjacent regions	.0289 (0.43)	.0474 (0.87)	.0066 (0.22)	.0006 (0.05)
Number of non-university research institutes in adjacent regions (ln)	−.0160 (0.32)	−.0307 (0.73)	.0914** (2.19)	.0499 (1.57)
Constant	1.7191*** (7.11)	1.3160*** (6.37)	2.8323*** (21.25)	3.8528*** (29.32)
Wald chi^2	176.90***	61.34***	186.70***	711.24***
Dummies for Federal States	Yes***	Yes***	Yes***	Yes***
Dummies for years	Yes***	Yes***	Yes***	Yes***
Number of observations (Number of zeros)	4550 (721)	4550 (443)	4550 (3)	4550 (0)
Log likelihood	−1946.5063	−2553.6038	−4628.1748	−5497.456
AIC	3959.013	5167.208	9322.35	11,058.91
Pseudo R^2	.5398	.3625	.4207	.3544
McFadden's R^2	.061	.023	.068	.066

Notes: Negative binomial panel regression with fixed effects. Z-values in parentheses. ***Statistically significant at the 1 % level; **Statistically significant at the 5 % level; *Statistically significant at the 10 % level

Table A.13 Total model for explaining innovative start-ups in different industries in regions with the middle third of population density

	High technology manufacturing	Technologically advanced manufacturing	Technology-oriented services	Non-innovative industries
Number of employed persons excluding R&D employees (ln)	.1626** (2.00)	.2078*** (3.16)	.1585*** (4.49)	1.8275*** (7.11)
Number of R&D employees (ln)	.4179* (1.64)	−.0283 (0.15)	.2346** (2.02)	.1248 (1.58)
Number of unemployed (ln)	−.1863* (1.66)	−.0345 (0.34)	−.0825** (2.36)	.0199*** (2.79)
Share of employees in high technology manufacturing industries (ln)	.1464*** (3.11)	–	–	–
Share of employees in technologically advanced manufacturing industries (ln)	–	.0194 (0.79)	–	–
Share of employees in technology oriented service industries (ln)	–	–	.0329** (2.18)	–
Share of employees in non-innovative industries	–	–	–	.0004 (0.04)
Share of employees in establishments with less than 50 employees (ln)	.0894* (1.76)	.1346* (1.63)	.1686*** (4.27)	.0855*** (8.16)
Number of R&D employees in surrounding districts	.1033 (1.05)	.0256 (0.30)	.0266 (0.86)	−.0239** (2.09)
Number of patents per 1000 employees (ln)	.0382 (0.97)	.0114 (0.42)	.0108 (0.77)	−.0158** (2.23)
Aggregate indicator for HEIs in the region	.1248** (2.35)	.0570 (1.46)	.0640** (2.42)	−.0018 (0.09)
Number non-university research Institutes (ln)	−.0462 (0.37)	.0595 (0.65)	.0586 (0.67)	.0492 (0.86)
Aggregate indicator for HEIs in adjacent regions	.0194 (0.34)	.0310 (0.65)	−.0122 (0.50)	.0578*** (3.59)
Number of non-university research institutes in adjacent regions (ln)	−.0323 (0.58)	−.0272 (0.67)	.0617 (1.58)	.0470* (1.89)
Constant	1.6998*** (9.61)	1.6764*** (11.34)	3.0702*** (27.84)	3.5538*** (25.32)
Wald chi^2	143.26***	139.07***	277.29***	577.49***
Dummies for Federal States	Yes***	Yes***	Yes***	Yes***
Dummies for years	Yes***	Yes***	Yes***	Yes***
Number of observations (Number of zeros)	4550 (422)	4550 (156)	4550 (0)	4550 (0)
Log likelihood	−2589.7331	−3223.7168	−5263.4282	−6940.5073

(continued)

Table A.13 (continued)

	High technology manufacturing	Technologically advanced manufacturing	Technology-oriented services	Non-innovative industries
AIC	5247.466	6509.434	10,594.86	13,947.01
Pseudo R^2	.4153	.3276	.4224	.4929
McFadden's R^2	.046	.031	.062	0.052

Notes: Negative binomial panel regression with fixed effects. Z-values in parentheses. ***Statistically significant at the 1 % level; **Statistically significant at the 5 % level; *Statistically significant at the 10 % level

Table A.14 Total model for explaining innovative start-ups in different industries in regions with the highest third of population density

	High technology manufacturing	Technologically advanced manufacturing	Technology-oriented services	Non-innovative industries
Number of employed persons excluding R&D employees (ln)	.0628 (0.88)	.1507*** (3.04)	.0963*** (3.70)	2.0413*** (8.96)
Number of R&D employees (ln)	.0136 (0.99)	−.0045 (0.45)	.0035 (0.58)	.0011 (0.34)
Number of unemployed (ln)	.1413 (1.48)	−.0072 (0.11)	−.0221 (1.07)	.0230*** (4.79)
Share of employees in high technology manufacturing industries (ln)	.2678*** (7.17)	–	–	–
Share of employees in technologically advanced manufacturing industries (ln)	–	.0364** (2.40)	–	–
Share of employees in technology oriented service industries (ln)	–	–	.0052 (0.43)	–
Share of employees in non-innovative industries	–	–	–	.0171*** (2.53)
Share of employees in establishments with less than 50 employees (ln)	.0584 (1.49)	.0278 (0.61)	.0963*** (3.27)	.0362*** (4.08)
Number of R&D employees in surrounding districts	−.0398 (0.58)	−.0420 (0.78)	−.0505*** (2.48)	−.0102 (0.92)
Number of patents per 1000 employees (ln)	−.0148 (0.42)	−.0355* (1.73)	.0706*** (5.50)	.0026 (0.42)
Aggregate indicator for HEIs in the region	.0314 (0.76)	.0852*** (2.69)	.0424** (2.26)	.0040 (0.23)
Number non-university research Institutes (ln)	.5342*** (7.03)	.4358*** (6.56)	.1793** (2.42)	−.1249* (1.63)
Aggregate indicator for HEIs in adjacent regions	.0362 (0.71)	.0800** (2.04)	−.0052 (0.26)	.0260* (1.67)

(continued)

Table A.14 (continued)

	High technology manufacturing	Technologically advanced manufacturing	Technology-oriented services	Non-innovative industries
Number of non-university research institutes in adjacent regions (ln)	.1137** (2.04)	.0963* (1.90)	.1337** (2.39)	.0251 (0.50)
Constant	1.4754*** (5.55)	2.3480*** (9.52)	3.7544*** (15.20)	3.6558*** (16.40)
Wald chi^2	397.21***	310.26***	488.41***	1180.64***
Dummies for Federal States	Yes***	Yes***	Yes***	Yes***
Dummies for years	Yes***	Yes***	Yes***	Yes***
Number of observations (Number of zeros)	4550 (121)	4550 (17)	4550 (0)	4550 (0)
Log likelihood	−3753.2226	−4232.6459	−6517.0252	−8072.6772
AIC	7578.445	8531.292	13,106.05	16,215.35
Pseudo R^2	.6286	.6213	.5857	.8098
McFadden's R^2	.104	.112	.135	.188

Notes: Negative binomial panel regression with fixed effects. Z-values in parentheses. ***Statistically significant at the 1 % level; **Statistically significant at the 5 % level; *Statistically significant at the 10 % level

Table A.15 Classification of scientific fields

Natural sciences	**Administration and political sciences**
Anthropology	Economics
Astronomy	Law
Biology	Management
Chemistry	Political science
Geosciences	Public administration
Informatics	Sociology
Mathematics	
Meteorology	
Mineralogy	
Oceanography	
Pharmacy	
Physics	
Applied sciences	**Others**
Architecture	Arts
Biotechnology	Cultural studies
Cybernetics	History
Engineering	Information science
Geodetics	Journalism
Machinery construction	Linguistics
Mechatronics	Pedagogics
Mining and metallurgy	Philosophy

(continued)

Table A.15 (continued)

Nuclear technology	Psychology
Optics	Sports
Medical science	Theology

Table A.16 Descriptive statistics for relevant variables in the baseline model

	Mean	Min	Max	Std. dev.
Number of start-ups in high-technology manufacturing industries	3	0	58	4.82
Number of start-ups in technologically advanced manufacturing industries	5	0	85	7.07
Number of start-ups in technology-intensive service industries	50	0	1386	95.30
Number of start-ups in non-innovative industries	700	75	13,904	1065
Number of start-ups in all private industries	758	78	14,992	1165
Number of employed persons, excluding R&D employees	63,110	7090	982,295	91,112
Number of unemployed persons	12,652	1323	310,661	18,839
Number of R&D employees	2331	60	62,469	5315
Number of R&D employees in neighboring regions	12,205	126	245,205	18,882
Share of employees in high-technology manufacturing industries	.010	0	.221	.024
Share of employees in technologically advanced manufacturing industries	.037	0	.692	.069
Share of employees in technology-oriented service industries	.035	0	.200	.048
Share of employees in non-innovative industries	.915	0.245	1	.120
Number of patentsper 1000 employees	1.94	.01	16.72	1.57
Share of employees in establishments with fewer than 50 employees	.51	.13	.77	.09

Table A.17 Descriptive statistics for relevant variables of HEIs

	Mean	Minimum	Maximum	Standard deviation
Natural sciences				
Number of professors	1.320	0	82	6.5063
Number of students	1354	0	24,401	2660
Number of PhD graduates	29.27	0	817	71.68
Amount of external funds	3452	0	109,988	8832
Applied sciences				
Number of professors	.7736	0	75	4.913
Number of students	1344	0	21,466	2738
Number of PhD graduates	9.386	0	404	33.62
Amount of external funds	2974	0	122,170	10,233

(continued)

Table A.17 (continued)

	Mean	Minimum	Maximum	Standard deviation
Medicine				
Number of professors	.6568	0	40	3.831
Number of students	163.67	0	7731	879.77
Number of PhD graduates	12.605	0	732	73.026
Amount of external funds	19,413	0	136,176	19,279
Administration and political sciences				
Number of professors	.9652	0	61	4.767
Number of students	2520	0	43,420	4688
Number of PhD graduates	13.57	0	460	33.697
Amount of external funds	716.37	0	24,562	1916
Regular universities				
Number of professors	11.98	0	275	35.780
Number of students	13,408	0	113,324	16,085
Number of PhD graduates	231.15	0	2306	330.08
Amount of external funds	22,963	0	295,084	33,811
Universities of applied sciences				
Number of professors	.4658	0	48	2.854
Number of students	2476	0	34,090	3375
Number of PhD graduates	.0019	0	1	.0431
Amount of external funds	787.32	0	22,586	1544
Arts colleges				
Number of professors	4.641	0	144	16.661
Number of students	740.74	0	6144	896.12
Number of PhD graduates	.2648	0	11	1.0366
Amount of external funds	266.281	0	3648	496.61
Universities of public administration				
Number of professors	.0099	0	2	.1193
Number of students	526.86	0	4824	652.22
Number of PhD graduates	0	0	0	0
Amount of external funds	32.199	0	5295.85	329.751

Table A.18 Correlations between variables in the baseline model

		1	2	3	4	5	6	7	8	9	10	11	12	13
1	Number of start-ups in high-technology industries	1.00												
2	Number of start-ups in technologically advanced industries	**.755**	1.00											
3	Number of start-ups in technology-intensive service industries	**.786**	**.834**	1.00										
4	Number of employed persons, excluding R&D employees	**.160**	**.174**	**.179**	1.00									
5	Number of R&D employees	**.645**	**.693**	**.807**	**.286**	1.00								
6	Number of unemployed persons	**.119**	**.053**	**.127**	**.392**	**.174**	1.00							
7	Share of employees in high-technology manufacturing industries	**.108**	−.013	*.032*	**−.295**	**−.055**	**.063**	1.00						
8	Share of employees in technologically advanced manufacturing industries	**.088**	*−.034*	.009	**−.292**	**−.065**	**.053**	**.917**	1.00					
9	Share of employees in technology-oriented service industries	**.096**	−.025	*.030*	**−.308**	**−.065**	**.069**	**.947**	**.908**	1.00				
10	Share of employees in establishment with fewer than 50 employees	**−.088**	**−.182**	**−.106**	**.180**	**−.094**	**.625**	**.266**	**.245**	**.287**	1.00			
11	Number of R&D employees in neighboring regions	**.112**	**.111**	**.133**	**.595**	**.257**	**.672**	**−.184**	**−.187**	**−.204**	**.358**	1.00		
12	Number of patents per 1000 employees	**.160**	**.084**	**.109**	**.274**	**.133**	**.163**	**.190**	**.193**	**.175**	**.209**	**.149**	1.00	
13	Aggregate indicator of HEIs in the region	**.413**	**.421**	**.448**	**.305**	**.465**	**.303**	**−.039**	**−.073**	*−.033*	**−.042**	**.323**	*.033*	1.00
14	Number of non-university public research institutes in the region	**.594**	**.596**	**.744**	**.073**	**.596**	**.097**	.022	−.023	*.036*	**−.109**	**.071**	.011	**.488**

Notes: Coefficients statistically significant at the 1 % level in bold. Coefficients statistically significant at the 5 % level in italic

Table A.19 Correlations between indicators for universities and other pubic research institutes in the region

		1	2	3	4	5	6	7	8	9	10	11	12	13	14	15	16	17	18	19	20	21	22	23
1	prof	1.00																						
2	stud	**.9543**	1.00																					
3	PhD	**.8794**	**.8496**	1.00																				
4	exfund	**.8704**	**.8330**	**.8878**	1.00																			
5	prof_ns	**.9618**	**.9217**	**.8750**	**.8728**	1.00																		
6	stud_ns	**.9084**	**.9615**	**.8412**	**.8476**	**.9401**	1.00																	
7	PhD_ns	**.8775**	**.8615**	**.9590**	**.8774**	**.9108**	**.8939**	1.00																
8	exfund_ns	**.7996**	**.7890**	**.8043**	**.9221**	**.8592**	**.8332**	**.8695**	1.00															
9	prof_as	**.8396**	**.7815**	**.6290**	**.7427**	**.8173**	**.7724**	**.7066**	**.6702**	1.00														
10	stud_as	**.8008**	**.7944**	**.5970**	**.7591**	**.7988**	**.7955**	**.6952**	**.6604**	**.9380**	1.00													
11	PhD_as	**.1187**	**.1095**	**.3917**	**.1177**	**.1336**	**.1391**	**.1611**	**.1239**	**.3067**	**.2075**	1.00												
12	exfund_as	**.4936**	**.4688**	**.3526**	**.6768**	**.5319**	**.5286**	**.4936**	**.5542**	**.6847**	**.7804**	**.2356**	1.00											
13	prof_ap	**.9353**	**.9172**	**.7756**	**.7603**	**.8931**	**.8755**	**.8144**	**.7410**	**.7979**	**.7603**	**.1026**	**.4443**	1.00										
14	stud_ap	**.8781**	**.9616**	**.7277**	**.7147**	**.8616**	**.9255**	**.8020**	**.7327**	**.7445**	**.7430**	**.1029**	**.4169**	**.9203**	1.00									
15	PhD_ap	**.8497**	**.8684**	**.8450**	**.7480**	**.8547**	**.8531**	**.8795**	**.7855**	**.6248**	**.5917**	**.1097**	**.3082**	**.8544**	**.8550**	1.00								
16	exfund_ap	**.7148**	**.7133**	**.6380**	**.8146**	**.7100**	**.7228**	**.7105**	**.8138**	**.6634**	**.6364**	**.2143**	**.5426**	**.7393**	**.7023**	**.6877**	1.00							
17	prof_u	**.9539**	**.9022**	**.8874**	**.8033**	**.8750**	**.7700**	**.8029**	**.6966**	**.8154**	**.7272**	**.2865**	**.2667**	**.8259**	**.7328**	**.7919**	**.5885**	1.00						
18	stud_u	**.8670**	**.9665**	**.8372**	**.7615**	**.7860**	**.8766**	**.7493**	**.6367**	**.6974**	**.7289**	**.3665**	**.2619**	**.7789**	**.8547**	**.7384**	**.5814**	**.8946**	1.00					
19	PhD_u	**.8394**	**.8145**	**.9495**	**.9324**	**.7432**	**.7094**	**.8622**	**.7366**	**.7157**	**.7376**	**.5455**	**.4316**	**.7050**	**.5903**	**.7206**	**.6574**	**.8589**	**.8330**	1.00				
20	exfund_u	**.6391**	**.5999**	**.7393**	**.9192**	**.4885**	**.4909**	**.6022**	**.5701**	**.5611**	**.6162**	**.5594**	**.5124**	**.4723**	**.3377**	**.4247**	**.5719**	**.6531**	**.6414**	**.8472**	1.00			
21	prof_fh	**.8719**	**.8247**	**.6622**	**.7013**	**.7639**	**.7301**	**.6474**	**.5996**	**.8262**	**.7604**	**.1735**	**.4499**	**.8387**	**.7457**	**.6569**	**.6205**	**.7174**	**.7303**	**.6548**	**.6776**	1.00		
22	stud_fh	**.8504**	**.8565**	**.6449**	**.6984**	**.7287**	**.7395**	**.6289**	**.5753**	**.7483**	**.7344**	**.1367**	**.4304**	**.8215**	**.7773**	**.6697**	**.5974**	**.6970**	**.7630**	**.6479**	**.6670**	**.9505**	1.00	
23	PhD_fh	**.0908**	**.0686**	*.0797*	**.1542**	**.0854**	**.0665**	**.1008**	**.1625**	**.1179**	**.0851**	.0174	**.0745**	**.0801**	**.0618**	**.0679**	**.0938**	**.1362**	**.0911**	**.1393**	**.1622**	**.0851**	**.0622**	1.00
24	exfund_fh	**.5426**	**.5555**	**.4460**	**.5632**	**.4447**	**.4878**	**.4113**	**.4105**	**.4564**	**.4617**	**.1241**	**.3491**	**.4752**	**.4600**	**.4310**	**.4635**	**.3743**	**.4514**	**.4216**	**.5685**	**.6110**	**.6256**	**.0671**

Notes: Coefficients statistically significant at the 1 % level in bold. Coefficients statistically significant at the 5 % level in italic. Prof: number of professor; stud: number of students; PhD: number of PhD graduates; exfund: amount of external funds; ns: natural sciences; as: applied sciences; ss: administration and political sciences; u: regular universities; fh: universities of applied sciences

Table A.20 Factor loadings and unique variances after varimax rotation of variables representing regional HEIs according to scientific field

	Natural sciences		Applied sciences		Social sciences		Others	
Variable	Factor loading	Uniqueness	Factor loading	Uniqueness	Factor loading	Uniqueness	Factor loading	Uniqueness
Same region								
Professors	.9272	.1403	.8547	.2695	.8418	.2913	.8482	.2806
Students	.8884	.2107	.9553	.0873	.9328	.1299	.9381	.1200
Graduates	.9276	.1395	.9636	.0715	.9479	.1014	.9557	.0866
PhD students	.8777	.2297	.6226	.6124	.7906	.3749	.8281	.3143
External funds[a]	.7868	.3809	.8108	.3425	.8356	.3018	.9076	.1763
Variance	3.8989		3.6169		3.8006		4.0222	
Cronbach's alpha	.9339		.9014		.9122		.9268	
Adjacent regions								
Professors	.9957	.0086	.9982	.0037	.9942	.0115	.9754	.0487
Students	.9933	.0133	.9910	.0180	.9985	.0030	.9786	.0424
Graduates	.9924	.0152	.9908	.0183	.9984	.0033	.9627	.0733
PhD students	.9823	.0351	.8085	.3464	.9984	.0033	.8000	.3601
External funds[a]	.6896	.5245	.7010	.5086	.6833	.5332	.8487	.2796
Variance	4.4034		4.1050		4.4458		4.1959	
Cronbach's alpha	.9256		.9160		.9234		.9459	

Note: All variables are logged
[a]Amount in 1000 €

Table A.21 Descriptive statistics for different variables of quality of life

	Mean	Min	Max	Std. dev.
Human capital	.0633	.0187	.2399	.0316
I. Material well-being				
Income	24.13	12.69	108.39	13.213
Public spending	533.65	136.63	4097	312.20
Labor market	.0296	−.2908	.5170	.0575
Infrastructure	.0576	.0163	.1772	.0224
Housing	41.19	32.01	53.28	3.166
Internet	.4776	.0861	1.171	.1671
Unemployment	.0877	.0207	.2446	.0275
II. Protection				
Healthcare	.0059	.0005	.0210	.0023
Psychotherapy	.0010	.00004	.0053	.0008
Hazardous waste	.1474	.0036	3.078	.1606
Coal energy	.0201	.0000	.7604	.0871
Renewable energy	.0498	.00001	.7311	.0864
Crime	.0426	.0075	.3530	.0268
Accidents	.0060	.0030	.0130	.0009
III. Education and arts				
Schools	.024	.007	.087	.008
Universities	.0588	.0000	.6330	.1007
Arts	.0023	.0001	.0554	.0017
IV. Socio-political dimension				
Political participation	.7730	.2753	.8723	.0626
Political preferences	.3272	.1963	.5735	.0639
Kindergarten	.0370	.0249	.0539	.0048
Youth facilities	.0013	.00001	.0063	.0009
V. Amenities				
Consumer services	.0246	.0014	.1426	.0188
Recreation	.0123	.0015	.1013	.0154
Water area	.0216	.0023	.2823	.0243
Sunshine	1600	1220	1878	102
VI. Tolerance				
Foreigners	.0198	.0018	.0962	.0126
Diversity of foreigners	.3188	.2100	.8555	.0764

Table A.22 Correlation matrix for quality of life variables

		1	2	3	4	5	6	7	8	9	10	11	12	13	14	15	16	17	18	19	20	21	22	23	24	25	26	27
1	Income	1.00																										
2	Public spending	−.35	1.00																									
3	Labor market	.38	−.07	1.00																								
4	Infrastruture	.21	−.41	.30	1.00																							
5	Housing	−.18	.44	−.14	−.31	1.00																						
6	Internet	.08	.22	.14	*.00*	*.00*	1.00																					
7	Unemployment	*.01*	.14	.00	.33	−.10	*−.01*	1.00																				
8	Healthcare	.11	−.31	.07	.26	−.16	*−.05*	.18	1.00																			
9	Psychotherapy	*.04*	−.03	*.04*	*−.01*	−.09	.07	*−.01*	.49	1.00																		
10	Hazardous waste	*.04*	−.10	.07	.28	−.05	−.10	.23	.11	−.06	1.00																	
11	Coal energy	−.11	−.10	*.00*	.20	−.12	−.07	.17	.09	*.03*	.17	1.00																
12	Renewable energy	−.05	*.03*	*−.01*	*−.05*	.07	−.13	−.09	*−.01*	*.02*	−.07	*.00*	1.00															
13	Crime	.05	−.06	−.17	−.11	.40	−.11	.18	.30	−.07	*.03*	−.13	−.11	1.00														
14	Accidents	−.05	−.10	−.04	−.05	−.17	−.05	−.16	.22	.05	*−.02*	*−.03*	−.07	.33	1.00													
15	Schools	.12	−.14	.11	.27	.10	.11	.14	.28	.09	.08	.05	.04	*.17*	−.16	1.00												
16	Universities	.21	−.23	.16	.42	−.23	.07	.15	.43	.10	.12	*.04*	−.05	.11	.04	.41	1.00											
17	Arts	.28	−.04	.21	.19	−.14	.23	.07	.21	.06	.09	*−.03*	.03	*−.07*	*.01*	.26	.42	1.00										
18	Pol.-participation	*.00*	−.08	*.02*	*−.03*	−.21	.17	−.14	*−.05*	*.02*	−.10	*−.03*	−.01	*−.03*	.24	−.22	−.11	−.11	1.00									
19	Pol.-preferences	*−.06*	*−.04*	*.01*	*.05*	−.18	*.01*	.12	.06	*−.01*	−.09	*−.02*	−.02	*−.05*	*−.02*	*.05*	.18	.14	−.69	1.00								
20	Kindergarten	*.05*	.14	.02	*.01*	.02	.00	*−.39*	*−.25*	*.01*	.00	*.01*	.00	*.00*	*−.02*	*.08*	.01	.03	.05	*.00*	1.00							
21	Youth facilities	*−.07*	*.01*	*−.05*	*−.03*	*.05*	.14	*.05*	.07	*.01*	*.04*	*.02*	−.04	*.19*	*.03*	.21	.13	−.03	*.01*	*−.03*	.06	1.00						
22	Consumer services	.16	.44	.11	.32	.20	.51	.22	.09	*.03*	.13	−.01	−.15	.03	−.13	.32	.31	.36	−.17	.08	−.10	.08	1.00					
23	Recreation	.19	−.42	.28	.86	−.29	*.06*	.38	.25	*.01*	.26	.21	−.08	−.04	*−.04*	.24	.35	.26	−.03	.02	.00	−.03	.36	1.00				
24	Water areas	*−.02*	−.14	*.05*	.23	−.16	.10	.28	.14	*.00*	.16	.14	−.08	.08	.06	.08	.07	.11	*.00*	*−.04*	.01	.01	*.21*	.41	1.00			
25	Sunshine	−.04	*.00*	*−.02*	−.09	.11	−.08	−.03	*.00*	.05	*−.01*	−.14	−.02	*.08*	−.02	−.12	.05	*.00*	.00	−.02	.03	.01	*−.03*	*−.02*	−.04	1.00		
26	Foreigners	.41	−.32	.28	.45	−.43	.06	−.25	.04	*.03*	.10	*.03*	−.07	−.29	−.04	.12	.24	.31	−.08	.08	.22	−.12	*.10*	.38	.06	−.05	1.00	
26	For.-diversity	−.11	*−.02*	−.06	−.14	.09	.01	.09	−.09	*.00*	*.02*	.01	.00	.01	−.08	−.23	−.17	−.16	−.14	*−.06*	−.19	−.08	−.24	*−.05*	.04	.12	−.05	1.00
28	Population density	.27	−.20	.36	.89	−.42	.07	.27	.22	*.02*	.30	.21	−.09	−.17	−.08	.31	.38	.35	−.07	.10	−.14	−.07	.21	.91	.34	−.07	.52	−.06

Notes: Coefficients not statistically significant at the 5 % level in italic

Table A.23 Testing equality of coefficients for variables of material well-being (standardized direct effects)

		1	2	3	4	5	6
1	Income	–					
2	Public Spending	.01 (1) .9303	–				
3	Labor market	14.39 (1) .0001***	14.12 (1) .0002***	–			
4	Infrastructure	8.15 (1) .0043***	8.13 (1) .0044***	.24 (1) .6246	–		
5	Housing	1.98 (1) .1597	1.40 (1) .2373	19.29 (1) .0000***	10.13 (1) .0015***	–	
6	Internet	20.25 (1) .0000***	15.68 (1) .0001***	3.31 (1) .0690*	1.02 (1) .3130	20.00 (1) .0000***	–
7	Unemployment	49.25 (1) .0000***	35.06 (1) .0000***	28.79 (1) .0000***	4.69 (1) .0303**	49.72 (1) .0000***	2.75 (1) .0971*

Notes: First row: chi-squared and degrees of freedom in parentheses. Second row: p-value. ***Statistically significant at the 1 % level; **Statistically significant at the 5 % level; *Statistically significant at the 10 % level

Table A.24 Testing equality of coefficients for variables Model II

		1	2	3	4	5	6
1	Income	–					
2	Crime	125.87 (1) .0000***	–				
3	Universities	129.94 (1) .0000***	517.91 (1) .0000***	–			
4	Political participation	9.73 (1) .0018***	55.37 (1) .0000***	186.57 (1) .0000***	–		
5	Consumer services	72.14 (1) .0000***	549.98 (1) .0000***	5.85 (1) .0156**	170.27 (1) .0000***	–	
6	Foreigners	80.21 (1) .0000***	1077.6 (1) .0000***	.11 (1) .7357	182.78 (1) .0000***	4.99 (1) .0255**	–
7	Diversity of foreigners	106.22 (1) .0000***	10.24 (1) .0014***	659.44 (1) .0000***	29.33 (1) .0000***	749.06 (1) .0000***	536.80 (1) .0000***

Notes: First row: chi-squared and degrees of freedom in parentheses. Second row: p-value. ***Statistically significant at the 1 % level; **Statistically significant at the 5 % level; *Statistically significant at the 10 % level

Table A.25 Standardized SEM coefficient with population density

	Coef.	Indirect effects	Total effects
Human capital			
Income	.1169***	.1026***	.2195***
Crime	−.1469***	−.0783***	−.2252***
Universities	.3301***	.0275***	.3576***
Political participation	.0497**	−.0061	.0436**
Consumer services	.2869***	.0108***	.2977***
Foreigners	.3256***	.0021	.3277***
Diversity of foreigners	−.0934***	–	−.0934***
Population density	.1077***	.4446***	.5523***
Constant	.6076**	–	–
Income			
Population density	.2632***	–	.2632***
Constant	1.615***	–	1.615***
Crime			
Population density	−.1636***	–	−.1636***
Constant	1.741***	–	1.741***
Universities			
Population density	.3884***	–	.3884***
Constant	.2848***	–	.2848***
Political participation			
Population density	−.0752***	–	−.0752***
Constant	12.397***	–	12.397***
Consumer services			
Population density	.3022***	–	.3022***
Constant	1.297***	–	1.297***
Foreigners			
Income	.2927***	–	.2927***
Crime	−.2390***	–	−.2390***
Universities	.0556***	–	.0556***
Political participation	−.0571	–	−.0571
Consumer services	−.0731***	–	−.0731***
Population density	.3996***	.1199***	.5195***
Constant	1.899***	–	–
Diversity of foreigners			
Income	−.0710*	−.0065***	−.0775***
Crime	–	.0053***	.0053***
Universities	−.0997***	−.0012***	−.1009
Political participation	−.1349***	.0013**	−.1336***
Consumer services	−.3716***	.0016***	−.370***
Foreigners	−.0223	–	−.0223

(continued)

Table A.25 (continued)

	Coef.	Indirect effects	Total effects
Population density	.0700***	−.1711***	−.1011***
Constant	6.203***	–	–

Notes: chi^2(50) = 341.97 (p = .00); RMSEA = .034; CFI = .962; R^2 (Human capital) = .6601; R^2 (Foreigners) = .4159; R^2 (Foreigners diversity) = .1669; R^2 (Income) = .0693; R^2 (Crime) = .0268; R^2 (Universities) = .1508; R^2 (Political participation) = .0057; R^2 (Consumer services) = .0913; Number of observations = 4998
***Statistically significant at the 1 % level; **Statistically significant at the 5 % level; *Statistically significant at the 10 % level

Table A.26 Standardized SEM results for three groups of regions sorted according to population density

	Only regions with the lowest third of population density	Only regions with the middle third of population density	Only regions with the highest third of population density
Direct effect			
Income	.0556	.1115***	.1331***
Crime	−.1426***	−.1386***	−.1525***
Universities	.1983***	.3633***	.3190***
Political participation	.2482***	.4720***	.0052
Consumer services	.3418***	.1701***	.3918***
Foreigners	.1437***	.3640***	.2920***
Div.-foreigners	−.2280***	.0022	−.0751***
Constant	−.8835	−1.711	1.153
Indirect effect			
Income	.0818***	.0911***	.1236***
Crime	−.0583***	−.1715***	−.0497***
Universities	−.0135	−.0112	.0395***
Political participation	.0727***	−.1081***	−.0168
Consumer services	.0931***	−.1204***	.0600***
Foreigners	.0024	.0001*	.0031
Div.-foreigners	–	–	–
Total effect			
Income	.1374***	.2026***	.2568***
Crime	−.2009***	−.3101***	−.2023***
Universities	.1848***	.3520***	.3585***
Political participation	.3209***	.0620	−.0116

(continued)

Table A.26 (continued)

	Only regions with the lowest third of population density	Only regions with the middle third of population density	Only regions with the highest third of population density
Consumer services	.4349	.3516***	.4517***
Foreigners	.1461***	.3641***	.2952***
Div.-foreigners	−.2280***	.0022	−.0751**
Number of observations	1718	1613	1667
R^2	.3553	.4372	.5898
chi^2	.00 (35) (p = 1.00)	.00 (38) (p = 1.00)	.00 (38) (p = 1.00)
RMSEA	0.00	0.00	0.00
CFI	1.00	1.00	1.00

***Statistically significant at the 1 % level; **Statistically significant at the 5 % level; *Statistically significant at the 10 % level

Table A.27 Standardized SEM coefficients for medium-educated employees

	Share of medium-educated employees			Foreigners	Foreigners diversity
	Coef.	Indirect effects	Total effects	Coef.	Coef.
Income	−.0311	−.1633***	−.1944***	.3904***	−.0457
Crime	.1604***	.1506***	.3110***	−.3597***	–
Universities	.0646***	−.0805***	−.0159	1931***	−.0873***
Political participation	.0366	.0286**	.0652**	−.0671**	−.1516***
Consumer services	−.4852***	−.0063	−.4915***	.0182	−.3657***
Foreigners	−.4185***	−.00004	−.4185***	–	.0105
Diversity of foreigners	−.0036	–	−.0036	–	–
Constant	15.595***	–		2.081***	6.383***

Notes: $chi^2(38) = .00$ ($p = 1.00$); RMSEA = .00; CFI = 1.00; R^2 (Human capital) = .5024; R^2 (Foreigners) = .3276; R^2 (Foreigners diversity) = .1635; Number of observations = 4998

***Statistically significant at the 1 % level; **Statistically significant at the 5 % level; *Statistically significant at the 10 % level

Table A.28 Standardized SEM coefficients for low-educated employees

	Share of medium-educated employees			Foreigners	Foreigners diversity
	Coef.	Indirect effects	Total effects	Coef.	Coef.
Income	−.0941***	.1098***	.0157***	.3854***	−.0576
Crime	.0386	−.1097***	−.0711***	−.3729***	–

(continued)

Table A.28 (continued)

	Share of medium-educated employees			Foreigners	Foreigners diversity
	Coef.	Indirect effects	Total effects	Coef.	Coef.
Universities	−.1355***	.0513***	−.0841***	.1933***	−.0900***
Political participation	−.1495***	−.0303***	−.1797***	−.0699**	−.1581***
Consumer services	−.6351***	−.0191***	−.6541***	.0040	−.3277***
Foreigners	.2934***	.0007	.2941***	–	.0118
Diversity of foreigners	.0618***	–	.0617***	–	–
Constant	5.666***	–		2.173***	6.500***

Notes: chi^2(38) = .00 (p = 1.00); RMSEA = .00; CFI = 1.00; R^2 (Human capital) = .5191; R^2 (Foreigners) = .3358; R^2 (Foreigners diversity) = .1427; Number of observations = 4998
***Statistically significant at the 1 % level; **Statistically significant at the 5 % level; *Statistically significant at the 10 % level

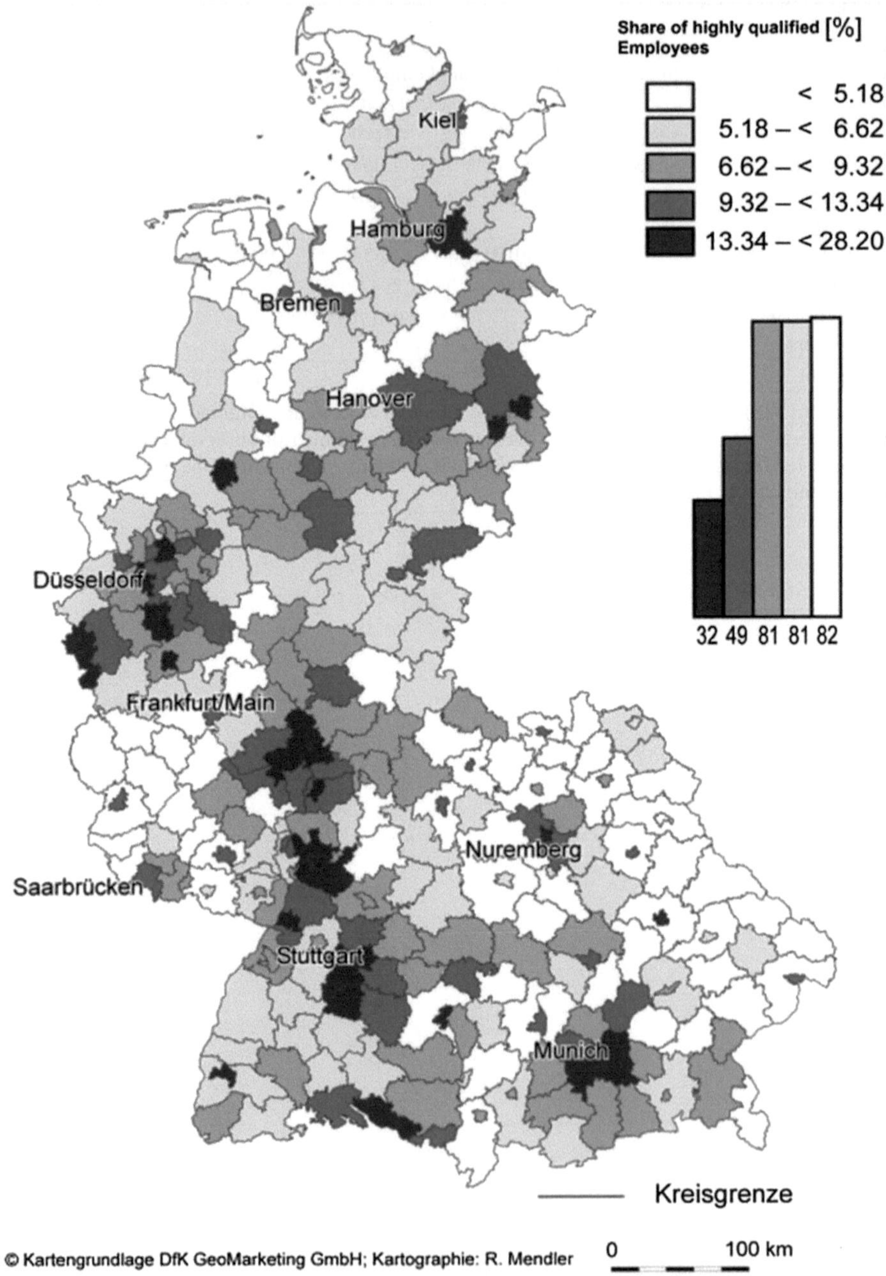

Fig. A.1 Average yearly share of employees with a tertiary degree 2005–2008

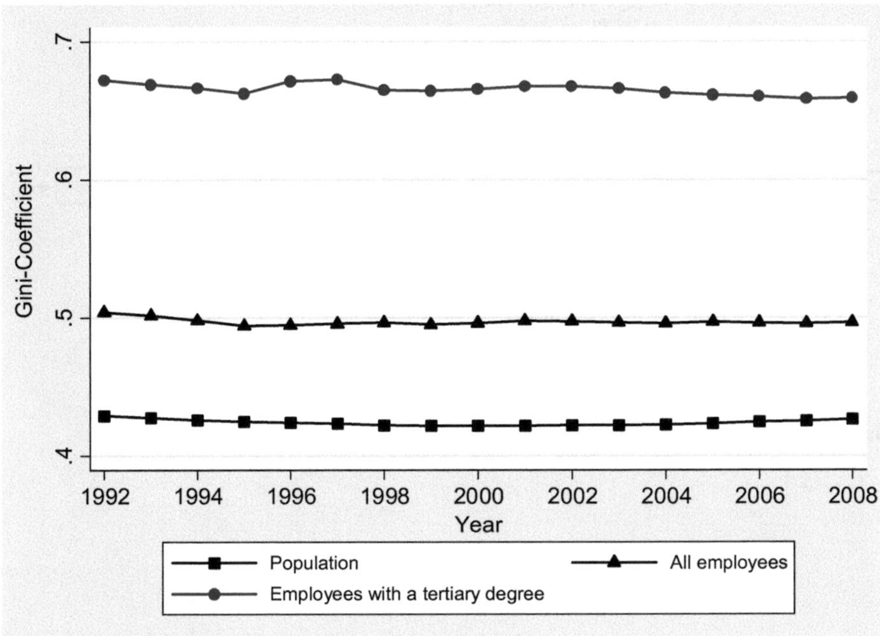

Fig. A.2 Development of Gini coefficient for human capital, all employees, and population between 1992 and 2008

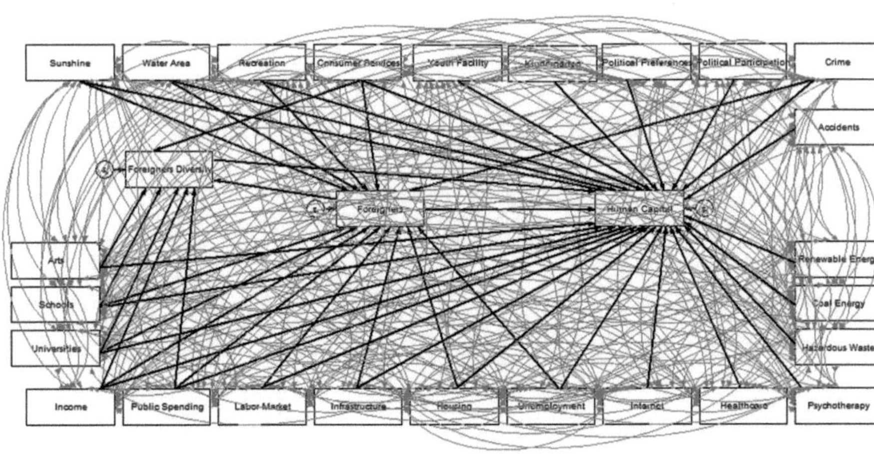

Fig. A.3 Path model for the effect of different dimensions of quality of life on human capital (Model I) with covariances

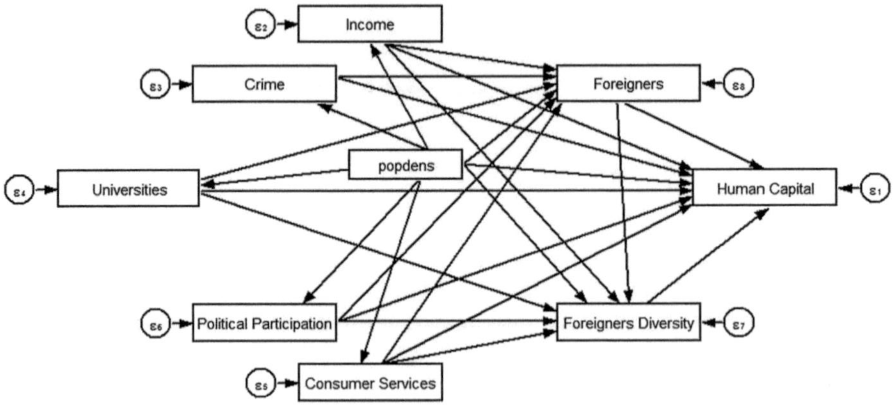

Fig. A.4 Path model with population density

Appendix B: German Summary—Deutschsprachige Zusammenfassung

Die vorliegende Dissertationsschrift beschäftigt sich mit den Determinanten der regionalen Entstehung und Verteilung innovativer Gründungen und des Humankapitals in Deutschland. Die grundlegende Hypothese ist, dass Wissen eine fundamentale Quelle der ökonomischen Entwicklung darstellt. Innovative Gründungen und Humankapital repräsentieren zwei Formen des Wissens und es wird dementsprechend in der Literatur angenommen, dass beide eine entscheidende Rolle für Entwicklung und Wachstum spielen. Das einführende Kapitel der Dissertationsschrift bietet zunächst einen Überblick über die unterschiedlichen Definitionen und Auswirkungen von innovativen Gründungen und Humankapital auf die regionale Entwicklung. Ferner zeigt dieses Kapitel einen Überblick über den Gegenstand und die Struktur dieser Dissertationsschrift.

Innovative Gründungen und Humankapital sind ungleichmäßig im Raum verteilt. Die Identifizierung der entsprechenden Ursachen stellt für die regionale Politik und die regionale Wachstumsforschung eine wichtige Frage dar. Diese Dissertationsschrift fokussiert dabei auf die regionale Ebene in Deutschland. Die regionale Ebene der Untersuchung ist aus mehreren Gründen wichtig. Vor allem Wissensflüsse sind oftmals räumlich gebunden. Ferner tendieren Gründer dazu, ihr Unternehmen in enger räumlicher Nähe ihres Wohnsitzes oder früheren Arbeitsplatzes anzusiedeln. Das lässt den Schluss zu, dass Entrepreneurship vor allem ein sehr regionaler Prozess ist.

Im Rahmen des zweiten und dritten Kapitels wird die Rolle der Hochschulen und anderen öffentlichen Forschungsinstituten für innovative Gründungen analysiert. Beide Kapitel basieren auf der sogenannten „Knowledge Spillover Theory of Entrepreneurship“. Die Grundidee dieser Theorie ist, dass innovative Gründungen eine Kombination von Wissen und unternehmerischer Initiative benötigen. Da ein großer Teil des Wissens in etablierten Unternehmen und akademischen Organisationen entsteht, sind innovative Gründungen, die das Wissen kommerzialisieren, als ein externer Effekt anzusehen. Mit anderen Worten, Entrepreneure schöpfen das ungenutzte Wissen der Universitäten und Unternehmen aus und vermarkten es im Rahmen einer neuen innovativen Gründung.

R. Aamoucke, *Innovative Start-Ups and the Distribution of Human Capital*, Contributions to Economics, DOI 10.1007/978-3-319-44462-8

Eine Reihe von Merkmalen der regionalen Wissensbasis beeinflusst das Auftreten von Wissens-Spillover. Hierbei sind u.a. das Niveau der Forschung und Entwicklung (FuE), Aktivitäten der Unternehmen in der Region sowie der Hochschulen und anderen öffentlichen Forschungseinrichtungen zu nennen. Der Fokus in dieser Dissertationsschrift ist auf akademische Institutionen gerichtet, die eine wichtige Quelle für die Schaffung von unternehmerischen Gelegenheiten darstellen. Hochschulen generieren, speichern und stellen Wissen in der Region zur Verfügung. Außerdem bilden Hochschulen Studenten aus, die später in den Arbeitsmarkt eintreten oder eigene Unternehmen gründen.

Im Rahmen des zweiten und dritten Kapitels werden anhand eines detaillierten Datensatzes die Auswirkungen verschiedener Indikatoren der Hochschulaktivitäten auf die Anzahl der innovativen Gründungen untersucht. Zunächst werden vier Gruppen von Gründungen nach ihrer Zugehörigkeit zu FuE-intensiven Branchen identifiziert: Spitzentechnologie, Hochwertige Technik, Technologieorientierte Dienstleistungen und nicht-innovative Branchen.

In den bisherigen empirischen Studien gibt es starke Hinweise, die auf positive Auswirkungen der regionalen akademischen Wissensbasis auf die Entstehung innovativer Gründungen hindeuten. Die Frage, welche spezifischen Merkmale der Hochschulen am wichtigsten für die Entstehung und Verteilung von innovativen Gründungen sind, ist nicht ohne weiteres zu beantworten. Ist es ihre bloße Präsenz in der Region, deren Größe oder Qualität? Unseren empirischen Ergebnissen nach (Kapitel 2), gibt es eine starke Beziehung zwischen der Präsenz von Hochschulen und der Entstehung innovativer Gründungen. Andere Indikatoren, die die Größe oder die Qualität dieser Institutionen widerspiegeln, haben eine geringere Auswirkung, sind aber dennoch statistisch signifikant. Die Auswirkungen der Hochschulen auf innovative Gründungen in benachbarten Regionen sind eher schwach ausgeprägt und dementsprechend auch statistisch insignifikant. Der Einfluss der Hochschulen ist für Spitzentechnologie und Hochwertige Technik am Größten. Für Technologieorientierte Dienstleistungen sind die Auswirkungen geringer. Kaum eine Auswirkung ist in Bezug auf nicht-innovative Gründungen feststellbar. Alles in allem, stehen unsere empirischen Ergebnisse im Einklang mit der Knowledge Spillover Theory.

Im Rahmen des dritten Kapitels gehen wir einen Schritt weiter und versuchen die Auswirkungen der Hochschulen nach Disziplin, Art der Hochschule und Transmissionskanal zu untersuchen. Im Hinblick auf die Disziplinen unterscheiden wir zwischen Naturwissenschaften, Ingenieurwissenschaften, Rechts-, Wirtschafts- und Sozialwissenschaften, Medizin und „anderen“ Disziplinen. Hinsichtlich der Art der Hochschule unterscheiden wir zwischen Universitäten, Universitätskliniken, Fachhochschulen, Verwaltungshochschulen, und Kunsthochschulen. Außerdem berücksichtigen wir die Anzahl der öffentlichen Forschungseinrichtungen. Im Hinblick auf den Transmissionskanal unterscheiden wir zwischen Professoren, Studenten, Promovierten und Drittmitteln.

Unsere Grundthese ist, dass von verschiedenen Disziplinen generiertes Wissen nicht von gleicher Bedeutung für innovative Gründungen ist. Unsere empirischen Ergebnisse zeigen, dass verschiedene wissenschaftliche Bereiche unterschiedliche

Auswirkungen auf die innovativen Gründungen haben. Ingenieurwissenschaften scheinen für die Förderung von innovativen Gründungen bedeutsamer zu sein als Naturwissenschaften. Die Wirkung von Sozialwissenschaften ist eher schwach ausgeprägt. Keine statistisch signifikanten Effekte können für die „anderen“ Disziplinen gefunden werden. Die Art der Hochschule spielt eine wichtige Rolle. Es scheint, dass Universitäten die stärksten Effekte aufweisen; vermutlich aufgrund ihrer relativ hohen Forschungsintensität. Außerdem zeigt die Zahl der Professoren den stärksten statistischen Zusammenhang mit der Anzahl der innovativen Gründungen. Diese Ergebnisse deuten darauf hin, dass Investitionen in akademische Institutionen, insbesondere im Bereich der angewandten Wissenschaften, eine effektive Art der Förderung der innovativen Gründungen darstellen.

Insgesamt lassen die Ergebnisse aus Kapitel 2 und 3 einen wichtigen Schluss zu. Dieser besagt, dass das generierte Wissen in akademischen Institutionen das Potenzial hat, kommerziell in Form von innovativen Gründungen ausgenutzt zu werden. Dieses Potential variiert jedoch je nach Disziplin, Art der Hochschule, und Transmissionskanal.

Im Rahmen des vierten Kapitels richten wir unseren Blick auf Humankapital als eine andere Form der Ausprägung von Wissen. Da Humankapital eine entscheidende Rolle für die wirtschaftliche Entwicklung zukommt, ist es unser Ziel, die regionale Verteilung von Humankapital zu untersuchen. Menschen mit höherer Bildung haben tendenziell mehr Wissen und relativ ausgeprägte Fähigkeiten, weiteres Wissen zu absorbieren und zu generieren. Außerdem zeichnen sie sich durch eine höhere Produktivität und eine höhere Neigung zur Gründung innovativer Unternehmen aus.

Humankapital ist definiert als Anteil der Beschäftigten mit einem Hochschulabschluss. Menschen versuchen normalerweise eine bessere Qualität des Lebens sowie mehr Freude, Genuss und Selbstverwirklichung zu erreichen. Lebensqualität ist ein Konzept, das versucht, verschiedene Aspekte des menschlichen Wohlbefindens durch einen Katalog von verschiedenen Faktoren zu berücksichtigen. Bisher hat die Literatur den Einfluss einzelner Elemente der Lebensqualität auf die regionale Verteilung von Humankapital untersucht. Es fehlt jedoch an Arbeiten, die versuchen Lebensqualität als mehrdimensionales Konzept zu untersuchen. Der Zweck des vierten Kapitels ist es deshalb, die Rolle der Lebensqualität für die Geographie von Humankapital darzulegen. Dazu setzen wir die regionalen Anteile an Humankapital in Bezug zu einer Vielzahl regionaler Indikatoren.

Die Haupterkenntnis des vierten Kapitels ist, dass die regionale Verteilung des Humankapitals eng mit den meisten Elementen der Lebensqualität verbunden ist. Aus praktischer Sicht kann dieses Ergebnis plausibel erscheinen, aber aus ökonometrischer Sicht kann es problematisch sein. Die empirische Analyse ist mit vielen Problemen und ökonometrischen Herausforderungen verbunden. Insbesondere Endogenitäten erschweren es, die empirischen Ergebnisse kausal zu interpretieren. In Anerkennung der Schwierigkeit, das Endogenitätsproblem vollständig zu lösen, wird versucht, es zumindest durch die Anwendung von

Pfadmodellen und Strukturgleichungen abzuschwächen. Dieses Verfahren ist mit Abstand die beste verfügbare Methode, um die Dynamik zwischen den Variablen auf der Grundlage ihrer Varianzen und Kovarianzen zu berücksichtigen.

Das fünfte und damit letzte Kapitel dieser Dissertationsschrift bietet zuerst eine Erweiterung der bisherigen Diskussionen in Form von einem Überblick über die Literatur, die den Zusammenhang zwischen Humankapital und innovativen Gründungen erforscht hat. Dabei wird das Konzept des Humankapitals um andere Elemente wie zum Beispiel „Erfahrung“ erweitert. Zudem werden die Entwicklung und der Erfolg der innovativen Gründungen betrachtet. Weiterhin bietet dieses Kapitel eine Zusammenfassung der empirischen Ergebnisse und nennt Implikationen für die Forschung und Politik, die sich aus den Analysen der Dissertationsschrift ergeben.

MIX
Papier aus verantwortungsvollen Quellen
Paper from responsible sources
FSC® C105338

If you have any concerns about our products,
you can contact us on
ProductSafety@springernature.com

In case Publisher is established outside the EU,
the EU authorized representative is:
Springer Nature Customer Service Center GmbH
Europaplatz 3, 69115 Heidelberg, Germany

Printed by Libri Plureos GmbH
in Hamburg, Germany